PETROLEUM INDUSTRY REGULATION WITHIN STABLE STATES

Petroleum Industry Regulation within Stable States

Edited by

SOLVEIG GLOMSRØD
Statistics Norway

PETTER OSMUNDSEN
Stavanger University College, Norway

Routledge
Taylor & Francis Group
LONDON AND NEW YORK

First published 2005 by Ashgate Publishing

Published 2016 by Routledge
2 Park Square, Milton Park, Abingdon, Oxon OX14 4RN
605 Third Avenue, New York, NY 10017

Routledge is an imprint of the Taylor & Francis Group, an informa business

British Library Cataloguing in Publication Data
Petroleum industry regulation within stable states. -
(Ashgate studies in environmental and natural resource economics)
1. Petroleum - Taxation 2. International business enterprises - Taxation 3. OECD countries - Economic policy 4. OECD countries - Economic conditions
I. Glomsrød, Solveig II. Osmundsen, Petter
336.2'786655'09177

Library of Congress Control Number: 2004117607

ISBN 13: 978-0-7546-4252-7 (hbk)
ISBN 13: 978-1-138-25904-1 (pbk)

Contents

List of Figures and Tables

Figures

Tables

List of Contributors

Nina Bjerkedal is Director General in the Tax Policy Department of the Ministry of Finance in Norway where she has worked since 1976. She was the Chairman of the Norwegian Petroleum Tax Commission in 2000.

Torbjørn Eika has worked as a researcher in the Division for Macroeconomics at Statistics Norway since he graduated (MSc) from the University of Oslo, Department of Economics, in 1986. His research fields are economic forecasting, business cycle analysis and macroeconomic modelling. His current position is Senior Adviser and his main tasks include macroeconomic short and medium term forecasts of the Norwegian economy and related macroeconomic analysis.

Solveig Glomsrød is Research Fellow at the Division for Natural Resource Economics at Statistics Norway. Her research relates to petroleum and energy markets, and environmental issues with particular focus on the interaction between general economic policies, natural resource use and environmental effects. She is a member of the steering committee of the Social Science Petroleum Research Programme (Petropol) of the Research Council of Norway.

Thomas A. Gresik is a Professor of Economics and Econometrics at the University of Notre Dame. He has also served on the faculties of Washington University at St. Louis and The Pennsylvania State University. He earned a BA in economics and mathematics from Northwestern University in 1981, an MSc in social sciences from the California Institute of Technology in 1982, and a PhD in managerial economics and decision sciences from Northwestern University in 1987. Professor Gresik's active research areas include mechanism design in economic environments with private information and international tax policy/competition.

Rögnvaldur Hannesson is Professor of Fisheries Economics at the Norwegian School of Economics and Business Administration, Bergen. He has a PhD in economics from the University of Lund, Sweden. His research has mainly been on the economics of fisheries, but he has also taken an interest in petroleum economics. He has written two books on petroleum economics and related subjects, *Petroleum Economics: Issues and Strategies of Oil and Natural Gas* and *Investing for Sustainability: The Management of Mineral Wealth.*

Torgeir Johnsen is Assistant Director General in the Tax Policy Department at the Ministry of Finance in Norway, where he has worked since 1993. Previously he did energy-economic analysis in the Research Department of Statistics Norway. He was a member of the Secretariat of the Petroleum Tax Commission.

Alex Kemp is Schlumberger Professor of Petroleum Economics at the University of Aberdeen, Scotland. For many years in his research he has specialised in the economics of North Sea oil and gas and has produced over 200 papers and books on this subject. Professor Kemp has advised many host governments and oil companies on economic aspects of contractual arrangements in the upstream industry. He is currently writing the Official History of North Sea Oil and Gas. He is a Fellow of the Royal Society of Edinburgh and a Fellow of the Royal Society of Arts.

Hans Jarle Kind is Associate Professor at the Norwegian School of Economics and Business Administration (NHH) in Bergen, Norway. He received his PhD from NHH in 1999. He previously held a position as Senior Researcher at the Institute for Research in Economics and Business Administration (SNF), affiliated with NHH. Today he holds an adjunct position as scientific advisor to SNF. His main research and teaching areas include Industrial Organization, Media Economics, International Trade, Regulation, and the Economics of Information and Communication Technology (ICT).

Knut Moum has been Deputy Director General in the Economics Department at the Ministry of Finance of Norway since 2001. Previously he was Research Fellow and later Director of Research in the Division for Macroeconomics at Statistics Norway.

Petter Osmundsen is Professor in Petroleum Economics at Stavanger University, where he is heading the Section of Petroleum Economics at The Department of Industrial Economics and Risk Management. He has a PhD from the Norwegian School of Economics and Business Administration (NHH) in Bergen. In 1992/93 he was a Research Fellow at MIT and Harvard. He has previously held positions as Associate Professor at NHH and Research Manager at the Institute for Research in Economics and Business Administration (SNF), affiliated with NHH. Today he holds an adjunct position as a scientific advisor to SNF.

Linda Stephen is Research Fellow in Petroleum Economics at the University of Aberdeen, Scotland. She has co-authored many papers on North Sea economics with Professor Kemp. She specialises in financial modelling of oil and gas exploration and production with emphasis on the effects of royalties and taxation.

Ragnar Tveterås is professor in Industrial Economics at Stavanger University. He has a PhD in economics from the Norwegian School of Economics and Business Administration, and a master's degree from the University of Bergen. His research has focused on natural resource based industries, primarily the petroleum, fisheries and aquaculture industries. Tveterås' international publications include econometric analyses of production risk, productivity growth, firm turnover, agglomeration economies and market structure.

Preface

This book, *Petroleum Industry Regulation within Stable States* is the second of three volumes based on research performed under the auspices of the Petropol Research Program, a Norwegian Research Council initiative. The two other volumes are *Oil in the Gulf* (published by Ashgate in 2004) and *The Changing World of Oil* (forthcoming 2005). The Petropol Research Program, a government/industry jointly funded initiative, started in 1996, is the latest in a series of Norwegian social science research efforts concerned with the policy making challenges presented to both government and industry by changes in the world of oil. The program's foci are wide ranging: Internationalization and industrial restructuring, the impact of geopolitical, national and cultural factors on the industry, the impact of human rights and democratization on corporate strategy and policy are but a few of the areas of research. While the primary objective of the program is to maintain and extend the knowledge base of the Norwegian social science research community working on petroleum-related issues, many of its research findings are of interest to a wider audience; hence the publication of these volumes by Ashgate.

This particular volume deals with national petroleum regulation aspects, which, perhaps unjustly, are given an interest secondary to the predominating focus on petroleum markets and business prospects. Regulatory issues are seldom given the necessary attention and analysis that they deserve given the sector's size, international character and planning horizon. Although the Petropol Research Program is the primary source of the research results presented in this volume, we have also had the privilege of including selected contributions from prominent researchers outside this research program.

We thank the Norwegian Research Council for its financial support, our contributors for their unstinting efforts, and the series editor, Professor Helge Hveem and publishing coordinator Maja Arnestad, for their efforts on our behalf. Finally we are very grateful to our Ashgate editors, Brendan George and Carolyn Court for their patience and support in helping us to complete this volume.

Solveig Glomsrød, Oslo
Petter Osmundsen, Stavanger

Chapter 1

Introduction

Solveig Glomsrød and Petter Osmundsen

Petroleum production partly takes place in politically young or unstable regimes where good governance can hardly be said to penetrate the societies. Under such circumstances the overall political uncertainty might dominate the minds and decisions of resource owners as well as petroleum companies while making efforts to create a niche for petroleum extraction. The evident curse of petroleum wealth under such political conditions is outlined by Gelb et al (1988), Karl (1997) and Auty and Mikesell (1998) among others. Social science petroleum research in a broader context has tended to respond by focusing on geopolitical affairs and petroleum company corporate behaviour (Yergin, 1991; Mitchell et al., 2001). However, there are petroleum producing countries where administrative capacity and political basis allow for a longertime perspective and more fine-tuning of petroleum taxes and regulations than is practised in many young and unstable regimes. The particular focus of this book is the challenge facing this kind of mature petroleum states in dealing with oil companies and oil revenues for the sake of general welfare in an experienced democracy. Our principal focus is petroleum, but the insights in resource administration generalize to other non-renewable natural resources.

Which are the stable states that we refer to? It is not the ambition here to come up with a definition of stability. Risk is a multiple faceted phenomenon, and even genuine ignorance about future outcomes should be kept in mind when considering the prevailing degree of stability in a petroleum province. A recent attempt to deal systematically with risk in petroleum producing countries has been presented by the HIS Energy Group. The HIS Energy Group developed a database for studies of risk elements and established indicators for total risk involved in operations. Risk was divided into three main categories: general political risk, fiscal risk and exploration and production risk. When the aggregate risk indicator was estimated by country, it turned out to assign the same total risk to operations in two countries as different as Norway and Nigeria. Norway ranks high on fiscal risk, and Nigeria ranks high on political risk.

Still, Norway is not Nigeria. Although perception of risk may vary considerably, it may be a baseline to assume that the OECD countries are major candidates to be listed as stable states in the petroleum regulation context. Countries like the UK, the Netherlands, Norway, Canada and the USA have considerable deposits of non-renewable and scarce natural resources. However, the OECD countries will see their share of petroleum reserves reduced in the coming decades. According to IEA (2003) the OECD countries' share of oil production will fall from 30 per cent in 2002 to only 11 per cent in 2030. The stable petroleum states are in the declining phase, whereas in recent years the new provinces outside the OECD area have come up with the most significant prospects of oil and gas reserves worldwide.

A first reaction to this development might be to expect less stability in the future global petroleum environment. However, regimes in several oil producing developing countries are now on the move towards more socially sustainable governance. This development is important to OECD countries, as 70 per cent of oil investments from now until 2030 will take place outside the OECD area, and about 40 per cent of these investment are made to serve demand from OECD countries. With support from the IMF, governments currently work to improve transparency in financial affairs in developing countries. Among the financial flows, oil revenues and taxes are of particular concern. Eventually, regimes that are rich in petroleum or other natural resources are likely to develop more sophisticated regulatory tools. Hence, in a dynamic context the petroleum management issues discussed in this book might become useful to petroleum resource owners beyond the petroleum states that may be characterized as stable today.

The degree of sophistication in petroleum management and taxation is not as much a question of the competence of the government officials as it is a question of the quality and reliability of the decentralized tax administration. Take royalties as an example. Royalties are used extensively in many countries, even if it is common knowledge that royalties are non-neutral and may convey detrimental incentives for reservoir management as well as cause petroleum fields to be closed down prematurely. A likely explanation for still relying on royalties is that this tax instrument – linked to extraction volumes – is easy to administer. Neutral tax devices, like a resource rent tax, call for detailed monitoring and control of income and costs, which are more challenging and less transparent tasks. The countries with less reliable administrations in many cases must see part of the petroleum rent lost in exchange for a tax system that works.

Tax Competition Between Producer Countries

The regulatory systems of stable states are also under pressure. Interaction among oil companies and governments can be perceived as a multi-dimensional game over licences, production efforts, taxes and information. There is a rent bargaining constellation between extraction firms and the government. There is also a tax competition between governments in different extraction countries, attempting to attract the most qualified firms. By their inherent global mobility, transnational oil companies may have a strong bargaining position towards resource extraction countries. The mobility and the presence of outside options give credibility to implicit threats of relocation. However, the effective bargaining power is reduced if the number of qualified firms is high, as collusion may be hard to sustain. Thus, the recent mergers and acquisitions in the petroleum industry pose a challenge to governments in petroleum host countries, which are confronting dominant giants like ExxonMobil, TotalFinaElf, BPAmoco and ConocoPhillips. A possible response to the reduction in bargaining power would be for the governments to co-operate in tax and regulatory design. An emerging example may be seen in recent talks between British and Norwegian governments over efficient use of infrastructure across the border, and indications of a reduction in the Norwegian/British tax rate gap.

Traditional tax theory argues that tax on natural resource rent is neutral and can be taxed 100 per cent without distorting economic decisions. However, we do not observe that governments tax 100 per cent of the resource rent, as pointed out by Stiglitz and Dasgupta (1971). Often, only half the rent is captured by taxes.

What factors may explain this tendency by governments to refrain from more thorough rent capture? A punitive tax regime may be detrimental to the oil companies' incentives. Multinational oil companies may focus more on tax management than on petroleum resource management. Transfer pricing activities – i.e. the allocation of costs to high tax regimes and revenue to low tax regimes – is one example. Also, the most productive resources and competence may be allocated to countries where the companies keep a larger fraction of the rent. The limitations of exorbitant taxation are often not accounted for in the simplest theoretical tax models.

Another reason for more lenient resource taxation is tax competition among various host countries. In an industry with economies of scale and barriers to entry there may be a host country concern that companies move to other provinces. The petroleum resources are immobile, but multinational oil companies can adjust their involvement from full presence to narrow physical field operations. Oil companies may consequently be considered as highly mobile. The petroleum companies decide on their degree of participation by means of global real investment portfolio decisions. By being mobile, the transnational oil companies can obtain lower taxes by threatening to move their scarce and valuable competence to another country, thus obtaining a mobility rent in an industry with substantial entry barriers (Osmundsen, Hagen and Schjelderup, 1998).

A third limiting factor on resource taxation is that the government typically lacks the necessary information to differentiate taxes so as to capture the entire rent, i.e. the extraction companies gain an information rent. The companies benefit from private information on economic and strategic conditions.

In this book, traditional resource taxation theory (e.g. Campbell and Linder, 1985) is combined with recent theory of international taxation (e.g. Zodrow and Mieszkowski, 1986; Kind, Knarvik and Schjelderup, 2000; Olsen and Osmundsen, 2003, 2001; and Gresik, 2001). In chapter 2, Petter Osmundsen pictures some of the new challenges facing the tax authorities. First of all, the high number of mergers and acquisitions has reduced the number of potential firms to attract, raising the stakes in tax bargaining. Second, the discovery of large petroleum reservoirs in West Africa and the Caspian region poses a serious challenge to other extraction countries. Third, the opening up for multinational enterprises in the Middle East and Russia represents additional options for the major oil companies. New options for private international companies may also emerge if state owned companies lose administrative privileges over rights to national reserves and more of these reserves become exposed to competition for contracts. All these changes imply enhanced international tax competition. On the other hand, the fear of acts of terror and the lack of confidence with respect to contractual and tax conditions in newly opened extraction countries may work in the favour of OECD extraction countries.

What strategies are feasible for OECD host countries facing enhanced tax competition? One obvious strategy is to implement measures that reduce entry barriers for new oil companies. A high number of companies will enhance the relative bargaining power of the government. This may to some extent alleviate the recent loss in bargaining power due to the considerable number of mergers and acquisitions in the petroleum industry. The challenge is to attract mid-size companies that have sufficient financial capacity. Also, the government may try to forestall collusion on the part of the companies. A relevant measure in this respect is to stimulate a heterogeneous corporate base, e.g. a diversity of companies in dimensions like size, geological focus and level of vertical integration. Heterogeneous company tax base may give the government some leeway for a conquer-and-rule strategy. Yet another strategy would be to initiate collusive behaviour over tax matters on behalf of various extraction countries. The latter may prove to be a difficult task due to political, cultural and economic differences. One example of important differences with respect to preferences over tax design is that whereas some countries are wealthy and patient tax collectors, other countries are in desperate need of current revenue. Some extraction countries like Australia and the UK may also have a more diverse objective function than simply revenue maximization. In addition to revenue they have objectives of self-sufficiency of petroleum.

Taxes and Agglomeration Economics

In design of taxes and regulations for petroleum extraction, the government needs to be alert to changes in corporate strategy. The petroleum companies are now pursuing focusing strategies through considerable portfolio adjustments in order to concentrate scarce resources on fewer activities and geographical areas where they have comparative advantages.

The financial volume of projects – or *materiality* in corporate lingo – is considered important. In return for a significant presence, they demand larger contributions after tax, measured in absolute value, from each of the selected activities. A stronger focus on the financial volume of projects is partly also a result of the mergers and acquisitions in the industry, with larger companies going for high materiality projects that can justify the relatively high level of indirect costs in large corporations. Implications of cluster externalities for optimal tax and regulatory design are discussed by Osmundsen, Emhjellen and Halleraker (2004).

Another regulation policy issue is the concept of industrial clusters. The literature on industrial clusters (e.g. Matsuyama, 1991 and Venables, 1996) discusses the possibility of *positive externalities*, or *agglomeration economies*, which give rise to geographical clustering of related production activities. The externalities offer competitive advantage, e.g. cost reductions, which are not obtained outside the geographical cluster. The size of the externalities is typically *a function of the size* of the industry.

Consider the starting point for offshore activities in two different provinces – the North Sea and the Caspian Sea. In the North Sea, initiating petroleum activity could benefit from a rich marine tradition and offshore suppliers, research institutions and consultancies. The Caspian Sea on the other hand was landlocked without the beneficial presence of an extensive marine/supply sector (although there was experience with on-shore oil production) or related suppliers with access to highly educated human capital. The unfavourable lack of an industrial cluster basis for the Caspian Sea was clearly negligible in comparison with the reserve prospects of the region. It was definitely found to be worthwhile to plunge into the Caspian Sea when the opportunity came up and step by step a growing sector built up the industrial environment to play within. However, the cluster externalities might be relatively more decisive for localization in other provinces than the Caspian region. Cluster advantages can be historically exogenous as in the examples above, or a result of the growth of the petroleum industry itself.

Presence of positive company and industry externalities may represent a source of dynamics in localization strategies. When considering leaving a producing region and moving to a newly opened province, it is less economical to be the first to do so. The activity level and the infrastructure in the current location work as mobility-preventers. However, as companies start to move, the economies of scale and agglomeration economics may rapidly change the relative attraction of migrating versus staying in the province. Threats of relocation should be considered in light of such dynamics embedded in scale and cluster externalities.

Chapter 3 focuses clustering incentives and the optimal government response to observed changes in localization strategy. As outlined by Hans Jarle Kind, Petter Osmundsen and Ragnar Tveterås, there are several reasons why the extent of interaction between agents – and therefore the potential for knowledge externalities – may be expected to be larger within the petroleum sector than within most other sectors. First, a number of remedial actions have been undertaken with respect to organization and communication in order to reduce transaction costs between different agents in petroleum production, e.g. standards have been set on issues ranging from technical specifications to design of procurement contracts. Second, geographical co-localization is widespread in the petroleum sector. Third, there is a tight integration between petroleum companies and their suppliers. For instance, even though the suppliers have changed to turnkey deliveries, the petroleum companies still have sizeable staffs of engineers working closely with the suppliers, sometimes even formalized as common project organizations. It should further be noted that parallel working processes, time-critical supply chains and mutually dependent R&D call for tight coordination between the different agents (petroleum companies, turnkey suppliers, and sub-contractors). Accordingly, there are substantial management and coordination challenges.

Transfer Issues

Given the relatively high rate of rent capture within the Norwegian petroleum tax system, the companies might benefit considerably from transferring revenue to other tax regimes. The Special Tax on petroleum revenue amounts to 50 per cent on top of the general corporate tax of 28 per cent that also applies to non-shelf activities. Consequently, both the non-shelf economy and foreign countries are attractive tax havens. The Petroleum Tax Commission of Norway identified transfer of shelf revenue to non-shelf activities as a major deficiency in the tax system. In chapter 8, Nina Bjerkedal and Torgeir Johnsen provide a summary of the proposals made by the Commission to deal with this and other deficiencies that were identified in its report, in particular barriers to entry due to lack of interest compensation for losses carried forward.

A tax regulator has to consider transfer pricing and profit shifting to tax havens – but avoid double taxation of ethically well-behaved companies. Since the oil companies are transnational and face a global variety of resource tax systems, transfer-pricing issues are pervasive. In chapter 4, Thomas Gresik argues that transnational corporations thrive for many reasons. Oft-stated reasons include proximity to customers and resources through vertical integration and operational economies of scale (e.g. in administration, R&D, and/or production activities). The economic advantage often conferred by these attributes is also attractive to many national and state governments. Transnational or foreign direct investment (FDI) not only creates direct economic benefits such as jobs and taxable income but significant indirect benefits such as knowledge spill-overs. However, the ability of individual governments to reap the benefits of transnational investment is compromised by a third characteristic of transnationals: the flexibility to shift production and resources across national boundaries. This flexibility not only helps transnationals minimize the cost of taxes and regulations imposed by individual governments, it can also aid them in pitting one government against another. Ultimately, the beneficiaries of such strategies are likely to be the transnationals and not the local jurisdictions. How these institutional and strategic factors limit the benefits governments earn from attracting FDI is the theme of chapter 4.

Social Versus Private Incentives

As petroleum provinces within OECD tend to mature, a need evolves to assess how the tax and incentive structure succeeds in matching the interests of the petroleum companies with that of the resource owner in the declining phase. If company incentives fail to get extracted as much as is optimal to the society at large there is a need to match the two set of interests.

It should be mentioned that genuine social value of petroleum resources is not easy to estimate. In the era of the Kyoto Protocol and deepened knowledge about pollution damages, an estimate of reserves taking these externalities into account could turn out to be smaller than what the industry is interested in extracting. However, it might also be opposite – the value of petroleum seen from a social perspective could also turn out higher than what corresponds to current oil price expectations if oil and particular gas increasingly replace coal for environmental reasons. Currently, however, in mature provinces, the concern among governments is that private extraction falls short of what they regard as socially optimal. The question for management is then how efficient higher oil prices or tax rebates are in getting more out of the fields.

In chapter 7, Alex Kemp and Linda Stephen present a model-based analysis that provides answers to this kind of question and thus may be very useful to the government as a tool to identify potential disharmony between private and public incentives concerning extraction activity. The UKCS is beyond the peak production and the rate of further decline is the key issue of policy design. The study of Kemp and Stephen is based on a detailed field account, distinguishing between sanctioned fields, current and future incremental fields, probable fields and technical reserves. Driven by a required return of 10 per cent on investments, the levels of exploration, development and production are determined endogenously by a Monte Carlo simulation to include the stochastics in field discoveries and development costs. Hence, the overall decline rate in oil and gas production can be studied under alternative price and tax scenarios. Further, the resource owner can obtain useful information like the time profile of investments and which field category the future production will rely on. Their analysis points to production from technical reserves as particularly price sensitive.

The maturing province dilemma also nurtures the debate over fiscal conditions on the Norwegian Continental Shelf (NCS). An industry initiative for improved fiscal terms to enhance end-tail production on the NCS was recently rejected by the Norwegian government in connection with the revised National Budget 2004. The government chose not to implement wide-ranging tax changes proposed by the industry but proposed minor adjustments in specific areas. The most significant of the proposals was the government's decision to pay back exploration expenditure in the same tax year as expenses are incurred, coupled with the guarantee that the full value of any losses incurred from operating on the NCS can be realized. This could act as a significant encouragement for potential new entrants to the sector. Company exploration strategy may change as cash flow is improved for those not yet in a full tax paying position and a greater degree of risk is removed from drilling smaller and more marginal developments. For medium-sized to large size companies that are not liquidity constrained, however, there were no significant fiscal improvements.

A high current oil price may seem to have eased the pressure for tax modifications. However, a high oil price may not be sufficient to secure enhanced exploration and production in mature provinces if tax competition works. High oil prices will raise the stakes in all provinces – a clear concern if company resources somehow are limited. At high oil prices, the provinces with the least progressive tax systems will improve their ranking in the transnational oil companies' investment allocations. The local prospects in a province need bench-marking against incentives worldwide. A tool for this purpose is found in a recently developed model of the oil market, where supply of oil is modelled based on detailed field data that are synthesized into reserves and production profiles in 13 provinces (Aune et al., 2004)

How to Manage High Oil Revenues

Government participation goes beyond tax rules. This book is not about Dutch Disease, which is the now famous name on the adverse macroeconomic effects of a resource boom. The oil booms of OECD countries are now mainly history, and the focus on macroeconomic management has now as its starting point an economy where petroleum revenues are generated and managed without seriously depressing other economic activities. Given this state of affairs, there are still important questions to deal with. There is the question of how to design macroeconomic policies in the presence of highly variable income from petroleum exports. What buffers should be constructed to shield the domestic economy against the volatility of the oil price and oil revenues? And if petroleum wealth is successfully transformed to financial wealth, how to prevent the fortune deteriorating?

Theoretical works provide analysis of the dynamic interaction between resource extraction and the economy, but generally lack the complexity of government challenges in this respect. A basic guideline to appropriate management is, however, to transfer natural resource wealth to other capital assets to maintain the capital base and thus be able to sustain the income flow from the petroleum wealth (Hartwick, 1977, Dixit et al., 1980). In a green accounting context it is a principle that rent from scarce natural resources should be subtracted from GDP to avoid the misunderstanding that rent is income. Increased transparency within accounting represents a step forward. However, how can we check if the accumulation of other assets has been sufficient to sustain future income after the petroleum extraction? Investments in produced capital and financial assets are fairly well depicted in the national accounts, but the investments in human capital and other even less tangible assets are harder to trace and to evaluate in terms of future revenue generating capacity. Thus there are loose ends when we leave the stylized theories and approach the making of a policy for sustainable income.

However, the theoretical basis delivers concepts that help mineral resource rich nations in structuring their management issues. One such concept is the permanent income concept. The permanent income may be defined in the tradition of Hicks (1939) as the maximum level of consumption that might be sustained endlessly from a given source of wealth like petroleum or other mineral resources. Hence the permanent income sets the limits to sustainable consumption.

In chapter 5 Torbjørn Eika and Knut Moum discuss the level of consumption in Norway on a background of the estimated permanent income from petroleum wealth. Even though the consumption level has been moderate in Norway in comparison with the total consumption potential so far, there still remains the problem that the level of consumption rests heavily upon the expected future oil and gas prices. In Norway, the estimated permanent income from petroleum amounts to 7.3 per cent of GDP in 2003 assuming the current oil price to last.

Thus, a significant share of total expenditure depends on a single market segment, and fluctuations in the oil price may be substantially higher than in more widely risk spread financial assets. This degree of dependency on petroleum exports of Norway is unique within the OECD, but meets counterparts in developing countries where the petroleum income might dominate in national value creation. Under such circumstances a downward adjustment of the permanent income estimate might necessitate a substantial readjustment of domestic spending to maintain a sustainable trade balance.

This challenge is the focus of Eika and Moum, who study how fiscal policy may work when there is need to adjust after a fall in expected permanent income from a resource. They take into account macroeconomic complexity by means of a mathematical simulation model for the national economy and question if the efficiency of fiscal policy to adjust differs between an inflation targeting regime and a fixed exchange rate regime.

It turns out that the answer is ambiguous, depending on the time horizon. However, over a 10-year period the efficiency of fiscal tightening turns out higher in the inflation targeting regime due to a quicker improvement in cost competitiveness so that production stays at a higher level. Although the overall differences are relatively small, this kind of study may be developed further and possibly reveal areas where the differences are more pronounced, for instance in relation to the income distribution effects.

Shifting wealth from the ground to productive capital may sound easy. However, the population of a resource rich developed nation is well aware of the wealth in its hands and the institutional capacity to lobby for a share of this rent is considerable. In Chapter 6 Rögnvaldur Hannesson presents three different institutional mechanisms for allocation and management of petroleum income funds with different degrees of defence against rent seeking and deterioration. These are the Alaska Permanent Fund, the Alberta Heritage Fund and the Norwegian Petroleum Fund. The Alaska Permanent Fund seems to have provided best hedging against the pressure to over-consume or over-invest in specific capital assets. It started out with a dividend scheme allocating about half the average earnings to individual dividends, creating an active wall of voters protecting the fund against spendthrift. The fund was established under law amendments and thus also had protection against political intervention.

The Alaska Permanent Fund is noteworthy for its contribution to sustainable wealth management. The fund might be an interesting role model for management of petroleum income in developing countries. If the population might receive their dividends directly and in person, the revenue could by-pass rent seeking and distortive investments and poverty alleviation might possibly gain some efficiency. This thought experiment may suggest that petroleum research and experiences within stable states may turn out to be useful to developing countries even in the short term, before their tax administration is functioning well.

Final Comments

Petroleum research treads in a landscape where the information is generally either private or strategically modified. Public funding provides some space for research with open access to the results. This book leans heavily on funding from the Social Science Research Programme PETROPOL of the Norwegian Research Council. The presence of independent and non-commercial petroleum research as contained in this book is an important source of information for the general public, and it may serve as an important reference point for consultancies and their customers among petroleum companies and ministries.

References

Aune, F.R., S. Glomsrød, L. Lindholt and K.E. Rosendahl (2004), 'The Oil Market Towards 2025 – Can OPEC Combine High Oil Prices with High Market Share?' Forthcoming as Discussion Paper, Statistics Norway.

Auty, R.M. and R.F. Mikesell (1998), *Sustainable Development in Mineral Economies*, Clarendon Press, London.

Campbell, H.F. and R.K. Linder (1985), 'A Model of Mineral Exploration and Resource Taxation', *The Economic Journal* 96, 146-160.

Conrad, J.M. and C.W. Clark (1987), *Natural Resource Economics, Notes and Problems*, Cambridge University Press.

Dasgupta, P.S. and G.M. Heal (1979), *Economic Theory and Exhaustible Resources*, Cambridge University Press.

Dixit, A., P. Hammond and M. Hoel (1980), 'On Hartwick's Rule for Regular Maximum Paths of Capital Accumulation and Resource Depletion', *The Review of Economic Studies* 47 no. 3, 551-556.

Gelb, A. and associates (1988), *Oil Windfalls: Blessing or Curse?* Oxford University Press, New York.

Gresik, T. A. (2001), 'The Taxing Task of Taxing Transnationals', *Journal of Economic Literature* 39, 800-838.

Hartwick, J.M. (1977), 'Intergenerational Equity and the Investments of Rents from Exhaustible Resources', *American Economic Review* 67 no.5, 972-974.

Hicks, J. R. (1939), 'Value and Capital', Second edition. Oxford University Press.

Karl, T.L. (1997), *The Paradox of Plenty*. University of California Press, Berkeley.

Kind, H.J., K.H.M. Knarvik and G. Schjelderup, (2000), 'Competing for Capital in a Lumpy World', *Journal of Public Economics* 78 (3), 253-274.

Kneese, A.V. and J.L. Sweeney (1993), *Handbook of Natural Resource and Energy Economics*, Elsevier.

Matsuyama, K. (1991), 'Increasing Returns, Industrialization, and Indeterminacy of Equilibrium', *Quarterly Journal of Economics* 106(2), 617-50.

Mitchell, J.V., K.Morita, N. Selly, and J. Stern (2001), *The New Economy of Oil: Impacts on Business, Geopolitics and Society*. Royal Institute of International Affairs, London.

OECD/IEA (2003), *World Energy Investment Outlook* 2003. Paris.

Olsen, T. and P. Osmundsen (2003), 'Spillovers and International Competition for Investments', *Journal of International Economics* 59, 211-238.

Olsen, T. and P. Osmundsen (2001), 'Strategic Tax Competition; Implications of National Ownership', *Journal of Public Economics* 81(2), 253-277.

Osmundsen, P., M. Emhjellen and M. Halleraker (2004), 'Transnational Oil Companies' Investment Allocation Decisions', forthcoming in Jerome Davis, ed. *The Changing World of Oil. An Analysis of Corporate Change and Adaptation.*

Osmundsen, P., K.P. Hagen and G. Schjelderup (1998), 'Internationally Mobile Firms and Tax Policy', *Journal of International Economics* 45, 1, 97-113.

Stiglitz, J. E. and P. Dasgupta (1971), 'Differential Taxation, Public Goods, and Economic Efficiency', *Review of Economic Studies*, 38, 151-174.

Venables, A. J. (1996), 'Equilibrium Locations of Vertically Linked Industries.' *International Economic Review*, 37, 341-359.

Yergin, D. (1991), *The Prize: The Epic Quest for Oil, Money and Power*, Simon and Schuster, New York.

Zodrow, G.R. and P. Mieszkowski (1986), 'Pigou, Tiebout, Property Taxation, and the Underprovision of Local Public Goods,, *Journal of Urban Economics* 19, 356-370.

Chapter 2

Optimal Petroleum Taxation Subject to Mobility and Information Constraints

Petter Osmundsen

Introduction

In most economic issues, decision makers are subject to constraints that limit the opportunity set. This is also the case when a government wants to design an optimal tax system for the petroleum sector, in order to promote the creation of high net values and to capture a high fraction of the resource rent for the benefit of the population in terms of public services or general tax cuts. The government is faced with participation and incentive constraints.

The participation constraints impose defined restrictions on taxation, licensing policy and regulation. The framework conditions must be sufficiently favourable for the companies to want to direct their efforts and expertise to the Norwegian Continental Shelf. In traditional resource economics, the participation constraints are often disregarded. This may be a convenient rough approach if fields that are offered are highly prospective. It may also be an approach for fields in operation, as these make up an immobile foundation for taxation. For existing fields, the challenge is to conduct a consistent tax policy in accordance with the expectations the companies were given at the point when the investments were made, in order to establish credibility concerning taxation. Tax design can be perceived as a repetitive game between governments and oil companies. Governments rely on the same group of companies to undertake future field developments, and current tax policy is a vital factor in forming the companies' expectations with respect to the future tax regime.[1]

For new fields and for additional investments on existing fields (e.g. in order to prolong the tail phase and increase the rate of recovery), Norway must compete with other oil and gas producing nations to attract competence and resources. This is partly an issue of the quantity of inputs we can attract and – since human resources are heterogeneous – partly an issue of quality. Tax competition is also present in industries that exploit non-mobile natural resources, since the input

[1] See Osmundsen (1999a).

factors and the companies are mobile.[2] Large discoveries in new basins, opening of established producing countries for transnational petroleum companies, and a reduction in the number of players through mergers and acquisitions, have increased competition between different producing countries to attract the most competent companies.[3] This is likely to make the fiscal terms more important, particularly in countries where the remaining acreage over time must be expected to yield economically marginal fields, i.e. where the resource rent experiences a decreasing trend.

One is thus confronted with participation constraints, and these will, over time, aggravate at falling prospects on the Norwegian Continental Shelf and improved opportunities in new or newly opened petroleum provinces. Competent companies have the possibility to reap parts of the petroleum rent in other countries, and will therefore demand a relatively high alternative rate of return on their scarce resources. These companies will require a corresponding profit on their activities in Norway. The international mobility of these companies entails that they acquire a mobility rent. The authorities will also lack complete information about the size of the petroleum rent and the behaviour of companies. They are thus faced with information constraints, also denoted as incentive conditions. This limits the authorities' ability to capture the petroleum rent, and the companies also acquire an information rent.[4] The potential for taxation is therefore to be found in the following relation: the petroleum rent less the mobility rent and the information rent. This explains why, in practice, it is impossible to tax one hundred per cent of the petroleum rent, as is often presumed in simple closed-economy resource tax models. With the prospect of falling petroleum rents and an increase in the mobility rent as a consequence of increased earning potential in other countries, the average taxation for new fields on the Norwegian Continental Shelf is likely to be reduced over time.

However, there are factors that are balancing this picture. Recently, a number of fairly large sized reserves have been discovered on the Norwegian Continental Shelf. Also, mergers among the largest oil companies might open up for new entrants, which may increase the relative bargaining power of governments in a bargaining game between governments and companies over the resource rent. Seen from the perspective of governments, it may be optimal to reduce entry barriers. Moreover, countries in which large new discoveries are made are likely to impose high taxes to capture a large fraction of the rent. Several of these countries are also associated with political risk. The obvious threat to the oil companies is the imposition of higher taxes or stricter regulation than expected after large irreversible investments have been sunk. In the last year, reports have been made

---

2 The companies do not need to move all of the operations physically to be internationally mobile. The transnational oil companies' international activities are to a considerable extent managed from the head office.

3 For a description of international tax and fiscal competition, see Zodrow and Mieszkowski (1986), Gresik (2001), and Olsen and Osmundsen (2001, 2003).

4 See Osmundsen (1995, 1998).

on a tougher regulatory regime in Angola, and tax increases have been announced in the Caspian area.

The challenge for tax designers is to promote the development of new marginal fields and at the same time capture a considerable share of the petroleum rent in previous and future prospective fields.[5] There are many practical monitoring and incentive obstacles to implementation of such tax differentiation.

The concept of neutrality will be different in an open as opposed to a closed economy. In a closed economy there is no desire to distort the investment level of domestic companies. True depreciation and domestic alternative cost for capital must therefore be deductible in the tax assessment. The objective of both the company and the authorities will be aligned, as both parties will want the highest national profit possible. In an open economy characterised by transnational companies, such concurrence will not occur, as the authorities will be concerned with the national profit while the company will be concerned with its global profit. In an open economy, the taxation system is neutral if the companies' decisions as to localization are not distorted. This implies that companies must be able to make tax deductions for the global alternative cost of their scarce resources, given by the profit the resources could have generated in other oil producing countries.

The objective of this article is to describe and clarify the implications of the different constraints in the petroleum industry that both authorities and companies are faced with.

Mobility and International Tax Competition

In what follows below, a description will be given of international tax competition theory. For high-tax nations, the fact that the tax base is increasingly more internationally mobile has become an ever-increasing problem. This applies especially to the corporate taxation. If conditions related to tax and regulation are not competitive, internationally mobile companies may move their activities to other countries. Competition may arise between various countries in attracting financially strong and competent companies, and this tax competition will typically lead to a pressure on the tax rates causing these to fall. This is dealt with in international taxation theory, see e.g. Zodrow and Mieszkowski (1986), Haaparanta (1996), Gresik (2001), and Olsen and Osmundsen (2001).

When parts of the tax base are internationally mobile, and thereby able to avoid high taxation, this tends to increase the tax pressure on immobile tax bases, e.g. property. Petroleum taxation is an interesting special case, in this regard. On the one hand, the petroleum resources are attached to their locality (immobile), which speaks in favour of these being good tax bases. (However, the tax potential is reduced in line with falling petroleum rent over time as a result of falling prospectivity, and the petroleum industry will over time come closer to other industries.) On the other hand, production requires substantial resources and competence, and these are possessed by transnational oil companies of very high

[5] See Osmundsen (1999b).

international mobility. Here, we must draw a distinction between new investments and investments that have already been made.

Petroleum investments already made are usually irreversible. The lack of mobility will therefore tempt the authorities to increase taxes after the time of the investment to a level beyond the level held out before the irreversible investments were made. This will, however, lead to an upwards adjustment of the companies' anticipated future level of tax, involve political risk and serve to substantially reduce the incentives to invest in new fields; see Osmundsen (1998). The optimal solution for the authorities is therefore to pursue a credible, predictable and time-consistent tax policy, which for existing fields will mean carrying forth the level of tax that was held out to the companies at the time of the investment.

Mobility may also play a practical role for existing production facilities, in the choice of the level of injection activity, scope of modifications and additional investments, the will to tie in smaller fields, with respect to the time of shutdown. A common feature of these projects – additional investments and extra efforts in the tail-end phase – is that they represent marginal projects. Problems may arise in that the companies' level of activity is lower (the rate of recovery gets lower) than what is preferable to the authorities. The reason for this discrepancy between business-economic and socio-economic profitability is, in part, that the companies are operating with a higher required rate of return and higher opportunity costs on other scarce inputs than the authorities and, in part, the companies' materiality requirement. Resource management considerations would therefore indicate that the authorities should, over time, improve the companies' incentives in IOR projects and development of marginal fields.

As regards investments in new fields, the companies' mobility comes into play in full. The companies will only go through with new investments on the NCS if anticipated, risk-adjusted rate of return is at least as high as for corresponding investments in other producing nations. It is worth noticing, in this regard, that the so-called Norwegian oil companies, Statoil and Norsk Hydro, have also become transnational companies, which in their portfolio evaluations of real investments are continuously holding the earning potential in Norway against the earning potential abroad. In their formulation of the framework conditions for the offshore sector, for new fields (and marginal IOR projects), the authorities are therefore facing a participation constraint, which involves an effective constraint on the tax level.

The participation constraint is modelled in Osmundsen, Hagen and Schjelderup (1998). Let $N_h(K_1,\ldots,K_n)$ denote the net income a transnational petroleum company will generate by allocation of the input factor vector $(K_1,\ldots,K_n)$ to the NCS. The input factors may consist of human, technological and financial resources. In order to arrive at the net income, we deduct national costs for the input factors. Somewhat oversimplified, we may for the purpose of our context say that $N_h(K_1,\ldots,K_n)$ corresponds to the petroleum rent in a closed economy. To consider the effect of an open economy with mobile companies, we introduce $N_f(K_1,\ldots,K_n)$, which stands for net income after source tax given the best alternative placement abroad for the same input factor vector, roughly corresponding to the petroleum rent that an oil company may realise by instead allocating its scarce resources to other producing nations. The effect of an open economy is that the input factors acquire several alternative applications. The companies' span of opportunities is extended, and the alternative payoff on scarce resources increases. Let T_h and T_f stand for the tax in Norway and the best alternative extraction country, respectively. The oil company will only allocate its scarce resources to Norway if after-tax rate of return is at least on a level with the return the companies could alternatively obtain by allocating these resources abroad. The participation constraint for the Norwegian Continental Shelf for a given transnational petroleum company is consequently given by the following:

$$(1) \quad \mathrm{N_h}(\mathrm{K}_1,\ldots,\mathrm{K}_n)-T_h \geq \mathrm{N_f}(\mathrm{K}_1,\ldots,\mathrm{K}_n)-T_f .$$

In a closed economy, the right-hand side of the participation constraint would have been 0. The companies' opportunities for resource rent-generating activities in other countries are, in other words, imposing additional constraints on the Norwegian level of tax if we would like to see the development of new fields in Norway. Norway can, in other words, not capture the entire petroleum rent, even if it had perfect information about the companies' profits on the Norwegian Continental Shelf.

Alternative rate of return on the resources, $\mathrm{N_f}(\mathrm{K}_1,\ldots,\mathrm{K}_n)-T_f$, given by the after-tax petroleum rent the company may realise by instead allocating its scarce resources abroad, can be perceived as the alternative costs for using the input vector $(\mathrm{K}_1,\ldots,\mathrm{K}_n)$ on the Norwegian Continental Shelf. Only the payoff in Norway, beyond the alternative payoff abroad, can be taxed by Norway. Payoff in Norway beyond international alternative payoff can be called country-specific rent or localisation rent, $\mathrm{L_h}(\mathrm{K}_1,\ldots,\mathrm{K}_n)$, given by

$$(2) \quad \mathrm{L_h}(\mathrm{K}_1,\ldots,\mathrm{K}_n)= \mathrm{N_h}(\mathrm{K}_1,\ldots,\mathrm{K}_n)- \left(\mathrm{N_f}(\mathrm{K}_1,\ldots,\mathrm{K}_n)-T_f\right).$$

It is the country-specific rent, and thus not the petroleum rent, that constitutes the potential tax base when the companies are mobile (that is to say for new fields or supplementary investments on existing fields). Foreign rate of return possibilities after tax for the company, $\mathrm{N_f}(\mathrm{K}_1,\ldots,\mathrm{K}_n)-T_f$, involve an efficient restraint on Norwegian taxation opportunities.

If we assume that Norwegian authorities have perfect information about the tax base, they will be able to capture all of the country-specific rent. The participation constraint (1) will accordingly be binding. Solving (1) with respect to T_h we derive that Norwegian petroleum tax from this company is equal to the country-specific rent:

(3) $T_h = N_h(K_1,\ldots,K_n) - (N_f(K_1,\ldots,K_n) - T_f)$.

Equation (3) gives a clear prediction of Norwegian tax revenues for new petroleum fields depending on the development in prospectivity on the Norwegian Continental Shelf, $N_h(K_1,\ldots,K_n)$, prospectivity abroad, $N_f(K_1,\ldots,K_n)$, and foreign taxation, T_f. Relevant features of development are here as follows:

1. NCS prospectivity is declining over time, with a greater presence of economically marginal fields, i.e. $N_h(K_1,\ldots,K_n)$ is falling.
2. The trend in prospectivity abroad, $N_f(K_1,\ldots,K_n)$, varies from one country to another. Essential new factors are that large-scale discoveries have been made in other producing nations, i.a. on the western coast of Africa and in the Caspian Sea. In addition, the countries of the Middle East have opened up for participation by transnational companies.
3. The effective tax on the producing activity, T_f, has over time been substantially reduced in the UK.[6] The situation in other countries is more varied, also involving tax increases.

There is also good news, however. Relatively large discoveries are still being made on the Norwegian Continental Shelf, and the discovery rate is high. In some cases, the development of additional reserves may also offer good commerciality by use of existing infrastructure. In addition, Norway may also have a strategic interest seen in relation to the large gas reserves relatively close to the EU nations, and the political risk is relatively low in Norway. A reduction in development costs and the possibilities for re-using existing pipelines improve profitability. Some of the countries in which large-scale discoveries are being made also have relatively severe taxation and lack essential infrastructure. The contractor contracts offered in the Middle East are reported to have limited upside potential.

All in all, however, there is no way of avoiding the conclusion that prospectivity over time will be falling on the NCS and that new discoveries in other countries and opening up of new countries have increased earning opportunities abroad. The competitiveness of the Norwegian Continental Shelf will, in other words, be weakened over time. The country-specific rent will fall, both as a consequence of falling prospectivity on the Norwegian Continental Shelf and of increasing opportunities abroad. In order to succeed in developing new fields in the Norwegian sector, it will therefore be necessary, in due time, to reduce the average taxation for new activity.

Another challenge to authorities in resource taxation is asymmetric information. We will, in actual fact, have asymmetrical information, i.e. the fact that the company will have better knowledge about its incomes and costs than the

6 The most recent change, however, was an increase in the tax rate. For new activity this was partly or fully compensated by allowing for immediate depreciation.

authorities, especially as regards the income opportunities in other countries. The companies will hence acquire an information rent, i.e. taxes paid will be lower than the country-specific rent. For a general discussion of information constraints and information rent, see Laffont and Tirole (1993) and Salanié (1998). Due to complex technology and a large number of intra-group and transnational economic transactions, information problems are particularly challenging in the petroleum industry; see Osmundsen (1995, 1998). There are thus two reasons why taxation of the petroleum rent ends up incomplete: (1) the participation constraint associated with internationally mobile companies, and (2) information problems complicating a perfect rent capture. In earlier resource taxation theory, these two constraints were not considered, and one was therefore unable to explain why, in practice, complete rent capture (a hundred per cent corporate income tax) is never observed.

In the presentation above, a number of simplifications have been made. First, the model is static. The net incomes and tax payments above, however, can be conceived of as present values. We have also left out effective resource constraints, such as, for example, the circumstance that development activities may be constrained by the availability of core personnel. Moreover, we have ignored fixed area-dependent costs. Resource constraints and fixed area-dependent costs may cause the companies to pose demands on minimum level of present value after tax for new projects, often referred to as materiality, critical mass, or financial volume; see Osmundsen, Emhjellen and Halleraker (2001).

Neutrality Concept in an Open Economy

Osmundsen, Hagen and Schjelderup (1998) emphasise that one has to employ a different neutrality concept in an open than in a closed economy. They are describing the recent years' tax reforms, which have assumed tax neutrality between different industries (including depreciation that reflects true depreciation) in order to secure equal marginal payoff in different industries so as to maximise the total profit before tax. The authors argue that this is based on theories developed under the assumption of a closed economy, and that adjustments need to be made in order to capture internationally mobile companies:

> The conventional line of reasoning is however based on two important assumptions. First, the desirability of a neutral corporate income tax was analysed within a closed economy setting. In an open economy context, tax neutrality would have to mean that the taxation of investment returns does not distort the location of mobile capital. Second, the tax authorities were taken to have complete information about the private and social profitability of firms' investment. As pointed out by among others Boadway and Bruce (1992), in an open economy the corporate income tax will in practice come close to a source tax on investment returns. With returns on mobile investments taxed at source the national government can tax away only domestic investment returns in excess of opportunity returns abroad net of mobility costs.

If the authorities are motivated by revenue considerations, the optimal tax base is, according to the authors, given by the country-specific profit, i.e. the companies are allowed deduction of both true depreciation and alternative payoff abroad on scarce factors. The latter means more generous depreciation arrangements for companies that have profitable business opportunities abroad. This also corresponds with the practice pursued in many countries. The implementation of tax neutrality, in other words, has different properties in connection with internationally mobile companies than for a closed economy.

Osmundsen, Hagen and Schjelderup (1998) deduce optimal depreciation for an internationally mobile industry, which implements the tax model. Total capital deductions, $D(K)$, are given by

$$(4) \quad D(K) = \partial K + rK + \left(\mathrm{N_f}(\mathrm{K_1},\ldots,\mathrm{K_n}) - T_f\right).$$

The first part of the capital deduction is compensation for value deterioration of the invested capital (depreciation). The second part is the alternative cost of capital in a closed economy, which in turn consists of interest expenses and alternative costs of equity. The latter will have a risk increment as compensation for systematic risk. In an open economy with mobile resources, neutrality will require taxation not to distort transnational companies' localisation and investment patterns.

Investment opportunities abroad mean that the home country can only tax payoff beyond the alternative payoff abroad, i.e. the companies must be offered capital deduction for extraordinary payoff opportunities in other countries, excluding foreign source tax. This deduction is given by the third part/factor of (4). By granting the companies this sort of deduction – i.e. by letting the tax base be equal to the country-specific rent – they will have incentives to maximise the home country's taxation potential. In the above reasoning, the authorities have been assumed to be solely interested in maximising tax revenues from the industry. If the government also assigns a positive welfare weight to the domestic profits in the industry, one will wish to turn investments in favour of the home country, which will mean more favourable capital deduction than (4).

It will be interesting to compare (4) with the capital deduction recommended by the Norwegian Petroleum Tax Commission, Government Report NOU 2000:18. The last factor in (4) is not included in the Commission's recommendations, the reason being that the Commission implicitly assumes the petroleum industry to be part of a closed mainland economy. The implication of the comparison is that the Commission is proposing too weak incentives for investments. The level of investments and tax revenues will thus end up lower than what is optimal from a socio-economic point of view.

Olsen and Osmundsen (1998) argue that, in regulating the petroleum industry, the Norwegian government faces two basic types of tax competition (tax is here widely defined as all economic conditions and regulations that affect the localisation decisions of petroleum companies). First, there is strategic tax competition between similar extraction countries, e.g. Norway, UK and Denmark, in which the national governments try to attract investments and human resources from competent companies. Second, the firms may have localisation options outside their present region, e.g. in emerging extraction countries. Recent empirical research shows that effective tax rates are important factors for determining the localisation decisions of multinational enterprises.[7] The particular setting of the model is as follows. We focus on multiple-principal regulation of multinational petroleum companies. The firm (the agent) divides its real investment portfolio and scarce human capital between two jurisdictions, and has an option of redirecting parts of its resources from one of the jurisdictions to the other. The firm has an additional option of investing in another region.

The relevant framework of analysis is strategic tax competition, i.e. in designing petroleum taxes the Norwegian government has to take into account that Norwegian petroleum taxes may affect petroleum tax design in other extraction countries. In tax design, a small country assumption is often made, thus ignoring strategic interaction. This approach may be valid for several Norwegian industries; Norway is indeed a small country. But we are a large country in terms of the petroleum industry, and strategic considerations have to be considered in designing taxes.

Behavioural Assumptions

Tax design can be perceived as a Stackelberg game. The government has the first move, designing a tax and regulatory regime. Thereafter, the oil companies make their moves, e.g. decide on the amounts to invest on the Norwegian Continental Shelf. The first mover – the Stackelberg leader – must, in its optimisation problem, try to figure out the optimal response functions of the followers, i.e. the government needs a model for the companies' actual investment behaviour.

An adequate model of corporate behaviour is also of vital importance for the formulation of a neutral taxation system. If one applies behavioural hypotheses that are not in accordance with the companies' actual behaviour, the tax system will generate unwanted tax-induced distortions.

A recent investigation into oil companies' project valuation practice found that the standard discounted cash flow method was the method most in use by petroleum companies for investment evaluations (Siew, 2001). For practical reasons the oil companies apply an average rate of return requirement for large development projects.[8] The decision making systems must be understood throughout the organisation, be used consistently, and practised in a decentralised manner. These concerns are in favour of a simple system that does not involve too

---

7 See e.g. Devereux and Freeman (1995).

8 However, for projects with regulated return, e.g. pipelines, some companies use a partial cash flow valuation approach.

much local assessment. The potential gains of more advanced decision and management systems are also often limited by the access of data.[9]

Recently the issue of distinct required rates of return when discounting individual cash flow streams of oil projects has been raised by the Petroleum Tax Commission. They implicitly propose that the oil companies should change their valuation method from discounting the aggregate net cashflow stream to a method where each cashflow is valued separately (NOU 2000:18). Partial cash flow discounting represents an active research agenda; see e.g. Laughton and Jacoby (1993); Laughton (1998a, 1998b); Emhjellen (1999); and Emhjellen and Osmundsen (2001). The same applies to real option theory; see e.g. Dixit and Pindyck (1994). It is therefore interesting and challenging to study optimal tax design subject to different behavioural assumptions. Since existing tax theory rests on the traditional NPV-assumption (average discount rates), there is no consensus on optimal tax design under alternative behavioural assumptions. The Petroleum Tax Commission only separates the cash flow of tax reductions due to tax depreciation. They do not discuss the issue of optimal tax design in the case that companies were to implement a full-fledged partial cash flow valuation approach.

Such research can be put to practical use in future tax design if the majority of the companies choose to adhere to new types of investment valuation models. Using it in current tax design analysis, however, is premature, since these types of analyses are in fact not yet widely used. Also, as reported by Siew (2001), the minority of companies that actually use new investment decision models do not use them in isolation, but rather as a supplement to the traditional NPV method.

The current view in the industry seems to be that it is an open question whether the precision is so accurate in the calculation of the 'correct' rate of return requirements for partial cash flow discounting that it is worth the effort of the calculations. The economic analysis departments of the oil companies prioritise the use of their limited resources. A common understanding is that the main challenges in terms of analysis are connected to structuring of the decision tree and a quantification of cash flows to find anticipated value, rather than to developing the risk premium for systematic risk exactly.

Focusing Strategies

To an increasing extent, transnational oil companies seem to choose a focusing strategy. Many functions are outsourced and the companies seek to concentrate their activities in a limited number of core countries, and even particular geological structures within the individual countries. The reasoning is that companies will become more competitive if they focus on particular core activities and core countries where they have a comparative advantage. One cannot excel at everything. Focusing on fewer areas also reduces monitoring and administrative costs. In the countries where the companies allocate their limited competence and

---

9 For a discussion of implementation challenges with NCS-data, see Emhjellen and Osmundsen (2001).

personnel, they want to have a considerable activity and a significant after tax present value, often denoted as materiality or financial volume.

A focusing strategy, however, may to some extent be in conflict with risk spreading. By being active in many countries and areas, a company reduces idiosyncratic risk like technical or political risk. By instead investing heavily in a few countries, on the other hand, the company will be vulnerable to different types of country specific risk. Portfolio theory prescribes that idiosyncratic risk will be drastically reduced if a firm invests in six or seven uncorrelated projects of about the same size. Thus, for the large transnational oil companies, which are present in a large number of projects around the world, additional risk spreading is not an issue. For small and medium sized oil companies, however, disproportional investments in a few projects or countries might be problematic.

Structural rationalisation in the petroleum industry and an increased focus on materiality are not considered in traditional tax theory. The Petroleum Tax Commission has made the conventional but unrealistic assumption that companies will realise any project with a positive present value, no matter the size, and that volume bears no significance for the behaviour of the companies.

The conventional models of investment view capital as the primary shortage factor, and the internal rate of return thus becomes the relevant criterion of decision. In designed examples based on internal rates of return, several simplifications and unreasonable assumptions are being made. However, one seems to disregard the fact that there are other shortage factors, one assumes that all relevant costs are included in the project calculations and that the projects are divisible. In reality, there are a limited number of large projects and many shortage factors and bottlenecks. One shortage factor is competent experts, i.e. human capital. For example, there is only a limited number of people who have the necessary skills and experience to manage the complex development projects in the North Sea. Furthermore, there is a shortage of competent geologists and geophysicists. Management capacity is also a shortage factor. The companies will thus consider the rate of profitability (present value) they may get back in relation to the contribution of competence and management capacity. The present value is then compared to the present value one would have received if the restricted resources had been invested in projects in other petroleum provinces where one would retain a greater portion of the valued added. Decisions about investments in transnational petroleum companies will thus consist of a ranking of many projects which show a positive present value, of which only a few will be realised. Other well known reasons for not developing all reserves with a positive NPV is that the partial project calculations do not account for all overhead costs, or that the NPV must exceed the value of the option to wait (irreversible investments).

Present value per shortage factor is not the only focus of the oil companies when they decide where to act. In addition to the evident points concerning prospectivity, cost level, tax level and access to acreage, they focus on getting a maximum of activity and creation of value added (large fields and parts) to carry the considerable fixed costs related to operating in the area, and not least to have a competitive understanding of the underground. The least profitable activity – critical mass – may thus be considerable. Furthermore, most companies find that a simple structure with a management focus on just a few factors is important. Areas that are profitable per se, but that do not create a lot of value added, may therefore be abandoned so that management and experts are able to focus on the areas creating value added for the company.

The impact of tax design on a transnational oil company's real investment portfolio decisions is shown in Osmundsen, Emhjellen and Halleraker (2001). They undertake portfolio analysis of an oil company, using real project data. The analysis clearly shows that extraction countries – if they believe that the oil companies will stick to their focusing strategies – need to curtail the tax system to the resource prospectivity. Less profitable fields call for more lenient taxation (lower average tax rates) for the country to maintain its competitiveness in attracting the most competent and internationally mobile oil companies.

Other factors influencing materiality, both at project and basin level, are the scope and prospect of exploration acreage, and the distribution of equity shares in the licences. A high marginal tax causes lower portions of the total cash flow to be retained by the companies. A similar reduction in cash flow is caused by the fact that companies often hold a limited equity share in the licence. Other companies' equity shares and the Norwegian State's share via the State's Direct Financial Interest (SDFI) reduce the share of the net cash flow (and the investments) to each individual company. This reduces the size of NPV to each company. The internal rate of return, however, remains unchanged provided the company is in a tax paying position or if there is perfect loss offset. Taxation thus does not reduce the rentability of the investment, but is instrumental in scaling down the project for each individual company. This reduces net present value after tax and thus the materiality of the project. The partial commercialisation of the SDFI (sale of equity shares from the state to privately run companies) could, in consequence, help bring about a substantial improvement in materiality for the companies on the Norwegian Continental Shelf, provided that the sale is done on a larger scale. A change in the licensing policies, involving larger equity shares for the privately run companies in new licences, has also improved the materiality conditions on the Norwegian Shelf.

There is reason to distinguish between localisation decisions faced by the company *before* and *after* they have built up a substantial organisation, infrastructure and specific competence in a certain producing nation. A company that has been present in a country for a long time has acquired substantial local competence that may not have the same value in a different country (specific investments). The company then has a number of irreversible investments that are immobile. The materiality consideration will therefore be different before and after a substantial activity has been established. This works in favour of established producing nations. This argument however, should not be overvalued since mobility can still be high provided that there is a second-hand market for oil leases and infrastructure. Also, there might be substantial area-dependent annual (avoidable) fixed costs associated with being established in a country.

Interesting to note, for governments, is that companies differ in their materiality requirements, with large companies typically having a higher demand for financial volume in projects than smaller companies. Thus, governments may be able to keep a larger share of the resource rent if they attract smaller petroleum companies. This is a policy currently pursued by Norwegian authorities. However, large and small companies differ in their financial strength and technical competence, and the authorities may have to trade off price (demand for financial volume) against quality (e.g. resource extraction rate). With a system of high marginal tax rates the state also carries a large share of new entrants' learning costs. We may expect to see a division of labour between larger and smaller companies, with the former developing larger reservoirs at deep water, whereas the latter focus on smaller, stand-alone reservoirs and tail extraction.

Conclusion

Petroleum extraction companies are facing stricter participation constraints due to three developments in the petroleum industry: 1) mergers and acquisitions have drastically reduced the number of integrated oil companies, 2) large discoveries in emerging extraction countries, and opening up of extraction countries that were previously closed for transnational oil companies, have increased the outside options, and 3) the oil companies are to a larger extent pursuing focusing strategies with emphasis on materiality conditions (financial volume).

The implications of these trends are that, more than previously, licensing and tax conditions need to be curtailed to the prospectivity in each extraction country or geological area. In particular, countries moving towards more marginal fields must improve overall framework conditions by increasing equity shares to participants in new licences, by selling state equity shares, and by reducing average tax rates. On the NCS we have seen an improvement in framework conditions, in particular with respect to equity shares and state ownership. At the same time discovery rates have improved.

References

Boadway, R. and N. Bruce (1992), 'Problems with Integrating Corporate and Personal Income Taxes in an Open Economy', *Journal of Public Economics* 48 (1), 39-66.

Devereux, M.P. and H. Freeman (1995), 'The Impact of Tax on Foreign Direct Investment: Empirical Evidence and the Implications for Tax Integration Schemes', *International Tax and Public Finance* 2, 85-106.

Dixit, A.K. and R.S. Pindyck (1994), *Investment under Uncertainty*, Princeton University Press.

Emhjellen, M. (1999), 'Valuation of Oil-Projects Using the Discounted Cashflow Method', *Doctor of Philosophy Thesis at the University of New South Wales*, March 1999.

Emhjellen, K. and P. Osmundsen (2001), 'Separate Cash Flow Evaluations – Applications to Investment Decisions and Tax Design', mimeo, Stavanger University College.

Gresik, T.A. (2001), 'The Taxing Task of Taxing Transnationals', *Journal of Economic Literature*, 39, 800-838.

Haaparanta, P. (1996), 'Competition for Foreign Direct Investments', *Journal of Public Economics* 63, 141-153.

Laffont, J.-J., and J. Tirole (1993), *A Theory of Incentives in Procurement and Regulation*, The MIT Press, Cambridge, Massachusetts.

Laughton, D. (1998a), 'The Management of Flexibility in the Upstream Petroleum Industry', *The Energy Journal*, 19, 83-114.

Laughton, D. (1998b), 'The Potential for Use of Modern Asset Pricing Methods for Upstream Petroleum Project Evaluation: Concluding Remarks', *The Energy Journal*, 19, 149-153.

Laughton, D. and H. Jacoby (1993), 'Reversion, Timing Options, and Long-Term Decision Making', *Financial Management*, . 22, 225-240.

NOU 2000: 18, *Skattlegging av petroleumsvirksomhet (Taxation of the Petroleum Industry)*, Report by the Petroleum Tax Commission, delivered to the Norwegian Ministry of Finance, 20 June 2000.

Olsen, T. and P. Osmundsen (2003), 'Spillovers and International Competition for Investments', *Journal of International Economics* 59, 211-238.

Olsen, T. and P. Osmundsen (2001), 'Strategic Tax Competition: Implications of National Ownership', *Journal of Public Economics,* 81(2), 253-277.

Olsen, T. and P. Osmundsen (1998), 'Strategic Tax Competition with Outside Options', *Discussion Paper 2/99,* Norwegian School of Economics and Business Administration.

Osmundsen, P. (1995), 'Taxation of Petroleum Companies Possessing Private Information', *Resource & Energy Economics*, 17, 357-377.

Osmundsen, P. (1999a), 'Risk Sharing and Incentives in Norwegian Petroleum Extraction', *Energy Policy* 27, 549-555.

Osmundsen, P. (1999b), 'Effektivitet, Insentiver og Proveny' (Efficiency, Incentives and Revenue), Report for the Norwegian Ministry of Oil and Energy, scientific attachment to the annual government report on the Norwegian oil industry, Oljemeldingen, St.meld. nr. 39 (1999-2000), 9. June 2000.

Osmundsen, P. (1998), 'Dynamic Taxation of Nonrenewable Natural Resources under Asymmetric Information about Reserves', *Canadian Journal of Economics*, 31, 4, 933-951.

Osmundsen, P., K.P. Hagen, and G. Schjelderup (1998), 'Internationally Mobile Firms and Tax Policy', *Journal of International Economics* 45, 1, 97-113.

Osmundsen, P., K. Emhjellen and M. Halleraker (2001), 'Transnational Energy Companies' Investment Allocation Decisions', Conference Proceedings, 24th IAEE International Conference. 25-27 April, 2001.

Salanié, B. (1998), *The Economics of Contracts. A Primer*, The MIT Press, Cambridge, Massachusetts.

Siew, Wei-Hun (2001), 'The Investment Appraisal Techniques Used to Assess Risk in the Oil Industry', *Conference Proceedings*, 24th IAEE International Conference. 25-27 April, 2001.

Zodrow, G.R. and P. Mieszkowski (1986), 'Pigou, Tiebout, Property Taxation, and the Underprovision of Local Public Goods', *Journal of Urban Economics* 19, 356-370.

Chapter 3

Critical Factors in Transnational Oil Companies' Localisation Decisions – Clusters and Portfolio Optimisation

Hans Jarle Kind, Petter Osmundsen and Ragnar Tveterås

Introduction

As the Norwegian Continental Shelf is approaching a status as a mature oil province, the issue of continued presence of transnational oil companies is becoming more pressing. There are several factors that make the presence of these companies attractive. Because of their resources and experience, transnational companies can develop and operate petroleum fields efficiently, and thereby generate a large tax revenue base for the government. In addition, they have created highly paid jobs, and are large customers for domestic offshore suppliers, both in Norway and abroad. Through their purchase experiences in Norway, transnational companies act as international door-openers, either as direct customers or reference customers in other oil provinces. Furthermore, it may be beneficial to have a large number of competent oil companies operating in Norway to ensure competition and supply of capital and new technologies. One should add that the Norwegian oil companies Norsk Hydro and Statoil have become transnational, and a significant share of their investments are allocated to other countries.

It is important to understand the factors explaining transnational oil companies' localisation decisions in order to be able to ensure the presence of both large oil companies and smaller companies specialising in marginal fields and tail production. To shed some light on this issue we will exploit two theoretical approaches – the theory of industrial clusters and materiality theories. These two approaches both represent potentially fruitful explanatory models for localisation decisions.

The literature on industrial clusters discusses the possibility of *positive externalities*, or *agglomeration economies*, which give rise to geographical clustering of related production activities. The size of the externalities is typically *a function of the size* of the industry, and the externalities lead to competitive advantages, e.g. cost reductions, which are not obtained outside the geographical cluster. Agglomeration economies in the Norwegian petroleum sector may lead to reduced costs in exploration, development and production, and thereby increase the attractiveness of the Norwegian Continental Shelf for transnational companies as long as these economies are still present. A petroleum cluster may include oil companies, offshore suppliers, parts of the maritime sector, consultancy firms, research institutions and universities.

The concept of materiality is linked to selection of investment projects when the firm has a given investment budget and has limited organisational and human capital resources, such as management and highly specialised expertise (e.g. geologists and engineers). Materiality implies that projects must be of a certain minimum size in order to be interesting investment objects for transnational companies. This is supported by statements from large oil companies suggesting that they will reduce their activity in Norway if the after-tax values of new projects, or ownership shares in these, become too small.

The Importance of Agglomeration Forces for Investment and Localisation Decisions

The dimension of the Norwegian petroleum sector, and its ability to attract high-competent foreign firms, has been closely connected to the allotment of licences and platform constructions on the Norwegian Continental Shelf. However, this linkage has become less strong as Norwegian petroleum companies and suppliers have increased the scale of their foreign activities and developed specialized knowledge that is demanded by multinational petroleum firms.[1] This development has been caused partly by substantial reductions in the technical costs of trading petroleum services, and a less protectionist attitude in most countries. As the Norwegian Continental Shelf matures, it thus becomes increasingly important to analyze the consequences of both inward and outward investments connected to the Norwegian petroleum sector (broadly defined).

It seems to be particularly central to take the extent of trade liberalisation in services and the strength of the alleged agglomeration forces in the petroleum sector into account when discussing the investment and localisation decisions of multinational petroleum companies. In the following we shall focus on how these factors may affect:

1. the competitiveness of the Norwegian Continental Shelf in particular, and the prospects for profitable development of petroleum fields in general;
2. the ability of Norwegian petroleum companies and their suppliers to compete in other petroleum regions.

Major technological innovations, and development of a large variety of specialised intermediate goods, are required in order to make it profitable to invest in marginal petroleum fields on the Norwegian Continental Shelf. Additionally, the sizes of the

---

[1] See Osmundsen (1999a, 1999b, 1999c) for a more detailed discussion on contractual and organisational arrangements related to exploitation of petroleum fields on the Continental Shelf.

stages in the value chain (e.g. R&D and engineering) must be above some critical level. One reason for this is that R&D is a stochastic process where the probability of success tends to be increasing in the number of research centres, the degree of interaction between different research centres, and the interaction between research centres and end-users (downstream and upstream firms in the petroleum sector). Since the Norwegian Continental Shelf is relatively exceptional with respect to weather conditions, water depth, and structure of the reservoirs, among other things, the use of knowledge capital from other petroleum regions is only possible to a limited extent. The knowledge that is created within the Norwegian petroleum sector, on the other hand, may prove to be an important competitive factor in future developments of complex and technologically demanding petroleum fields in, for instance, Azerbaijan, Kazakhstan, Brazil and West Africa (Dalen et al, 1999).

It is interesting to analyze the petroleum sector in relation to knowledge externalities. Indeed, there are several reasons why the extent of interaction between agents – and therefore the potential for knowledge externalities – may be expected to be larger within the petroleum sector than within most other sectors. First, a number of remedial actions have been undertaken with respect to organisation and communication in order to reduce transaction costs between different petroleum agents. Second, geographical co-localisation is widespread in the petroleum sector. Third, there are some aspects of the division of labour within this sector that indicate a tight integration between petroleum companies and their suppliers. For instance, even though the firms have changed to turnkey deliveries, the petroleum companies still have sizeable staffs of engineers that work closely with the suppliers. In some circumstances this cooperation is even formalised as common project organisations. It should further be noted that parallel working processes, time-critical supply chains and mutually dependent R&D call for tight coordination between the different agents (petroleum companies, turnkey suppliers, and sub-contractors). These characteristics of the petroleum sector indicate complex organisational relationships that allow for major changes during the development and manufacturing process. Accordingly, there are substantial management and coordination challenges.[2]

Below, we shall first discuss why investment decisions in industries where agglomeration forces exist may be fundamentally different from those in traditional industries, and why there may be a coordination problem between different investors. We shall then go on to show how the agglomeration forces may influence the choice of localisation for multinational petroleum companies, and in particular discuss possible consequences of trade liberalisation in petroleum-related services. Finally some policy related issues will be discussed.

---

2 This is in contrast to some kinds of conventional shipbuilding, for instance, which is characterised by large physical distance between customer and suppliers, low R&D intensity, sequential working processes, and few changes during the production process.

Coordinated Investment Decisions

Traditional economic theory predicts that a given industrial sector is less profitable, the larger the number of active firms, other things being equal. If we observe that firms in a particular sector typically have a return on invested capital below average, we thus have an indication that there is an over-establishment of firms. In a situation like this, we should certainly not expect to observe new entries. On the contrary, we should expect firms to exit the market until there are so few competitors left that the remaining firms achieve the same profitability as those in other sectors. But suppose that there are agglomeration forces in the sector that we consider. In this case the story above may almost be reversed: if a sector is unprofitable, the reason may actually be that there are too *few* active firms. Up to a critical point, increased entry may therefore be a premise for a sufficiently high profitability.

In order to understand why the existence of agglomeration forces may imply that we have a 'reversed' relationship between the number of firms and sector profitability, it is useful to imagine that we have only one factor of production that is mobile between the sectors – labour – and two possible industries: the petroleum sector and the 'traditional' sector.[3] Assume further that there are agglomeration forces only in the petroleum sector, while we follow neoclassical theory and assume that there are decreasing returns to scale for labour in the traditional sector. The latter implies that the wage ability of the traditional sector is higher the lower the level of employment in the sector. This is illustrated by the curve labelled T in Figure 3.1, where we measure wages on the vertical axis, and employment in the traditional sector from the right to the left. Employment in the petroleum sector is accordingly measured from the left to the right, and the wage ability of this sector is illustrated by the curve labelled P. This curve is upward-sloping, reflecting the fact that the higher the employment in this sector, the higher the wage level it is able to pay. This is in sharp contrast to neoclassical theory, and the explanation for this, as will be discussed below, is the presence of agglomeration forces.[4]

Before we enter into a more detailed discussion of what Figure 3.1 really tells us, and the implications for investment decisions, it is useful to look at some of the characteristics of the petroleum sector. According to Nordås and Kvaløy (1999) the petroleum sector is among the most R&D intensive sectors in Norwegian manufacturing, with very high expenditures on research and development per worker in some of the segments. A large share of these costs can be ascribed to external purchases of highly specialised intermediate goods (typically in the form of services); the share of external purchases for the petroleum sector is as high as 43 per cent, compared to an average of 20 per cent for all industries exclusive of petroleum. Nordås and Kvaløy (op cit) and Nordås (2000) further argue that these intermediates are complementary, in the sense that the higher the agglomeration of

---

3 This labour force is not meant to include the complete labour force of the country. It is presumably most relevant to consider technologically highly skilled labour, which is used intensively by the petroleum sector.

4 See Matsuyama (1991, 1995) for a formal analysis.

specialised intermediate goods, the higher the productivity of each single good. Thereby the market value for any given intermediate good, and thus the sustainable wage level, is increasing in the number of other specialised intermediates that are already produced. Making the reasonable assumption that there is a positive relationship between employment in the petroleum sector and the agglomeration of intermediate goods producers, we consequently end up with the upward-sloping curve P in Figure 3.1.

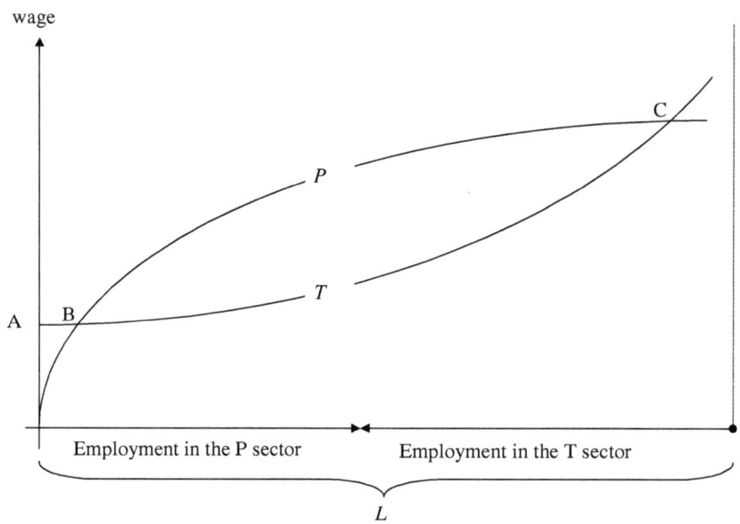

Figure 3.1 Agglomeration forces in the petroleum sector

In order to find possible equilibrium allocations of labour in Figure 3.1, and thereby the size and wage ability of the petroleum sector, we assume that labour is employed in the sector that pays the highest wages. We further assume that each intermediate good in the petroleum sector is produced under increasing returns to scale, due to significant investments in R&D.[5]

As a point of departure, suppose that the economy is initially at point A. Here the whole labour force is employed in the traditional sector, and therefore wages are relatively low (due to the fact that there are decreasing returns to labour). Nonetheless, the wage level in the traditional sector is higher than in the petroleum

[5] Note that we are actually considering economies of scale at two different levels. First, each single firm produces under increasing returns to scale due to large investments in R&D. Average costs are thus falling if production increases. Second, the complementarity implies that there are economies of scale at a sector-wide level, since the productivity increases when the number of differentiated intermediate goods increases.

sector; despite the low wage level it is not profitable for this sector to employ workers and develop specialised intermediate goods. However, the Figure shows that at point B – where the wage level is higher than at A – the petroleum sector is actually able to pay the same wage level as the traditional sector. There are two things that are worth noting here. First, the traditional sector employs a smaller share of the labour force than at point A, and therefore has higher wage ability. Further, the size of the petroleum sector is so *large* in B that this sector is also able to pay relatively high wages. More precisely, the supply of specialised intermediate goods is so large in B that the productivity of this sector is high enough to be able to compete against the traditional sector for labour. Second, it should be noted that B is a so-called unstable equilibrium: if the employment in the petroleum sector is a bit larger, it will have a wage ability that is higher than the traditional sector. If point B is passed, the agglomeration forces therefore imply that there are highly profitable petroleum investment opportunities. In this case the petroleum sector will continue to grow endogenously until the economy reaches point C, where the wage ability in the traditional sector once more is equally high as in the petroleum sector. In practice this implies that the positive agglomeration forces are exhausted, and that further investments in the petroleum sector are unprofitable. We thus have two stable equilibria in Figure 3.1. The economy will either be at point A, where the petroleum sector is not operative, or at point C, where a relatively large share of the labour force is employed in the petroleum sector. The wage level, and presumably also national welfare, is highest in the latter equilibrium.

The above analysis is, of course, highly stylised, but it underscores that the existence of agglomeration forces may turn out to be a double-edged sword. On the one hand, the agglomeration forces may imply that the profitability of investing is very high if the activity level is sufficiently large, but on the other hand it may be unprofitable to invest unless a sufficiently large number of other firms also invest. Consequently, there may exist a coordination problem between firms that are capable of making intermediate goods. This problem seems to be particularly relevant for the petroleum sector, not least since a high share of the intermediates is bought externally rather than produced internally in each firm. In other industries, where there is a smaller need for specialised intermediates, each single firm may be able to produce the intermediates on their own if the goods do not exist on the market. In the latter case there will be no coordination problem.

The need for a coordinated entry may help explain why some republics of the former Soviet Union and other inadequately developed countries have problems in exploiting potentially rich oil fields. Besides obvious political risks and lack of experience with market economies, it is a fact that domestic entrepreneurs are short both of financial and human capital and that they are poorly coordinated. On this background the countries are interested in attracting foreign petroleum companies. However, the petroleum sector is so intensive in knowledge, and requires such large varieties of intermediate goods and specialised services, that it is typically not profitable for just one or a few multinational petroleum companies to operate on their own. The governments therefore need a policy that induces a coordinated entry of foreign firms, a task that becomes particularly difficult when political and juridical institutions are weak and unpredictable.

How Trade in Services may Affect the Choice of Localisation

Consider two countries that are initially symmetric, and assume that they have large as well as small (marginal) petroleum fields that potentially may be set into production. Should we expect that the network of sub-contractors will be of the same size in the two countries, or should we expect to observe a relative concentration into one of the countries (which then goes on to export services and other inputs to the other country)?

The answer to this question is in many ways given if the countries have restrictive requirements on local content in deliveries to the domestic petroleum sector: the two countries will remain symmetric, and have the same size of their petroleum related activities. However, due to WTO agreements and other international accords, most countries have become less protectionist in recent years,[6] at the same time as technological progress has made trade in intermediate goods (not least services) profitable to a larger extent than was previously the case.[7] However, for most intermediates the level of international trade costs will still be significant. And it is precisely the fact that transaction costs are higher between than within petroleum agglomerations which implies that increased trade may have large consequences for the localisation choices of petroleum companies. Actually, it may happen that one of the two intrinsically symmetric countries is only able to profitably invest in the largest petroleum fields, while the other country may find it profitable to invest in even relatively marginal petroleum fields. The point of departure for the discussion that follows is a theoretical field of economics labelled New Economic Geography, which was developed by Paul Krugman and Anthony Venables in the early 1990s.[8]

In what follows we have to distinguish between upstream and downstream activities. Downstream firms purchase specialised intermediate goods from a number of different suppliers. As discussed above, investments in, for example, R&D and the need for complementary inputs imply that there are economies of scale internally for each firm as well as externally. We further assume that there are transaction costs related to trade in upstream goods, and that many of the petroleum fields have only a marginal profitability. This means that we have demand and cost linkages, which possibly implies that trade in intermediate goods will have dramatic consequences.

In Figure 3.2 trade costs (transaction costs) are measured on the horizontal axis, while the *share* of the total petroleum related activity that takes place in country 1 is measured on the vertical axis. If trade costs on intermediate goods are very high, the two countries will to a large extent be self-sufficient and have

---

6 In the case of Norway, this is reflected in the fact that the new Petroleum Law of 1996, in contrast to the Petroleum Law of 1985, does not explicitly require that Norwegian suppliers must be chosen if they are ‘competitive’.

7 See also Nordås and Kvaløy (1999) for a discussion on the relationship between technological changes and liberalisation of trade in petroleum related services.

8 Our discussion will be informal; see Venables (1996) and Fujita, Krugman and Venables (1999) for formal analyses.

exactly 50 per cent each of the total petroleum related activity in the two countries.[9] The solid line to the right of t_{high} in Figure 3.2 illustrates this situation. There may be some trade in intermediates between the countries, but net export will be equal to zero. In short, there will be a unique symmetric equilibrium when trade costs are high.

Since the countries are assumed to be intrinsically identical, the symmetric equilibrium will certainly always exist. However, as trade costs are reduced it becomes more profitable to export and less important to serve each market locally. Therefore the symmetric equilibrium may become unstable when trade costs are sufficiently low, and one of the countries may end up with a much larger petroleum sector than the other. To see the intuition for this, assume that country 1 for some exogenous reason is able to attract a few more upstream firms than country 2. This tends to make country 1 a net exporter of petroleum related services, and to reduce the cost level for downstream producers in country 1. Thereby it may be profitable to invest in more marginal petroleum fields in country 1 than in country 2 (given that trade costs are positive). Since the upstream firms produce under increasing returns to scale (decreasing average costs), such that the size of the market matters, the subsequent increased demand in country 1 possibly makes it even more profitable to invest in this country. Thereby we may end up in a situation where self-reinforcing agglomeration forces lead to a flourishing of the petroleum sector in country 1, with investments taking place in increasingly more marginal petroleum fields and domestic production of a larger and larger set of specialised intermediate goods.[10] In Figure 3.2 we have illustrated this by assuming that country 1 ends up with 70 per cent of the total petroleum related activities when $t < t_{high}$.[11] Note also that we have drawn a solid curve that indicates that country 1 has only 30 per cent of the activity. The reason for this is that we assumed that the countries are intrinsically symmetric, such that it is more or less accidental which of the countries ends up with the largest activity in the petroleum sector. We will comment further on this below, when discussing the importance of the public policy towards the petroleum sector.

---

9 Requirement on local content – as was prevalent in the previous Norwegian Petroleum Law – implies de facto that trade costs for certain intermediates are infinitely high.

10 Note that we are here considering the same kind of mechanisms as in Figure 3.1.

11 In principle it is possible that the countries end up with the same structure again if trade costs become sufficiently low. The reason is that if it is approximately costless to trade intermediates internationally, then geographical location is relatively unimportant. However, when transaction costs of the petroleum sector are taken into consideration, this possibility seems to have a larger theoretical than practical interest.

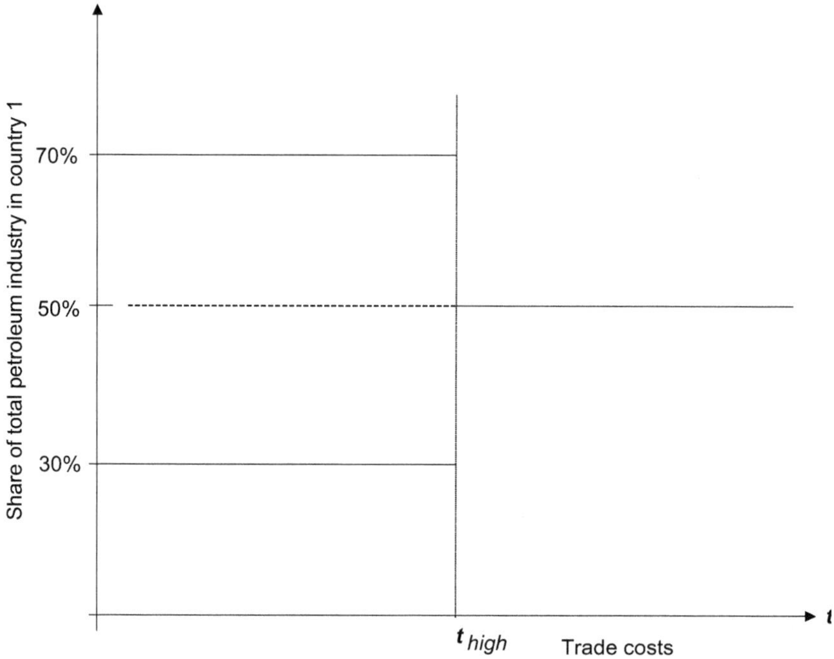

Figure 3.2 Consequences of increased international trade in intermediate goods

Public Policy

The political milieu has become increasingly concerned over the importance of developing and maintaining industrial agglomeration through an attractive public policy, not least within sectors such as petroleum, shipping and ICT-related industries. The discussion above makes it clear that it is important to focus on policy issues in such industries. Tax policy, for instance, may be decisive for whether it is country 1 or country 2 that ends up with the largest petroleum agglomeration in Figure 3.2. However, the sensitivity towards the tax policy should not be exaggerated. Actually, if a self-reinforcing petroleum agglomeration is established, the tax policy may turn out to be relatively unimportant. The reason is that the agglomeration forces create a kind of pure rent for the firm (in addition to the petroleum rent), such that the advantages of being located in an agglomeration are larger than the disadvantages of relatively high taxes. It is further important to stress that the maximum tax rates can indeed be higher if the transaction costs outside the agglomeration are reduced. The intuition for this result, which may seem a bit surprising, is that with lower international transaction costs it becomes less beneficial for other countries to set low taxes in order to attract the agglomeration. This is a fact that the government in a country that hosts an agglomeration can utilise by increasing the tax rate. Thereby it is possible that

Norway, for instance, will be able to impose high taxes on the petroleum sector even if international trade costs on petroleum services fall (see Kind, Knarvik and Schjelderup, 1998 and 2000, for a more detailed discussion). However, as shown by Venables (1997), a tax rate that is only slightly too high may imply that the whole agglomeration breaks down. This indicates that it is better to be on the safe side by setting a relatively low tax rate, due to the negative welfare effects of losing an industrial agglomeration.[12]

Concentration versus dispersion The possibility of a self-reinforcing petroleum agglomeration has normative implications for the public policy towards localisation. Since many of the positive linkages between petroleum firms are related to geographical proximity, it is important that the policy in general, and the regulation policy in particular, aims at a certain geographical concentration of the petroleum sector. Since agglomeration effects are based on externalities, it follows that each single petroleum firm will not internalise all effects of their choice of localisation. It is therefore possible (though not necessarily true) that a stronger geographical concentration than the petroleum companies tend to prefer is socially optimal. What we have seen in Norway, however, is that the government, due to an active regional policy, has instead followed a policy of spreading the petroleum sector more than what would be the market outcome. This is perhaps one reason why the Norwegian petroleum sector seems to have weaker linkages than the British petroleum sector (see Reve and Jakobsen, 2001).

A smoother investment trend The Norwegian petroleum sector is characterised by large fluctuations in the activity level. This has implied that the cost budgets have been significantly overstepped during booms, as discussed by Osmundsen (1999c). The reason is that when the firms are beyond their natural capacity limits they will have to hire workers (often with insufficient skill levels) at high wage rates, they will have to use less qualified sub-contractors, and the administrative management becomes too thin and spread over too many activities. When the activity level is low, on the other hand, we observe that high-competent labour migrates to other industries. The stock of human capital specific to the petroleum sector erodes, and it is difficult to find enough skilled labour when the activity level increases again. Large fluctuation in the activity level thus reduces the possibility of building up a strong and knowledge intensive petroleum agglomeration.

There are certain factors beyond the control of the petroleum firms that govern the fluctuation of the activity level on the Norwegian Shelf, such as the government's allotment of investment licences across time. The government should try to reduce rather than increase these fluctuations (parallel investments in several large gas fields are one explanation for the investment boom in 1998).

[12] The research literature on agglomeration uses the term 'catastrophic scenario' to describe cases where a small increase in the tax rate implies that the agglomeration dissolves and the pure rent disappears. Note that we shall never have such catastrophic scenarios in 'traditional' industries, where a marginal increase in the tax rate has only a marginal influence on the activity level.

However, one should be careful in implementing new criteria in allocation mechanisms that are primarily meant to serve other needs. There are many examples of public interventions in the economy that are intended to reduce the cycles, but that have actually increased the fluctuations because the interventions have been implemented too late. Fine-tuning of the petroleum activity level, as for the economy in general, is unlikely to be successful.

Materiality

To secure the presence of large transnational oil companies on the Norwegian Continental Shelf, as well as to promote entry of smaller companies specialised in developing marginal fields and to undertake tail-end production, it is vital to understand factors that determine the transnational companies' allocation of activity among countries. In discretionary licensing decisions, it is not sufficient for authorities only to ascertain the companies' competence. They must also take into consideration the after-tax remuneration each individual company requires to operate in the country. To the extent that the best companies are also the ones with the highest requirements, there may be a trade-off between competence on the one hand and remuneration on the other hand. This is of particular interest for marginal fields, where the materiality potential may be insufficient for large companies at the general fiscal conditions.

Materiality is a concept which is linked to selection of investment projects when the company has a given investment budget and limited resources in the form of management and employees with specialised competence. Materiality – also referred to as financial volume or critical mass – implies that projects need to be above a certain size (in terms of after-tax net present value) in order for them to be interesting to multinational oil companies. A small project can be unattractive even if it is able to show a high expected return (internal rate of return).

Materiality requirements – requirements for minimum level of after-tax net present value – can be justified on the basis of different academic disciplines. Corporate strategy, accounting, corporate finance, management and investment analysis can all provide arguments for there to be a certain critical mass in connection with investment decisions. The petroleum companies' increasing materiality requirement is closely connected with their focusing strategies. They concentrate scarce resources on fewer activities, focus on those areas where they have comparative advantages. In return, they demand larger contributions after tax, measured in absolute value, from each of these selected activities. Thus, a positive net present value is, in connection with such allocation strategies, only an entrance ticket to transnational companies' ranking of projects on a global basis. It is a necessary yet not sufficient condition for realisation. The materiality requirements may also be looked upon from a finance and management theory setting. There is an increasing recognition that corporations incur certain amount of costs that for different reasons are not included in the expected project cash flow. One way to make allowances for these extra costs generated by a project is to demand a certain minimum size for the present value of projects.[13] One may envisage far more sophisticated methods by which to rectify this problem, but simple, implementable management systems are often the preferred solution by companies.

Materiality requirements may also follow directly from traditional economic decision analysis, if one recognises the fact that the real decision problem is non-linear and non-divisible, with a number of scarce factors and fixed costs. This is shown in Osmundsen, Emhjellen and Halleraker (2001); a portfolio analysis employing data from actual petroleum projects on the Norwegian Continental Shelf.

Materiality is particularly important in the petroleum industry, an industry dominated by a few profitable players. Through their international mobility and access to private information,[14] these companies succeed in capturing part of the resource rent generated from scarce petroleum resources. The taxation never reaches 100 per cent, the companies keep a mobility rent and an information rent; see Osmundsen, Hagen and Schjelderup (1998). This is also valid for industries that exploit non-mobile natural resources, since the input factors and the companies are mobile.[15] Large discoveries in new basins, opening of established, producing countries for transnational petroleum companies, and a reduction in the number of players through mergers and acquisitions, have increased competition between different producing countries to attract the most competent companies.[16] This is likely to make the fiscal terms more important, particularly in countries where the remaining acreage over time must be expected to yield economically marginal fields, i.e. where the resource rent experiences a decreasing trend.

However, there are factors that are balancing this picture. Mergers among the largest oil companies might open up for new entrants, which may increase the relative bargaining power of governments in a bargaining game between governments and companies over the resource rent. Seen from the perspective of governments, it may be optimal to reduce entry barriers. Moreover, countries where large new discoveries are made are likely to impose high taxes to capture a large fraction of the rent. Several of these countries are also associated with political risk. The obvious threat to the oil companies is the imposition of higher taxes than expected after large irreversible investments have been sunk. In the last year, reports have been made on a tougher regulatory regime in Angola, and tax increases have been announced in the Caspi area.

13 See for instance Zimmerman (1979).

14 See Osmundsen (1995, 1998).

15 The companies do not need to move all of the operations physically. The transnational oil companies' international activity is to a considerable extent managed from the head office.

16 For a description of international tax and fiscal competition, see Zodrow and Mieszkowski (1986), Gresik (2001), and Olsen and Osmundsen (2001).

Non-linear Optimisation

Materiality is not modelled in elementary investment analysis or in existing taxation theory. These models consider capital to be the primary scarce factor, in which case the internal rate of return becomes the relevant decision-making criteria. In conventional examples based on internal rate of return, however, a number of simplifying and unrealistic assumptions are made. One assumes that other scarce factors are fully reflected in prices, one assumes full divisibility of projects and that all relevant costs are included in the calculation. In reality, there is often a small number of larger projects, and many scarce factors and bottlenecks. One such relevant scarce factor is qualified experienced professionals. For example, only a few individuals possess the necessary qualifications and experience to manage complex development projects in the North Sea. Furthermore, competent geologists and geophysicists are scarce. Usually, managerial capacity is also a scarce factor. The companies will, in consequence, look at what values (present value after tax) the companies can retain, compared to the input of professional resources and managerial capacity which could, alternatively, have been invested in projects in countries where the companies are allowed to retain a larger portion of the value created. The various projects also have to bear all area-dependent fixed costs and make contributions to the payment of overhead costs at the corporate level. An analytical approach to this decision problem will be to use portfolio analysis to arrive at the portfolio of projects with greatest combined present value for the company, with consideration to fixed costs and resource and capital constraints. For practical reasons however, one often uses simpler decision-making tools. One important reason is that recommendations and often decisions are made, not at the corporate level, but at a divisional level where not all constraints and costs are known. A practical way of paying consideration to scarce factors and area-dependent costs is therefore for the head office to demand a minimum size for a project's net present value after tax. Even though portfolio models are not necessarily used explicitly to deduce the optimal investment portfolio, such considerations may – via materiality requirements – be underpinning the choice of what core geographical areas the companies wish to invest in and how large equity shares the companies wish to go for. Simple capital allocation models, like a fixed investment budget and requirements of a certain financial volume, may act as a proxy or as an implementation mechanism for more advanced portfolio models.

Why, then, are these inputs scarce? If managers or professionals create values beyond the costs generated by them, one would think the companies would hire more staff until the last employee just barely satisfies his or her marginal cost. One reason why this is not automatically possible is that scarcity often does not concern professionals or managers as a group, but those that are highly qualified. It is argued that companies typically have a limited number of professionals and managers that are crucial to success and others that are important in completing the task to be undertaken. Due to asymmetric information – the fact that the individual employee knows more about his or her own skills than potential employers – it may be difficult to provide such new staff as and when required. Most likely one has to overstaff in order to be reasonably sure to capture some of the best individuals. Given a relatively rigid labour market, this is an expensive strategy, which is why the companies prefer to keep their organisation slim. Due to fluctuating levels of activity and costs of restructuring, one is reluctant to build up capacity that will subsequently have to be down-scaled.

Not only present value per scarce factor is important when companies decide where to invest. Besides the obvious elements such as prospectivity, level of cost, tax burden and acreage availability, the costs associated with being present in a region or country may be substantial and therefore the minimum profitable activity must be of a certain volume. Furthermore, most companies learn that a simple structure with management focus on a few matters is important. Areas which as such are commercial, but which do not generate much value after tax (make small contributions to payment of overhead costs) can thus be rejected so as to allow management and professional employees to focus on those areas where values are generated for the company. Reference is often made to materiality considerations, and there is reason to take these seriously. Norwegian branches or subsidiaries of transnational companies are arguing that projects of a small scale in a corporate context, often represented by expected present value after tax being low, have difficulties in attracting attention – and thus investment funds – from the head office. This line of reasoning has also gained a foothold in Norwegian companies, in parallel with their growing international activity. Note that even though the total project may be large, materiality can nonetheless be limited viewed from the perspective of a large international corporation if the company holds a low equity share.

Factors Determining the Materiality of a Project

Materiality can be analysed at two main levels: 1) project level, and 2) basin level. Both issues are argued to be relevant. For example, as far as the project level on the Norwegian Continental Shelf is concerned, there is a development towards smaller fields. In an international context, though, these fields will still be considered large. New Norwegian fields are, on average, several times the size of fields on the UK Continental Shelf. Recently, there has been a marked shift to positive exploration results, also including large discoveries.

The fact that in a mature area there will gradually be vacant capacity within processing and pipeline transportation, as established fields are phased out, may make it highly profitable to develop satellite fields. This presupposes that one is able to keep down the costs of operation and maintenance on old production facilities. However, in some new potential discovery areas, one is facing problems with long distances from existing infrastructure. Tightened cost control in development projects will also be of importance for the profitability of new field developments.

Improved Fiscal Conditions

Other factors influencing materiality, both at project and basin level, are the scope and prospect of exploration acreage, the tax system and the distribution of equity shares in the licences. A high marginal tax causes lower portions of the total cash flow to be retained by the companies. A similar reduction in cash flow is caused by the fact that companies most often hold a limited equity share in the licence. Other companies' equity shares and the Norwegian state share via the State's Direct Financial Interest (SDFI) reduce the share of the net cash flow (and the investments) to each individual company. This reduces the size of NPV to each company. The internal rate of return, however, remains unchanged provided the company is in a tax paying position. Thus taxation does not reduce the profitability of the investment, but is instrumental in scaling down the project for each individual company. This reduces net present value after tax and thus the materiality of the project. The present commercialisation of the SDFI (sale of equity shares from the state to privately run companies) could potentially – if escalated – help bring about a substantial improvement in materiality for the companies on the Norwegian Continental Shelf. A change in the licensing policies, involving larger equity shares for the privately run companies, has also improved the materiality conditions on the Shelf.

There is reason to distinguish between localisation decisions faced by the company *before* and *after* they have built up a substantial organisation, infrastructure and specific competence in a certain producing nation. A company that has been present in a country for a long time and has acquired substantial local competence may find that these factors may not have the same value in a different country. The company then has a number of irreversible investments that are immobile. The materiality consideration will therefore be different before and after a substantial activity has been established. This works in the favour of established producing nations. This argument however, should not be overvalued since mobility can still be high to the extent that there is a second-hand market for oil leases and infrastructure. Also, there might be substantial area-dependent annual (avoidable) fixed costs associated with being established in a country.

Entry

Interesting to note, for governments, is that companies differ in their materiality requirements, with large companies typically having a higher demand for financial volume in projects than smaller companies. Thus, governments may be able to keep a larger share of the resource rent if they attract smaller petroleum companies. This is a policy currently pursued by Norwegian authorities. However, large and small companies differ in their financial strength and technical competence, and the authorities would have to trade off price (demand for financial volume) against quality (e.g. resource extraction rate).[17] We may expect to see a division of labour between larger and smaller companies, with the former developing larger reservoirs at deep water, whereas the latter focus on smaller, stand-alone reservoirs and tail extraction.

The Behavioural Hypotheses of Tax Theory

Economic tax theory typically presumes that a company will realise any project with a positive net present value (materiality is irrelevant). If the capital is scarce, the company will allocate its investments where the profitability (internal rate of return) is highest. According to these behavioural assumptions,[18] the fact that the company's cash flow is scaled down should have no negative impact on the investment decision. However, somewhat more sophisticated portfolio investment theory does not prescribe the use of internal rate of return as decision-making criterion, but rather the use of portfolio models to arrive at the portfolio of projects with the largest accumulated present value to the company (with consideration paid to resource and capital constraints). This theory is also more in line with company practice.[19] Several scarce factors, fixed costs and divisibility problems may favour projects with good materiality. In order to secure the participation of competent companies one must – in situations of reduced expected basin profitability – give the companies higher equity shares and gradually lower average tax for new fields. This is simply to state that the tax and licensing conditions must be curtailed to the present level of resource rents generated.

Summary and Conclusions

Norway has succeeded in building a petroleum cluster, which includes oil companies, an offshore supply industry, parts of the maritime sector, consultancy firms, research institutions and universities. The degree of interaction between agents in the value chain, and consequently the potential for knowledge externalities, is larger in the petroleum industry than in many other industries.

The ability to develop marginal petroleum fields will to a large extent depend on the presence of a significant offshore supply industry. Large fluctuations in activity levels reduce the possibilities for maintaining a petroleum cluster, and thereby reduce the economic attractiveness of the Norwegian Continental Shelf. Through improved liquidity management in the companies, it is possible to reduce

[17] One should not forget that a particular feature of the Norwegian tax code with a high marginal tax is that the learning costs of new entrants to a large extent will be borne by the state.

[18] This neutrality property is only valid if we can ignore the probability that the company, for instance due to low oil prices, falls out of tax position, or if the tax system has perfect loss offset. These conditions are not satisfied in practice.

[19] Simplified approaches – like NPV per unit of scarce factor – is used in some companies to rank investment opportunities.

the importance of short term liquidity considerations in investment decisions, and long term investment programmes can be sustained.

Materiality considerations, leading to geographic concentrations of activities, are relevant for oil companies' localisation decisions due to limited management resources and other highly specialised expertise. The companies will choose regions with significant materiality. This may even be confined to regions within a country. Mergers and acquisitions have improved the materiality for companies operating in Norway. Changes in the Norwegian government's licensing policies and the partial sale of state equity shares in licences, leading to larger ownership shares for the oil companies, have also contributed in a positive direction.

References

Dalen, D.M., E. Jakobsen, E.R. Moen, T. Reve and C. Riis (1999), 'Perspektiver på norsk oljeindustri som næringsklynge' (In Norwegian: 'Perspectives on the Norwegian Oil Industry as a Cluster'), mimeo, Handelshøyskolen BI.

Fujita, M., P. R. Krugman and A. J. Venables (1999), *The Spatial Economy*, MIT-Press.

Gresik, T. A. (2001), 'The Taxing Task of Taxing Transnationals', *Journal of Economic Literature* 39, 800-838.

Kind, H.J., K.H.M. Knarvik and G. Schjelderup (1998), 'Industrial Agglomeration and Capital Taxation', NHH Discussion Paper 7/98.

Kind, H.J., K.H.M. Knarvik, and G. Schjelderup, (2000), 'Competing for Capital in a Lumpy World', *Journal of Public Economics*, 78 (3), 253-274.

Matsuyama, K. (1991), 'Increasing Returns, Industrialization, and Indeterminacy of Equilibrium', *Quarterly Journal of Economics* 106(2); 617-50.

Matsuyama, K. (1995), 'Complementarities and Cumulative Processes', *Economic Literature* 33(2), 701-729.

Nesheim, T. 1998, 'Outsourcing og bedriftens effektive grenser' (In Norwegian: 'Outsourcing and the Effective Boundaries of the Firm') *Praktisk Økonomi og Ledelse*, 1, pp. 77-86.

Nordås, H. K. and O. Kvaløy (1999), 'Oljerelaterte produsenttjenester' (In Norwegian: 'Oil Related Producer Services', mimeo.

Nordås, H. K. (2000), 'Liberalization of Trade in Services and Choice of Technology in the Norwegian Petroleum Sector', CMI working paper 2000:1.

Norman, V. (1996), 'Teori om næringsklynger' (In Norwegian: 'A Theory of Industrial Clusters', Appendix 3 in NOU 1996:17, *I Norge - for tiden?*

Olsen, T. and P. Osmundsen (2001), 'Strategic Tax Competition: Implications of National Ownership', *Journal of Public Economic*, 81(2), 253-277.

Osmundsen, P. (1995), 'Taxation of Petroleum Companies Possessing Private Information', *Resource & Energy Economics*, 17, 357-377.

Osmundsen, P. (1996), 'Dynamisk Petroleumsbeskatning og Bindingsproblemer' (In Norwegian: 'Dynamic Petroleum Taxations and Holdup Problems'), *Norsk Økonomisk Tidsskrift* 110, 35-53.

Osmundsen, P. (1998), 'Dynamic Taxation of Nonrenewable Natural Resources under Asymmetric Information about Reserves', *Canadian Journal of Economics*, 31, 4, 933-951.

Osmundsen, P. (1999a), 'Norsok og kostnadsoverskridelser sett ut i fra økonomisk kontrakts- og insentivteori' (In Norwegian: 'Norsok and Cost Overruns from the

Perspective of Contract- and Incentive Theory), Scientific Attachement to 'Analyse av investeringsutviklingen på kontinentalsokkelen', NOU 1999: 11, commissioned by the Ministry of Petroleum and Energy, 28. August 1998.

Osmundsen, P. (1999b), 'Risikodeling og anbudsstrategier ved utbyggingsprosjekter i Nordsjøen; en spillteoretisk og insentivteoretisk tilnærming' (In Norwegian: 'Risk Sharing and Bidding Strategies in the North Sea: A Game Theoretical and Incentive Theoretical Approach'), *Praktisk Økonomi & Finans* 1, 94-103.

Osmundsen, P. (1999c), 'Kostnadsoverskridelser på sokkelen; noen betraktninger ut i fra kontrakts- og insentivteori' (In Norwegian: 'Cost Overruns on the Norwegian Shelf; some Reflections Based on Contract- and Incentive Theory'), *Beta, Tidsskrift for Bedriftsøkonomi,* 1, 13-28.

Osmundsen, P., K. Emhjellen and M. Halleraker (2001), 'Transnational Energy Companies' Investment Allocation Decisions', Working Paper 92/2001. Conference Proceedings, Annual Conference for International Association of Energy Economics (IAEE), Houston, 25-27 april 2001.

Osmundsen, P., K.P. Hagen and G. Schjelderup (1998), 'Internationally Mobile Firms and Tax Policy', *Journal of International Economics* 45, 1, 97-113.

Reve, T., and E.W. Jakobsen (2001), *Et verdiskapende* Norge, Universitetsforlaget.

Venables, A. J. (1996). 'Equilibrium Locations of Vertically Linked Industries', *International Economic Review*, 37, 341-359.

Venables, A. J. (1997), 'Economic Policy and the Manufacturing Base: Hysteresis in Location', mimeo, London School of Economics.

Zimmerman, J. (1979), 'The Cost and Benefits of Cost Allocations', *The Accounting Review*, July, 504-521.

Zodrow, G.R. and P. Mieszkowski (1986), 'Pigou, Tiebout, Property Taxation, and the Underprovision of Local Public Goods', *Journal of Urban Economics* 19, 356-370.

Chapter 4

The Taxing Task of Taxing Transnationals[1]

Thomas A. Gresik

Godel and Miller's Tax Proposition: No finite and feasible system of business taxation can collect positive revenues. (Stephen Ross, *Journal of Economic Perspectives*, 1988)

Introduction

Transnational corporations thrive for many reasons. Oft-stated reasons include proximity to customers and resources through vertical integration and operational economies of scale (e.g. in administration, R&D, and/or production activities).[2] The economic advantage often conferred by these attributes is also attractive to many national and state governments. Transnational or foreign direct investment (FDI) not only creates direct economic benefits such as jobs and taxable income but significant indirect benefits such as knowledge spillovers. However, the ability of individual governments to reap the benefits of transnational investment is compromised by a third characteristic of transnationals: the flexibility to shift production and resources across national boundaries. This flexibility not only helps transnationals minimize the cost of taxes and regulations imposed by individual governments; it can also aid them in pitting one government against another. Ultimately, the beneficiaries of such strategies are likely to be the transnationals and not the local jurisdictions. How these institutional and strategic factors limit the benefits governments earn from attracting FDI is the theme of this paper.

The focus of this survey is on the role of corporate income tax laws and investment policies in influencing the nature and composition of FDI and on their strategic role as tax competition instruments. I take as given the existence of transnational companies and focus only on corporate income tax competition, as opposed to commodity tax competition. This focus away from the issues of transnational formation and commodity tax competition should not be construed to

---

[1] The permission to include this chapter, which was first published in the *Journal of Economic Literature* (39) no.3, 800-839, is gratefully acknowledged.

[2] See G. Peter Wilson (1993) for examples from field studies.

imply that they are less important. Instead, I prefer to see this paper as complementing existing surveys of these literatures.[3]

One benefit of focusing on corporate income tax policy is that it helps identify three dimensions of transnational investment and taxation that challenge the ability of governments to raise tax revenues and extract rents: financial and real investment flexibility, tax competition, and informational advantage. The first exists because of characteristics common to many commercial tax codes that encourage transnationals to manipulate production and financial flows to reduce tax liabilities. Tax competition pressures not only help explain why such characteristics persist, they also introduce additional strategic effects that influence the level of investment and the ability of governments to collect transnational tax revenues. A natural response to these first two sources of transnational power would be to consider cooperative agreements between countries. I will argue that informational asymmetries between governments and transnationals and across governments add a third layer of strategic effects that further impedes efforts by governments to benefit from transnational activity. In the extreme, the combined impact of these three dimensions suggests what one might consider a corollary to Godel and Miller's Tax Proposition: Governments cannot accurately measure transnational profits they plan on taxing.

In practice, many countries seem to have responded to these economic pressures by formulating very complex tax codes. In section 2, I offer a taxonomy that reduces some of this complexity by organizing observed commercial tax and investment policies associated with FDI, both within and across countries, into four basic categories: deferral rules, double taxation rules, apportionment rules, and trade policies. This taxonomy is applied in section 3 to show how the corporate tax codes themselves often endow transnationals with the ability to structure investment flows in ways that not only reduce taxes but increase a government's informational disadvantage. It is here that I also summarize some of the empirical research on the impact of various policies on FDI.[4]

One seemingly simple response that circumvents the three dimensions of transnational advantage is to have no corporate income taxes. In section 4, I show that one rationale for corporate income taxes arises when there exists asymmetric information, either between foreign and domestic investors or between transnationals and their governments. This suggests that corporate taxes are an imperfect solution to the information problem. I return to a more detailed

[3] James Markusen (1995) discusses the various economic environments in which transnational investment can arise. The impact of endogenous transnational formation on strategic trade theory is also developed in Markusen and Anthony Venables (1998). For a broader review of tax competition issues, including commodity tax competition, see the recent survey by John Wilson (1999).

[4] Most of the empirical studies I will summarize utilize data on U.S. based transnationals. Rather than reflecting a national bias, it instead reflects a bias in the availability of individual tax data for research studies. James Hines, Jr. (1999), which provides a more comprehensive survey of transnational responses to international tax provisions, offers a similar caveat. The Hines survey, however, does not address tax competition or informational concerns.

discussion of the impact of asymmetric information in section 7. The introduction itself of corporate income taxes in an open economy also raises new economic tradeoffs and these economic tradeoffs ultimately impact the design of tax policies. These tradeoffs are introduced and discussed in section 5.

The issue of tax competition is taken up in section 6. One thing section 6 will try to make evident is the significant difference between the complexity of commercial policies reflected in sections 2 and 3 and those that are incorporated in tax competition models. Filling this gap, I argue, is an important research direction that in some cases will require new theoretical tools. Section 7 outlines some of the outstanding theoretical issues involved in understanding the role of asymmetric information in open economy models with transnational investment. Consistent with the need to include tax competition effects as expressed in section 6, particular attention is paid to the development of common agency (multiple principal) models. Section 8 offers some brief, forward-looking comments.

Common Features of Corporate Tax and Investment Policies

In practice, countries vary considerably in how they interact with transnational enterprises. Since a transnational will look at the aggregate effect of a country's policies on its investment, seemingly innocuous details can often affect how well a country competes for and benefits from FDI. However, with regard to trade and tax policies intended to stimulate or moderate aggregate levels of inbound and outbound FDI and/or to generate revenues from these flows, there appears to be a fair amount of policy convergence. Some of this convergence is due to cooperative efforts such as OECD conventions or the GATT, some has been a response to financial structuring strategies adopted by transnationals, and some has been the result of changes in U.S. policy that other countries have felt compelled to mimic. It is upon these most prevalent components of tax and commercial policies that I focus.

One can think of the major components of national corporate income tax/commercial policies in terms of four important categories: deferral of taxes on foreign-source income, double taxation rules, expense apportionment rules, and trade policies. All four categories influence the financial and economic structure of FDI as well as the ongoing decisions of established transnationals. At the simplest level, transnational investment creates two sources of income: domestic-source income or income attributed to investments made in the home country of the transnational's parent corporation and foreign-source income or income attributed to investments made outside the parent's home country. The first two categories determine when and how a transnational's home country taxes the transnational's foreign-source income. The last two categories relate to the definition of domestic-source and foreign-source income for the purpose of calculating home tax liabilities. Together these four categories span the critical dimensions along which transnationals can structure transactions to enhance the marginal benefit of advantageous regulations (e.g. deferral, revenue sourcing rules) and to mitigate the impact of costly regulations (e.g, taxes, environmental restrictions). Table 4.1

summarizes how some of these policies vary across several developed countries. The terms used in the table will be explained as each category is discussed.

Table 4.1 Transnational income tax policies

Country	Double taxation: Dividend income	Distribution of parent costs	Parent interest deductions	Domestic R&D subsidies	Foreign sales corporations
Australia	Exemption	Allocation	Tracing	Deduction	No
Canada	Exemption	Tracing	Share	Credit	No
France	Exemption	Allocation	Share	MIC	No
Germany	Exemption	-	Share	-	No
Italy	Credit	Tracing	Share	-	No
Japan	Credit	Allocation	Tracing	MIC	No
Netherlands	Exemption	Tracing	Tracing	Deduction	No
Norway	Credit	Allocation	Allocation	-	No
Sweden	Exemption	-	Share	-	No
UK	Credit	-	-	-	No
US	Credit	Allocation	Allocation	MIC	Yes

Notes: Most countries have separate double tax rules for different classes of foreign income. Since transnationals can usually structure intrafirm transactions to earn the most favorable tax treatment, the tax treatment pertaining to dividend income is listed. Information about parent interest deductions comes from Brian Arnold (1994). Information on cost distribution rules and R&D subsidies comes from Price Waterhouse (1995) and Coopers and Lybrand (1998). MIC denotes 'marginal investment credit.' Blank cells denote the lack of an explicit policy.

Deferral[5]

Many countries tax their residents, including resident corporations, based on worldwide income. For residents with foreign-source income, the calculation of foreign-source income depends on the specific corporate structure of the foreign sources. While branch income is generally taxed when earned by the branch, deferral allows income from subsidiaries classified as controlled foreign corporations (CFCs) to be taxed only when it is remitted to the resident corporation.[6] One rationale for home countries to allow deferral is the idea of

---

5 I treat the issue of deferral/accrual as distinct, although obviously not independent, from the issue of double taxation. Until recently the economic and strategic impact of deferral has received relatively less attention than double tax rules. Presumably this is due to the fact that one can study double taxation issues in static models while deferral policies require dynamic analysis. Two recent efforts to focus on the dynamic aspects of deferral are Rosanne Altshuler and Harry Grubert (1996) and Alfons Weichenrieder (1996a).

6 A number of countries have exceptions to this repatriation rule for earnings from passive investments, e.g. U.S. Subpart F regulations.

capital import neutrality. Without deferral, a country's foreign investments would be placed at a competitive disadvantage to host investors who face only one set of tax rates. Minimum equity rules are used to distinguish active foreign investment from portfolio investment. For instance, for tax purposes the United States considers a foreign corporation to be controlled by U.S. citizens if U.S. citizens individually controlling at least 10 per cent of the foreign firm together own at least 50 per cent.

The main advantage of deferral to transnationals is the ability to avoid paying home taxes on foreign earnings that are reinvested in the foreign operations. This same feature is often criticized because it creates an incentive for transnationals to park foreign earnings abroad. Hines and R. Glenn Hubbard (1990) lend credibility to this concern with their study of income repatriation patterns based on 1984 returns which found that 84 per cent of all U.S. controlled foreign corporations paid no dividends to their U.S. parents. This figure corresponds to 62 per cent of all parent corporations in their sample.

Double Taxation Rules

Dividend payments from a CFC represent repatriated earnings on which the CFC has already paid taxes to its host country. In countries that allow deferral, it is at this point that a home tax liability is created. Double taxation rules specify the extent to which the home country provides some relief from double taxation; the most common methods either exempt foreign-source income from home taxation or provide a tax credit for the host taxes.[7] All of the countries represented in Table 4.1 use one of these two rules.[8] In fact, current OECD and UN treaty conventions, rather than advocating a specific method, only proscribe the use of deductions. A possible rationale for such conventions will be discussed in section 6. For now, the important feature of credit and exemption rules to note is that their proper application requires the parent to divide its income into foreign-source and domestic-source as only the former is eligible for double tax relief.

---

7 In practice, the actual calculation of home taxes due on foreign source income is complicated by variations in how CFC earnings are taxed by host countries. These include the use of split-rate systems that tax distributed and undistributed earnings at different rates or imputation systems that provide relief to domestic investors from paying both corporate and individual income taxes on the same dividend. Altshuler and T. Scott Newlon (1993) derive marginal tax prices for dividends that include these variations.

8 China, Columbia, the Czech Republic, Egypt, Lebanon, and Peru are among the few countries that use deductions as their main method of double tax relief. Angola, Bolivia, Congo, Libya, Myanmar, Nigeria, Uruguay, and Venezuela offer no relief from double taxation.

Expense Apportionment Rules

During the oil crisis of the late 1970s and early 1980s, U.S. airlines adopted the strategy of topping off a plane's fuel tank in cities with low fuel prices and unloading this same excess fuel in cities with high fuel costs. Because of substantial variations in fuel prices across the United States, this strategy provided some relief from historically high fuel costs. In an analogous fashion, double taxation rules can create an incentive for one subsidiary to bear expenses on behalf of another subsidiary or its parent because doing so converts domestic-source income into foreign-source or vice versa.

For countries that exempt foreign income, like Australia, each dollar of cost borne by the parent reduces its global tax liability by its marginal home tax rate. For tax credit countries like Japan, the savings depends on whether the home tax rate is larger or smaller than the host rate. In the first instance, such cost shifting has no effect on home tax liabilities. In the second instance, the parent has excess credits because it can generally claim a tax credit only up to the value of (pre-credit) home taxes due on its foreign income.[9] With excess credits, the effective marginal home tax rate on foreign income is zero, making the tax savings the same as under an exemption system. Two approaches for distributing parent expenses to calculate domestic-source and foreign-source income are 'tracing' and 'allocation.' The first attempts to trace the actual source of the costs so that only those costs that are directly linked to foreign operations are labeled foreign-source. The second gets around the cumbersome and complicated tracking of expenses by employing a formula based on various financial ratios. The way tracing and allocation methods work will be made clearer in the next section. Column three of Table 4.1 reports the preferred method for general costs. In addition, these rules may be supplemented with special provisions for costs associated with parent debt and R&D expenses. The range of special rules is reported in columns four and five and will also be discussed in the next section.

Trade Policies

In addition to opportunities to classify costs for tax purposes, special rules that create export zones or foreign sales corporations provide transnationals with some flexibility in how they structure or classify their revenues. In general, a parent corporation's domestic income from foreign operations can take the form of either exports or royalties.[10] To the extent that countries offer rules that give firms discretion in classifying income sources, they involve allowing firms to classify some domestic-source income as foreign-source. For firms with excess credits, shifting domestic-source income to foreign-source income allows them to use their excess credits and lower their net tax payments.

---

9 Some countries have provisions for applying any excess tax credits on earlier or future tax returns.

10 A third source, service income, does usually not qualify for special treatment under standard sourcing rules.

Financial and Real Investment Flexibility in an Open Economy

Deferral and the distinction between domestic-source and foreign-source income necessitated by the use of exemption or credit methods create opportunities for both income-shifting and production-shifting. Some details of the common rules used to combat such tax induced behavior and related empirical evidence are presented in this section.

Interest Allocation Rules

One type of expense allocation rule specifies how a parent must allocate domestic interest expenses to calculate its domestic and foreign income. Suppose a transnational headquartered in an exemption country decides to borrow funds to finance a foreign subsidiary. If the subsidiary borrows on its own behalf, its interest expenses reduce its host profits and hence also the parent's eventual foreign income. Since foreign income is not taxed by its home country, this borrowing has no effect on the transnational's home taxes. However, if the parent borrows the funds, the interest expense reduces the parent's net domestic income and its home taxes. In effect, the lower home taxes indirectly subsidize the transnational's foreign investment. To prevent this type of subsidization, some exemption countries – Australia, Luxembourg, and the Netherlands – deny all parent interest deductions for which one can trace or find a paper trail to foreign investments. Other exemption countries allow such interest deductions if the funds are used for purchasing shares in the subsidiary. Examples of such countries are denoted by the term 'share' in column four of Table 4.1. A similar situation exists when the parent is located in a credit country and it has excess credits. Among credit countries, Japan denies a deduction for debt traced to foreign investments. Norway and the United States require parent corporations to allocate domestic interest expenses between domestic-source and foreign-source income based on asset and sales ratios. For example, if 25 per cent of a Norwegian transnational's assets are titled in Norway, then only 25 per cent of interest expenses incurred by the parent can be expensed against the parent's domestic income. The other 75 per cent must be expensed against the parent's foreign-source income.

Since subsidiaries are typically financed with a combination of debt and equity (as well as retained earnings for mature subsidiaries), changes in either deductibility policies or allocation rules can influence both the composition of subsidiary financing as well as the marginal cost of FDI. Empirical evidence of these effects related to changes in the allocation rules in the Tax Reform Act of 1986 (TRA) has been found by Julie Collins and Douglas Shackelford (1992), Altshuler and Jack Mintz (1995), and Kenneth Froot and Hines (1995).

In his seminal work on the composition of subsidiary financing, Thomas Horst (1977) reported that by 1974 U.S. manufacturing firms had made roughly \$21 billion in foreign investments of which only \$2.7 billion involved new equity and U.S. debt. The remaining \$18.3 billion consisted of foreign debt (debt acquired by the subsidiary in its host country) and retained earnings. More recently Martin Feldstein (1995) reports that, according to the 1989 Benchmark Survey of U.S.

Investment Abroad, investment in non-bank CFCs of non-bank U.S. firms totaled $1,237 billion. Of this amount, U.S. equity amounted to $203 billion; U.S. debt, $47 billion; non-U.S. equity, $92 billion; non-U.S. debt, $567 billion; and retained earnings, $328 billion. Not only do foreign debt and retained earnings still account for a significant percentage of subsidiary financing but these 1989 figures also indicate that foreign debt, by itself, is an important source of investment funds.

Prior to 1986, U.S. rules required interest expenses to be allocated on an individual company basis based on the ratio of domestic to foreign assets. Since 1986, interest expense allocations have been determined on a consolidated basis. Froot and Hines (1995) explain that, without this change, a U.S. parent corporation could set up a U.S. subsidiary that controlled all the transnational's foreign assets. By doing all the borrowing for the transnational and paying the borrowed funds to the subsidiary as equity, the parent could deduct all of its interest expenses against domestic-source income. With the TRA and subsequent revisions, domestic interest expenses must now be allocated between domestic- and foreign-source income based on the ratio of domestic assets to foreign assets less foreign borrowing. Using 1986 and 1991 data, Froot and Hines (1995) show that not only did these rules increase the marginal cost of domestic debt financed investment for parents in excess credit positions, they also increased the relative return to domestic investment. Collins and Shackelford (1992) document a shift toward the use of preferred stock to finance subsidiaries.

The Horst and Feldstein data suggest a third effect – a decrease in the marginal cost of foreign debt. As one increases the proportion of foreign debt financing for a given level of FDI, the ratio of foreign assets less foreign borrowing to domestic assets falls and a U.S. parent can expense more of its domestic interest expenses against domestic-source income. Unfortunately, data on the distribution of transnational debt is difficult to come by. Using a special data base describing the financial structure of a small number of large transnationals compiled by Price Waterhouse, Altshuler and Mintz (1995) find some support for a shift towards foreign debt from 1986 to 1991. First, for each 1 per cent increase in the allocation of domestic interest expenses to foreign-source income, the ratio of foreign debt to worldwide debt increased by 1.7 per cent. Second, the post-1986 rules increased the effective tax rate on outbound U.S. FDI to Canada, Japan, and the United Kingdom from 7 per cent to 10 per cent while only increasing the effective tax rate on U.S. investment by 5 per cent.

R&D Expense Allocation Rules

A second type of expense for which cost shifting tax strategies can arise is R&D. Many countries offer some form of tax incentive to encourage R&D investments. The rationale is that R&D investment not only generates specific benefits to the investor but also generates spillover benefits to the economy at large. Because the spillovers do not accrue to individual investors, the aggregate level of R&D will be below the socially optimal level unless some type of Pigouvian subsidy is offered. Generally the subsidies take the form of a tax credit (e.g. France, Japan, and the United States offer tax credits for marginal increases in R&D spending) or an enhanced deduction for expenses (e.g. Australia allows a deduction for 125 per cent of R&D expenses). The specific policies for the countries covered in Table 4.1 are reported in column five. Of course, to the extent that some of the domestically undertaken R&D is targeted for application in another country, such subsidies end up promoting increased investment for which some of the spillover benefits accrue to foreigners. The stochastic link between R&D spending and actual product or production improvements makes tracing difficult and leaves countries with only one active option – allocation formulas.

To the best of my knowledge, the United States is the only country that explicitly imposes allocation rules on R&D spending in an attempt to limit the subsidization of R&D to R&D with domestic applications. For economists the use of apportionment rules is interesting because, as with the interest allocation rules discussed above, the R&D apportionment rules only affect the marginal tax rate on R&D activity for firms in excess credit. Thus, changes in the apportionment formula creates natural experiments for assessing the tax sensitivity of R&D investment. According to Hines (1993), the U.S. tax rules on R&D expense apportionment changed frequently in the 1980s, in part because of unanticipated responses by transnationals gaming the rules. In 1977 when the first apportionment rule was codified, firms were required to allocate a portion of their domestic R&D expenses against foreign-source income. In 1981, ostensibly out of concern for declining R&D investment in the United States relative to that in other countries, Congress introduced a 25 per cent tax credit for domestic R&D expenses based upon moving three-year averages and allowed for 100 per cent apportionment against domestic source income.[11,12] The TRA required partial allocations again, but under more generous rules than in 1977, and reduced the value of the tax credits. Since 1986, the apportionment formulas have been modified numerous times – mainly due to unintended responses to the rules. Current rules require U.S. transnationals to allocate 50 per cent of R&D expenses against domestic-source income with the remainder either allocated against foreign-source income or apportioned between both income sources based on relative sales or asset levels.

The response of U.S. transnationals to the changes in tax credit provisions and apportionment rules during the 1980s is documented in several papers by Hines. Hines (1993) reports an after-tax price elasticity of 1.2 to 1.6 for R&D expenses. Hines (1994b) reports that the TRA changes had little effect on the location of R&D abroad relative to in the United States in part because of unfavorable tax treatment for foreign R&D expenses. As a result, most R&D used by subsidiaries of U. S. firms is performed in the United States and licensed to the subsidiary. In 1989, subsidiaries of U.S. transnationals received only $54 million in royalty payments from their U.S. parents while making $9.8 billion in royalty payments to U.S. parents. Finally, Hines (1995) examines the role of withholding

---

[11] It should be noted that, at about the same time, the Carter administration pushed through patent law reforms that reversed an almost thirty-year deterioration in patent protection in U.S. courts.

[12] The use of moving average formulas creates incentives for transnationals to time R&D investment to take advantage of tax benefits.

taxes on technology transfer since higher withholding taxes raise the cost of imported technologies. A withholding tax is a tax paid to a host country when a subsidiary makes a dividend or royalty payment to its parent. It is intended to capture the income taxes that would have been paid had the dividend or royalty been received by a host citizen. He estimates an elasticity of royalty payments to the withholding rate of -0.4. This reduction in royalty payments occurs because the higher withholding tax both discourages the use of imported technologies and it reduces incentives for engaging in pre-tax profit shifting via the royalty rate.

Transfer Pricing

When one subsidiary transfers an asset or provides a service to another subsidiary of the same transnational, the separate legal identities of the subsidiaries require that a value be placed on the transfer. If a well-functioning market for the intermediate good exists, the appropriate value to place on the transfer is rather easy for tax authorities to determine. However, with transnationals the transferred assets are specialized enough that comparable products produced by firms not related to the transnational do not exist or they are intangible in nature, e.g. technical knowledge. Such features mean that accurate economic information on the asset's value will be difficult to find and that the transnational may have considerable discretion in setting its transfer price. When the transfer takes place between subsidiaries in different tax jurisdictions charging different marginal tax rates, one important objective the transnational may pursue is tax minimization. As with the last two examples, transfer pricing strategies create both real and financial effects.

Since the seminal work by Lawrence Copithorne (1971) and Horst (1971), considerable time and effort has been invested, by both researchers and governments, studying this potential for transnationals to use transfer prices to shift the apparent location of profits. The evidence of tax-induced transfer price behavior is not uniform across industries. Studies of Colombian affiliates of U.S. transnationals by W. Erwin Diewert (1985) and Lorraine Eden (1985) suggest markups ranging from 25 per cent in the chemical industry to 155 per cent in the pharmaceutical industry. Grubert and John Mutti (1991) also offer evidence of strategic transfer pricing using industry level data. Among their results they show that transfer prices are affected by tax differentials as well as other aspects of the commercial policies the transnational faces, such as tariffs. However, Jean-Thomas Bernard and Robert Weiner (1990) do not find evidence of transfer pricing by U.S. transnationals in the petroleum industry despite the absence of spot markets for crude oil and significant industry concentration during the time period covered by their data (1973-1984). K. Hung Chan and Lynne Chow's (1997) study of transfer pricing regulation in the PRC also finds little evidence of tax-induced transfer pricing, although they do find evidence of transfer price manipulations due to foreign exchange control and devaluation risk.

More recently, research using firm-level data by Grubert, Timothy Goodspeed, and Deborah Swenson (1993) and David Harris, Randall Morck, Joel Slemrod, and Bernard Yeung (1993) report evidence consistent with tax-induced transfer pricing behavior. For example, Harris et al. find that U.S. transnationals with subsidiaries in low-tax countries have lower U.S. tax liabilities (i.e. low net domestic-source income associated with foreign operations) per dollar of assets or sales than those with subsidiaries in high tax countries. This general result can be consistent with several explanations besides tax-induced transfer pricing, including higher-tax countries provide better investment opportunities for U.S. transnationals (their evidence suggests that this is only true for Japan); deferral (the economics of benefitting from deferral suggest the opposite of the observed pattern); debt-shifting (the levels of debt placement appear to be too small to explain differences in tax liabilities for the largest transnationals); and transitory macroeconomic conditions (again the evidence suggests that this may only be true of Japan). Overall their evidence suggests that while transnationals do not set up foreign operations to benefit from transfer pricing opportunities, neither do they ignore these opportunities when they exist. It appears that the bulk of the transfer pricing distortions are generated by the largest U.S. transnationals. Harris et al. estimate that these transnationals end up reducing their U.S. tax liabilities from foreign operations by 52 per cent. Finally, Grubert and Slemrod (1998) report that income shifting appears to be the primary reason for U.S. investment in Puerto Rico. Because of special rules related to the tax treatment of income from U.S. possessions, income earned in Puerto Rico is effectively exempt from U.S. taxes.

From the perspective of national or state governments, the economic impact of tax-motivated transfer pricing goes beyond lost tax revenues. It can also result in economic distortions in production decisions.[13] How obvious these distortions are depends on the type of transfer price regulation adopted. Currently the norm is to adopt procedures for identifying transfer price abuses that explicitly disregard the potentially significant distortions in production and investment they might create. Harris (1993) offers one indication that such distortions exist. He finds strong evidence of both income shifting and investment shifting behavior by U.S. transnationals in response to the TRA.

The issue of transfer pricing also arises between states or provinces and the method for addressing transfer price concerns can be very different. In the United States, most states use apportionment formulas to allocate a firm's profits for the purpose of calculating state taxes. The most common apportionment formulas use a weighted average of relative amounts of sales, payroll, and property attributable to a firm's operations within each state. As one might expect, such rules distort a firm's production and pricing decisions. The precise general equilibrium distortions are derived by Gordon and John Wilson (1986). Empirically, the location and level of inbound FDI is quite sensitive to variations in such rules. In his study of the distribution of inbound FDI for the United States, Hines (1996) estimates that a 1 per cent reduction in a state income tax rate could increase capital investment by 10 per cent. Thus, the issue of transfer pricing cannot be viewed solely as a distributional issue. The incentives tax differentials create also produce real investment effects.

---

[13] Enforcement costs can also exceed tax revenues, as Roger Gordon and Slemrod (1998) document in the case of U.S. taxes on capital income.

Reflecting the economic importance of transfer price regulations are several high profile government studies conducted over the last several decades, including UNCTAD (1978), OECD (1984), and U.S. Treasury (1988). The last two studies form the basis for revised transfer price rules (OECD, 1995, and U.S. Treasury, 1994). The impact of these rules (which are very similar) is due to the introduction of two ideas: a 'best methods' rule recognizing that the most reliable method for evaluating a company's transfer prices will vary from industry to industry as well as across companies and across product lines (prior to the 1994 rules a more rigid assignment of procedures was mandated) and 'advanced pricing agreements' (APAs) which give transnationals an opportunity to negotiate with the IRS over how best to calculate transfer prices before being audited.[14]

The 'best method' provisions legally obligate the transnational to prove its method best approximates an arm's-length price, i.e. the price at which two independent firms would carry out a similar transaction. Certainly in competitive markets such a price would reflect true economic value. However, for many transactions, the market is anything but perfectly competitive and the extent to which the environment in which the transfers occur is imperfect may bear on the assessment of the value of a transfer. Several examples illustrate some of the problems that accompany arm's-length standards.

In imperfectly competitive markets both the targeted or tested firm and the firms providing comparable data are all likely to have some market power. Robert Halperin and Bin Srinidhi (1996) show that, when the tested and comparable firms compete in an oligopoly, transfer price rules that use comparable data can distort market prices. Vibhas Madan (1998) and Guttorm Schjelderup and Weichenrieder (1999) also demonstrate that arm's-length transfer price rules can interact with a country's trade policies and result in perverse outcomes.

It may also be inappropriate to compare data from non-integrated firms to judge the appropriateness of transfer prices of integrated firms. One motivation for a transnational to form is that vertical integration eliminates incentives for opportunistic behavior when efficient production requires investment in relationship-specific investments. If a supplier needs to install highly specialized equipment to serve a customer, once the initial equipment investment is made the customer can seek to renegotiate prices in order to appropriate the rents from the specialized investment. Vertical integration eliminates the incentive for this type of behavior and as a result also helps the integrated firm realize operating efficiencies it otherwise would not. Thus, vertically integrated firms can be expected to have a different cost structure than non-integrated entities. Yet arm's-length regulations sometimes require an integrated firm to justify its transfer prices by comparison with non-integrated firms. Harris and Richard Sansing (1998) demonstrate that, as a result, arm's-length prices can distort the investment decisions (both levels and distributions) of both divisions in a transnational.

---

14 Many European countries remain reluctant to use APAs. Australia on the other hand has a treaty with the U.S. which allows for joint APAs.

Categorizing Income

Mutti and Grubert (1998) analyze the cost and benefits of a firm's selection of income sources. If a transnational chooses to produce its product at home and export it to the foreign market, foreign sales corporation rules, if available, would allow it to categorize some of its export income as foreign source. This would benefit the transnational if the parent has excess credits. However, the decision to export the product as opposed to producing it in the foreign country would subject the parent to tariff payments. Mutti and Grubert's calculations indicate that the benefits of the sourcing rules would outweigh the cost of the tariffs only if the firm's gross profit margins are high enough. Alternatively, the attractiveness of subsidiary production and the attendant royalty payments depends on the host country's withholding rate. For firms in excess credit, the benefits from royalty payments is most pronounced when royalties represent a significant proportion of foreign-source income and withholding rates are low. The first condition arises when intangible assets comprise a large proportion of asset transfers to the subsidiary. Thus, Mutti and Grubert suggest that export production is most attractive for high margin goods while affiliate production is most attractive when intangibles represent a large component of production. For low-margin goods with small intangible components, service income appears to be the best alternative.

Why Tax Corporate Income?

Given the numerous difficulties associated with designing corporate tax policy in an open economy, it is important to ask from a normative perspective: Should corporate income be taxed? In a large open economy, the use of corporate taxes to distort capital flows by influencing international rates of return on capital can create a beneficial 'terms of trade' effect. What about in a small open economy? Are there additional economic rationales beyond market power for taxing corporate income? For closed economies, the seminal work of Peter Diamond and James Mirrlees (1971) shows that combinations of income and commodity taxation are consistent with national welfare maximization and productive efficiency given either constant returns to scale or pure profit taxes. Since then the work of others (e.g. Alan Auerbach, 1979, and Kåre Hagen and Vesa Kanniainen, 1995) suggests that features common to international investment, such as heterogenous capital or international differences in intertemporal marginal rates of substitution, may require some efficiency-welfare compromises that modify our understanding of optimal tax policies. In fact, by extending Diamond and Mirrlees' analysis to the case of small open economies with mobile capital and immobile labor, Gordon (1986) presents a strong argument against corporate income taxation. Not only does a positive corporate income tax rate result in inefficient levels of capital investment, the economic burden of the tax ultimately falls on labor income. It would be more efficient to simply tax labor income directly.

An important role for corporate income taxes arises in A. Lars Bovenberg and Gordon (1996) where informational asymmetries between domestic and foreign investors about the value of domestic investments in a small capital-importing country creates a lemons effect which, on the margin, discourages inbound foreign investment. Bovenberg and Gordon show that a corporate income tax coupled with a net subsidy to foreign investors corrects this distortion and equalizes foreign and domestic equilibrium rates of return.

Gordon and Jeffrey MacKie-Mason (1995) offer a second, and in my opinion, more fundamental reason for corporate income taxation: corporate taxes help limit the extent to which managers might substitute between wage and non-wage forms of compensation or analogously the extent to which tax differentials between corporate and personal income distort career path decisions. The following simple model illustrates this effect. Consider a competitive economy with free entry in which output is produced with labor via a constant returns to scale technology. Employees can be compensated in two ways: with wage income taxed at the personal rate τ^* and with alternative compensation taxed at the corporate rate t^*. If a fraction s of the worker's compensation w is taxed at the corporate rate, then the after-tax wage is

(1) $$w_n = w[(1 - \tau^*)(1 - s) + (1 - t^*)s] .$$

To a firm, non-wage income is more costly than wage income. Denote this added cost by $b(s)$ where $b(0)=0$, $b'(\cdot) > 0$, and $b''(\cdot) > 0$. For a given share s, total wage costs are $c_w = w(1+b(s))$. Minimizing total wage costs associated with a given after-tax wage, w_n, requires the firm to substitute non-wage income for wage income as long as the higher cost of non-wage income can be offset by a sufficient reduction in the workers' total compensation. This substitution is possible only when an increase in s benefits workers through a lower marginal tax burden, i.e. when $\tau^* > t^*$. The optimal share of non-wage income satisfies

(2) $$b'(s) = (\tau^* - t^*)(1 + b(s))/(1 - \tau^* + s(\tau^* - t^*))$$

meaning employers will prefer to use non-wage income when the personal tax rate is higher than the corporate tax rate.

Because firms earn zero profit in equilibrium, total equilibrium tax revenues equal

(3) $$R = w[\tau^*(1 - s) + t^* s]$$

where the total supply of labor is normalized to 1. The individual's indirect utility from any tax regime (τ^*, t^*) is $V(w_n)$ and the government's objective is to set tax rates to maximize utility subject to $R \geq R^*$, where R^* is a tax revenue level. For a given value of w_n, the cost of the non-wage income, $b(s)$, represents a deadweight loss. Notice that by setting $t^* = \tau^*$ the government can induce the firm to lower s to 0 and raise w to $w_n/(1-\tau^*)$. These changes reduce the deadweight loss and relax the revenue constraint. So although the model is that of a closed economy, corporate taxation can be viewed as a tool for eliminating socially inefficient compensation.

In an open economy, this same need for a corporate income tax persists but now tax differentials between countries can compromise its effectiveness. For instance, suppose that the firms in this previously-closed economy are subsidiaries of corporations located in another country and that the subsidiary output is sold to the parent corporations which use it for final good production. As is common with transnational transactions, these intermediate inputs provided by the subsidiaries do not have close substitutes that freely trade. Yet, for tax purposes, the transnational must set an appropriate transfer price. If corporate profits are taxed at different rates in the two countries, a transnational can use its transfer price to shift income into the lower tax jurisdiction. For the higher-tax country, reducing its corporate rate to reduce the transfer price distortions reintroduces the compensation distortions.

To demonstrate how this tension between compensation-shifting and profit-shifting via transfer prices arises, consider a modified version of a model developed by Gordon and MacKie-Mason (1995).[15] There are two countries and many similar transnationals. The parent corporation of each transnational produces a final good at a price q. For simplicity, each unit of the final good requires one unit of an intermediate good, X, which is produced by a subsidiary in the host country with a constant returns to scale technology.[16] Labor is the only input so unit cost is c_w. The transfer price is p^*. The home country corporate rate, t, is less than the host country corporate rate, t^*. This gives the transnational an incentive to set the transfer price below c_w in order to shift profits out of the host country.

If the intermediate good was freely traded in a competitive market, the equilibrium price would be c_w. With no trade in X between independent parties, the host government cannot easily observe c_w and instead uses an imperfect auditing procedure to evaluate each transnational's transfer price. If auditing identifies underpricing, a tax penalty is imposed by the host government on the subsidiary. Denote the expected value of this additional per unit tax liability by the convex function $\Gamma(t^*, c_w - p^*)$ where $\Gamma(\cdot,0)=0$, $\Gamma(\cdot, c_w - p^*) > 0$ if $p^* < c_w$, $\Gamma_1(\cdot,\cdot) > 0$ if $p^* < c_w$, and $\Gamma_2(\cdot,\cdot) > 0$ if $t^* > 0$. Thus, the expected penalty is strictly positive only if the transnational's transfer price is less than its host wage cost. Increases in the host tax rate increase the expected penalty for any given transfer price while increases in the transfer price are consistent with both a higher probability that the audit uncovers a manipulated transfer price and a larger penalty. Together these assumptions imply that the transnational's global post-tax profit is

[15] In a related paper that presupposes the use of corporate taxes, Andrea Haufler and Schjelderup (2000) show that when small open countries choose both the size of the tax base (by specifying the deductibility of investment costs) and the tax rate, first-best policies call for full deductibility of investment costs while, in an open economy, transfer pricing effects necessitate a partial deductibility policy.

[16] This assumption results in multiple equilibria as the number of firms and X are indeterminate. However, all equilibria exhibit the same qualitative transfer pricing behavior.

(4) $$\pi_n = (1-t)(q - p^*)X + (1-t^*)(p^* - c_w)X - \Gamma(t, c_w - p^*)X$$

and the host country's tax revenue from each unit of X is

(5) $$w[\tau^*(1-s) + t^* s] - t^*(c_w - p^*).$$

For any given tax rates, t, t^*, and τ^*, each transnational chooses s, w, X and p^* to maximize (4) subject again to a given after-host-tax reservation wage. A firm's choice of s and w is separable from its choice of X and p^* as the latter two variables do not influence the firm's margins on the first two. Thus, (2) still defines the optimal value of s. If $t=t^*$, the first-order conditions imply $p^*=c_w$ and $q = c_w$. However, when $t^* > t$, the optimal transfer price implies $p^* < c_w$, and, because $\Gamma(\cdot,\cdot)$ is convex, zero profits imply

(6) $$q = c_w + [(t^* - t)(p^* - c_w) + \Gamma]/(1-t) < c_w.$$

Comparing (5) with (3) also shows that increasing the corporate rate, t^*, to equal the labor tax rate, τ^*, eliminates the deadweight loss from income-shifting but increases the welfare losses from profit-shifting. Thus, for fixed values of τ^* and t such that $\tau^* > t$, transfer pricing opportunities limit the effectiveness of a corporate tax in addressing income-shifting distortions and vice versa. While the general equilibrium implications of this rent-shifting are not well understood, a variety of partial equilibrium effects have been studied. I will return to a discussion of these in section 6. For the present discussion, it is hopefully clear that the ability of transnationals to shift resources across national borders places additional demands on a country's corporate tax structure.

Two Basic Problems of Transnational Taxation

Once one accepts the need for a corporate income tax in an open economy, two basic issues concerning the scope of a country's corporate tax policy arise. The first is, 'What corporate income should be taxed?' For citizens, the typical options are tax worldwide income or tax only domestic income. For foreign investors, the income they earn in a host country is generally subject to host taxation although in some optimal tax models host countries are assumed to have the discretion to exempt such income. The second issue is, 'Does the form of double taxation relief matter?' Both of these questions arise because operating in an open economy endows transnationals with financing and investment strategies that can help deflect the intended impact of national tax policies.[17] The answers to these two

[17] Gordon's important (1986) study of taxation in an open economy explicitly ignores issues arising from transnational corporate structures.

questions are not independent. Moreover, for the double taxation question, we will again see that the ability to use transfer prices for income shifting will be important.

A Basic Model of Transnational Taxes

Two frequently studied polar cases of transnational tax policies are the pure source and pure residence systems. Under the first system, a country taxes the returns to domestic investment regardless of the nationality of the investor. Under the second system, a country taxes the global income of its residents and does not tax the returns to domestic investment by foreign investors. A simplified version of a model due to Mintz and Henry Tulkens (1996) can be used to evaluate these and other hybrid systems.

Consider two economically small countries *A* and *B*. A representative individual (referred to as *a* and *b*) in each country makes an investment decision. Individual *a* is endowed with *K* units of capital which can be invested in either country and *L* units of immobile labor. Let κ equal the amount *a* invests in *B* so that K-κ is the amount *a* invests in *A*. Denote similar variables for *b* by use of an asterisk. Consistent with the tax competition models discussed in the next section as well as the early optimal taxation models of George MacDougall (1960) and Murray Kemp (1964), we only consider the possibility of one-way capital flows. Both capital and labor endowments are inelastically supplied, *A* is the capital-exporting or home country, and *B* is the capital-importing or host country. Thus, the total invested in country *A* is K-κ and the total invested in country *B* is $K^* + \kappa$. Output is defined by the quasi-concave, constant returns to scale production functions, $f(\cdot,\cdot)$, in *A*, and $f^*(\cdot,\cdot)$ in *B*. Output and factor markets are assumed to be perfectly competitive.

This presents each country with two distinct capital income flows and scope for two possible capital income tax rates, t_{Aa} and t_{Ba}, where t_{ij} denotes the tax rate levied by *A* on capital income earned in country *i* by investor *j*. Using the same notational convention, *B*'s relevant tax rates are t^*_{Bb} and t^*_{Ba}. National sovereignty implies that $t_{Bb} = t^*_{Aa} = 0$, that is, neither country has the ability to tax the domestic income of the other country's residents. Using the terminology of Mintz and Tulkens (1996), a pure source system of taxation in *A* means that investor *a* pays taxes to country *A* only on its domestic income or that $t_{Ba} = 0$. A pure residence system in *A* allows country *A* to tax investor *a* on its worldwide income or that $t_{Ba} > 0$. It is also possible under a residence system that $t_{Ba} \neq t_{Aa}$. With transnational investment, the distinction between source and residency principles becomes a little fuzzy. If a transnational based in *A* makes direct foreign investments through a subsidiary incorporated in *B*, the subsidiary is considered a legal resident of *B*. As such, income from the subsidiary is technically not earned by the parent in *A* until it is repatriated to the parent. Thus, a transnational in *A* could circumvent residence taxes on foreign income by leaving the income in *B*.[18] Finally, assume that each country sets its tax rates before *a* decides where to invest its capital. Because of the one-way capital flow assumption, all of *b*'s capital is invested in *B*.

The issue of double taxation becomes relevant if a home country adopts residence-based taxes (pure or combined with some source taxation) and a host country adopts a source-based tax system.[19] Denote *A*'s adjustment policy by the function $\alpha(t_{Ba}, t^*_{Ba})$. For investor *a*, its effective tax rate on investments in *B* is $T_{Ba} \equiv t_{Ba} + t^*_{Ba} - \alpha(t_{Ba}, t^*_{Ba})$. With this notation, the three generic double taxation rules can be defined: exemption, $\alpha(\cdot,\cdot)=t_{Ba}$, which effectively converts a residence system into a source system; deduction, $\alpha(\cdot;\cdot) = t_{Ba} t^*_{Ba}$, which treats *B* taxes as a cost of business and makes the after-tax return on a dollar of foreign investment income $(1 - t_{Ba})(1 - t^*_{Ba})$; and credit, $\alpha(\cdot;\cdot) = t^*_{Ba}$ if $t^*_{Ba} \leq t_{Ba}$ and $\alpha(\cdot,\cdot) = t_{Ba}$ if $t^*_{Ba} > t_{Ba}$, which makes the investor's effective tax rate on foreign investment income equal to $\max\{t_{Ba}, t^*_{Ba}\}$.[20] In the first credit case *a* is said to be in an excess limit position, while in the second credit case *a* is said to be in an excess credit position. Without the second part of the credit rule definition, *a*'s net liability to *A* from its investments in *B*, $t_{Ba} - t^*_{Ba}$, could be negative.

In a static, non-strategic model with inelastic capital supply and no consumption, Koichi Hamada (1966) showed that for any given set of tax rates from a capital exporting country and a capital importing country, FDI flows are higher with either credits or exemptions than with deductions. This is because the after-tax return from a dollar of FDI with a deduction rule is $(1 - t_{Ba})(1 - t^*_{Ba})$ while with a credit or exemption rule it is either $1 - t_{Ba}$ or $1 - t^*_{Ba}$. Thus for any given set of tax rates, a deduction rule distorts the marginal return on FDI the most.

[18] Active investment rules such as Subpart F rules in the United States are designed to limit the use of this strategy.

[19] A further complication that, for the sake of simplicity, will be ignored is the role of withholding taxes which were briefly introduced in section 3.

[20] Which rule a transnational investor can or must use will often depend upon two characteristics of the foreign investment: control and corporate structure. First, if an investor does not own a significant percentage of shares in the foreign operations, the income is treated as portfolio income. Portfolio investment income and direct investment income are often subject to different tax rules. Second, foreign operations of transnationals can be set up either as a branch of parent operations or as a subsidiary. In the former case, the foreign office is considered an extension of the parent investor's domestic operations, and its income is treated as domestic income of the parent regardless of its actual disposition (repatriation or reinvestment). In the latter case, the foreign office is a legally incorporated resident of the foreign country and as such has income that is not subject to taxation by the parent's home country until it is not actively reinvested or it is repatriated to the parent via a dividend, royalty, or interest payment. For simplicity, I will assume that all investment is direct and controlled and that foreign offices are subsidiaries. The latter assumption will not become relevant until the next section.

From a national welfare perspective, a credit rule has been strongly criticized on the grounds that it allows a capital-importing country to effectively appropriate tax revenues from the capital-exporting country by setting its corporate income tax rate at or above the capital-exporting country's rate. Additionally, Peggy Musgrave (1969) has argued that a credit rule encourages too much outbound FDI. If a is the capital exporter and b inelastically supplies all of her capital for B production, excessive FDI is encouraged because a will invest domestically and abroad to equate after-tax rates of return,

$$(1 - t_{Aa}) f_K(K - \kappa, L) = (1 - \max\{t_{Ba}, t^*_{Ba}\}) f^*_K(K^* + \kappa, L^*).$$[21]

Alternatively, if country A's goal is to maximize national income, equal to output in A plus after-tax income from investments in B, the nationally optimal levels of domestic and foreign investment should equate the after-tax foreign return with the pre-tax domestic return,

$$f_K(K - \kappa, L) = (1 - \max\{t_{Ba}, t^*_{Ba}\}) f^*_K(K^* + \kappa, L^*)$$

as t_{Aa} has only distributional effects. In general, a's FDI choice will not maximize national income under credits but, as Musgrave shows, it will under deductions.

Source Versus Residence Taxation?

Interest in studying the economic implications of source and residence systems is motivated by two facts: relative simplicity and capital-export neutrality. Capital-export neutrality of a single country's tax system arises if the effective tax rates on domestic and foreign investment do not distort the allocation of capital. If a's capital is internationally mobile, then in equilibrium

$$(7) \qquad (1 - t_{Aa}) f_K(K - \kappa, L) = (1 - t_{Ba} - t^*_{Ba} + \alpha(t_{Ba}, t^*_{Ba})) f^*_K(K^* + \kappa, L^*).$$

Under a residence system with a full credit ($\alpha(\cdot, t^*_{Ba}) = t^*_{Ba}$) in A, (7) simplifies to

$$(8) \qquad (1 - t_{Aa}) f_K(K - \kappa, L) = (1 - t_{Ba}) f^*_K(K^* + \kappa, L^*).$$

If $t_{Aa} = t_{Ba}$, then the capital supplied at those tax rates will be efficiently allocated in A. Under a source system, the same is true only if $t_{Aa} = 0$. However, under a residence system in A without full crediting (full crediting is not observed in practice), the capital flow, κ, that solves (7) for any arbitrary tax rates need not imply efficient capital flows. For example, with a deduction rule (7) becomes

$$(1 - t_{Aa}) f_K(K - \kappa, L) = (1 - t_{Ba})(1 - t^*_{Ba}) f^*_K(K^* + \kappa, L^*).$$

Now A can induce efficient capital flows only if $t_{Aa} > t_{Ba}$.

Another way to appreciate the differences between source and residence systems is to look at a's effective home marginal tax rate on outbound foreign

[21] Subscripts denote marginal products.

investment, T_{Ba}. With source taxation, $T_{Ba} = t^*_{Ba}$, and with residence taxation (and full crediting), $T_{Ba} = t_{Ba}$. Unless economic assumptions imply that $T_{Ba} = t^*_{Ba}$ is nationally optimal for *A*, source taxation restricts *A*'s ability to maximize national welfare.[22] Thus, pure source taxes appear to be (weakly) dominated by pure residence taxes.

The point of this discussion is that a country's choice of what transnational income to tax is not independent of its choice of a double taxation rule. Moreover, with the possibility of two-way capital flows, Assaf Razin and Efraim Sadka (1990) demonstrate that transnational capital investment not only increases the complexity of capital income taxation for individual countries, it also introduces global conditions on taxes to eliminate arbitrage opportunities between countries. These global conditions may require some degree of tax coordination.

Whether such coordination can be achieved without distorting capital flows depends in large part on the tax-setting incentives transnational investment presents each country. A simple comparison of the residence and source systems suggests countries may prefer residence systems. By taxing the worldwide income of one's residents, the economic burden of a tax increase is distributed globally, and by not taxing the domestic investment income of foreigners, the supply of foreign capital is maximized. On the other hand, adopting source taxes results in a country internalizing any tax-induced economic distortions. In a model in which foreign-paid taxes are deducted, Razin and Sadka (1991) confirm that a residence system arises in a Nash equilibrium of a tax competition game between two countries.

In reality, most countries adopt tax policies that involve both residence and source taxes, and I would argue they do so for reasons intimately associated with the corporate structure under which domestic and foreign investments occur. That is why, so far in this section, no attention has been given to the manner in which investments are made. Once one does pay attention to these issues, the significance of tax competition or investment models with pure source or residence taxes is suspect.

The model I have just sketched out, which is representative of many of the models employed in the study of tax competition with mobile capital, is really a model of capital income tax competition and not corporate income tax competition. Yet the ability to construct the legal structure of one's investments can have important tax implications. Consider the following strategy (which is now neutralized by the tax laws in most countries). Suppose that *A* levies only residence taxes and that *B* does not tax corporate income. If *a* sets up a corporation in *B*, which I will call corporation β, any income from this investment will be taxable in *A* upon repatriation. Suppose also that β invests its capital in investments located in *A*. Since β is not a resident of *A*, it will pay no taxes to *A* on its income. Instead, from its *A* income β funds new investments and only pays a dividend to *a* if *a*'s direct domestic investments are inadequate to cover its consumption needs. In this case, the existence of a low-tax country like *B* creates an opportunity for *a* to

[22] Mintz and Tulkens (1996) show that with two-way capital flows and additively separable production functions source taxation can be nationally optimal.

reduce the taxes it pays on domestic investment through creative corporate structuring. Razin, Sadka, and Chi-Wa Yuen (1998) show that this same basic idea applies if, instead of manipulating corporate structure, an investor has several sources of investment capital other than equity, e.g. retained earnings and debt, and if the investor has strict preferences over the various sources (perhaps associated with internal risk differences such as moral hazard). In such a case, they show that a pure residence policy is no longer nationally optimal and hence that countries should think about using both source and residence taxes.

Does the Double Taxation Remedy Matter?

Despite the exogeneity of tax rates, the Hamada/Musgrave debate highlights the potentially important interaction between tax rates and double tax rules. Yet Hans-Werner Sinn (1984) and David Hartman (1985) dispute the Hamada/Musgrave conclusion that double tax rules necessarily have real economic effects by showing that the investment and dividend decisions of mature foreign subsidiaries, that is, subsidiaries that can finance new projects out of retained earnings, are unaffected by home country tax rates and double taxation rules as long as the parent company is allowed to defer home taxes on subsidiary profits until these profits are repatriated. Hartman uses a simple two-period model to illustrate his argument. Assume that a foreign subsidiary has $1 of post-host-tax profit. It can either pay out this dollar to its parent as a dividend now or reinvest the dollar and pay out the dollar plus the post-host-tax return later. Let t denote the rate at which foreign source income is taxed by the home government and let t^* denote the rate at which this income was taxed in the host country. For simplicity assume that $t > t^*$. With a credit for foreign paid taxes, the home tax liability on a dollar of foreign source income is calculated in three steps. First, the foreign taxes associated with this dollar of post-host-tax subsidiary profit is added back in – a step referred to as 'grossing up.' Second, a home tax liability is calculated on these grossed-up profits. In this case, the liability equals $t/(1\text{-}t^*)$ dollars. Third, a credit for taxes paid to the host country, $t^*/(1\text{-}t^*)$ dollars, reduces the parent's domestic tax liability to $(t\text{-}t^*)/(1\text{-}t^*)$ dollars and leaves post-home-tax profits of $(1\text{-}t)/(1\text{-}t^*)$ dollars. If the net return on home investments is r, repatriating the dollar of subsidiary profit now is worth $(1\text{-}t)(1+r)/(1\text{-}t^*)$ dollars to the parent. On the other hand, if the dollar of subsidiary profit is reinvested in the host country with a net return of r^* and then repatriated, the parent's after-home-tax return equals $(1\text{-}t)(1+r^*(1\text{-}t^*))/(1\text{-}t^*)$ dollars. Equating these two post-tax returns shows that only the net returns and the host tax rate will affect the subsidiary's dividend/investment policy because a credit rule results in both the profit from investing repatriated funds, $1+r$, and the profit from reinvesting in the host country, $1+r^*(1\text{-}t^*)$, being taxed proportionately. Present values calculations are not relevant since, in both cases, one has to wait one period to reap the benefits of the investment. Given the proportional impact of home taxes under credits, delaying repatriation does not confer any tax benefit. Under a deduction policy, the only part of this argument that changes is that now a dollar dividend from a foreign subsidiary yields $(1\text{-}t)$ dollars after home taxes. Thus, the choice of the double taxation method also has no impact on dividend and investment policy.[23]

Theoretically the Hartman-Sinn result can be overturned by dynamic investment factors. Chad Leechor and Mintz (1993) show that differences in the definition of taxable income (e.g. differences in allowable depreciation schedules) can make repatriation and investment decisions sensitive to home tax rates. For instance, a slower depreciation of invested capital in the home country serves as an additional tax on repatriated foreign income, the effect of which on an investor's marginal cost of FDI depends on both countries' tax rates and the home country's double tax rule. Altshuler and Fulghieri (1993) point out that in a dynamic environment, a firm can also time its investments to take advantage of changes in tax rates. For example, when the TRA lowered corporate income tax rates in the United States, the benefit of earning tax credits from repatriating foreign income was increased because it increased the number of countries from which foreign income could be repatriated without incurring additional U.S. tax. Anticipating this change in tax laws would have encouraged some U.S. transnationals to delay repatriation until after passage of the act. Finally, Hines (1994a) uses a dynamic model with subsidiary debt, royalty payments, and investment tax credits (which affects tax base definitions) to demonstrate the importance of the home country rate in calculating the after-tax cost of FDI capital.

Several empirical studies help us gauge the importance of these dynamic factors. Hines and Hubbard (1990) report that in 1984 both home tax rates and the credit position of the parent division of the transnational influenced the level and form of repatriations. They found that U.S. parents in excess credit positions accounted for 53 per cent of dividends from subsidiaries while U.S. parents in excess limit positions accounted for 63 per cent of royalty payments and 58 per cent of Subpart F income (passive investment income subject to immediate U.S. taxation). They also found that parents with higher tax liability to asset ratios had significantly lower ratios of dividend plus Subpart F income to assets. Using 1986 data from U.S. returns, Altshuler and Newlon (1993) find a negative and highly significant relationship between the ratio of subsidiary dividends to subsidiary assets and the effective marginal tax rate on foreign source income: a 1 per cent increase in the tax price of dividends reduces dividends by 1.5 per cent. Additionally, Altshuler and Newlon (1993) identify a significant effect of a firm's expected future effective marginal tax rate on dividends associated with the likelihood of a parent switching from an excess credit position to an excess limit position or vice versa. This switching effect is shown to reinforce, rather than moderate, the direct tax rate effect. This is consistent with Harris (1993) who finds empirical evidence of both increased repatriations and increased FDI out of the United States due to the TRA. However, when Altshuler, Newlon, and William Randolph (1995) decompose variations in the effective marginal tax rates on repatriations into permanent and transitory components they find that the impact of home tax policy is due only to transitory rate changes. While this last result lends

---

[23] Note that this argument assumes that the home tax rate does not distort the equilibrium rate of returns, r and r^*.

more credence to the Hartman-Sinn theory, their analysis fails to account for important variations in financing opportunities available to transnationals, as in Hines (1994a), and thus to potential linkages between national welfare and home and host tax policies. I return to this issue when I discuss tax competition models.

A Connection Between Double Taxation Rules and Transfer Pricing

Consistent with the analysis in section 4, there is another component of transnational investment that circumscribes the Hartmann-Sinn result: transfer pricing. From the discussion of transfer pricing in section 4, the extent to which a transnational might distort transfer prices from their underlying economic values depends on both the tax rate differential and expected penalties. If a transnational headquartered in *A* operates a subsidiary in *B*, it would face the following investment decision. A dollar of subsidiary profit can now be put to three uses: repatriation via a dividend, repatriation via strategic transfer pricing, and reinvestment in the subsidiary. The first option yields a return of $(1 - T_{Ba})(1+r)$. The after-tax return on reinvestment is more complicated to calculate because of the role of transfer pricing. Let $\rho(T_{Ba}, t^*_{Ba})$ denote the fraction of subsidiary profits the transnational would repatriate via its transfer pricing channel. A dollar reinvested in the subsidiary would then yield a return of

$$(1 - T_{Ba})(1 + (1-\rho)r^*) + (1 - t_{Ba})\rho r^*$$

as the transnational avoids paying host tax on the percent of the return repatriated via transfer pricing. By equating these two returns, one can prove a weaker version of the Hartmann-Sinn result: If the firm does not engage in strategic transfer pricing, the capital-exporting country's tax policy is irrelevant in determining the distribution of capital. However, when transnationals do manipulate transfer prices, both the home tax rate and its double tax policy can affect capital decisions, in this case because transnationals have the flexibility to fund new investments both with additional capital as well as with retained earnings. This result, due to Weichenrieder (1996b), nicely illustrates the fact that the flexibility enjoyed by transnationals not only makes both home and host policies very relevant in the capital allocation decisions of the transnational, but also that this flexibility increases the strategic linkages between different components of a country's tax policies.[24] It is interesting to note that as the host or capital-importing country adopts practices or adjusts policies to limit the incentive for transnationals to manipulate their transfer prices, it also reduces the influence of home tax policies on FDI decisions.

[24] Mintz and Thomas Tsiopoulos (1994) show that similar linkages exist when transnationals need to evaluate tax holiday offers.

Tax Competition

From the Mintz-Tulkens model presented in section 5, it is clear that one country's choice of tax policy can impose fiscal externalities on another country. With more elaborate financial strategies available to transnational investors, the complexity of the externalities increases. This suggests the importance of considering models of tax competition to assess when the interests of home and host countries align and when and how they conflict. It also becomes important to pay attention to the timing of tax policy decisions. For example, tax treaties that follow the OECD (1997) convention stipulate policies like double tax rules while leaving signatories some latitude in setting tax rates. Thus, an alternative to analyzing tax competition incentives when governments choose all aspects of their tax policies simultaneously (such as Mintz and Tulkens, 1996), is to analyze dynamic models in which competition in tax rates is preceded by non-rate policy choices.

For most of the literature on transnational income tax competition, the policy focus has been on the choice of a double tax rule. Recall that from a static perspective, the proponents of foreign tax credits (e.g. Hamada, 1966) point to the FDI enhancing properties of credits while the opponents (e.g. Musgrave, 1969) point to the fact that, from a national perspective, credits induce overinvestment in FDI. The seminal work of Eric Bond and Larry Samuelson (1989) indicates that the conflict between national income maximization and world income maximization may not be as transparent as the Hamada-Musgrave positions suggest because the same properties of foreign tax credit systems that support high levels of world income for a given set of tax rates also result in higher equilibrium tax rates.[25] This can be understood more easily by observing how credit and deduction methods of double taxation relief influence effective tax rates on FDI.

The model developed in section 5 is essentially the Bond and Samuelson (1989) model. Both countries, *A* and *B*, are assumed to maximize national income. That, coupled with the inelastic supply of capital, implies that a home tax on domestic income has only distributional effects that have no impact on home welfare. For simplicity, this rate (t_{Aa}) is set to zero and we let t denote the home rate on foreign income, t_{Ba}. Similarly, since host citizens only earn domestic income, the sole relevant tax rate, t_{Bb}, is denoted by t^*. With these changes, (7) becomes

$$(9) \qquad f_K(K - \kappa, L) = (1 - T_{Ba}) f^*_K(K^* + \kappa, L^*)$$

where now $T_{Ba} = t + t^* - \alpha(t,t^*)$. Remember, T_{Ba} equals t^* with exemptions, $t + t^* - tt^*$ with deductions and $\max\{t,t^*\}$ with credits. Given any pair of tax rates and any double tax rule for the home country, a factor market equilibrium can be described

[25] Feldstein and Hartman (1979) present an early attempt to understand the implications of non-cooperative tax competition and the choice of a double taxation rule. Their results on non-cooperative tax competition assumed that the capital importing country was small relative to the capital exporter, implying a Stackelberg framework, and required specific functional form assumptions on the aggregate production functions.

by the solution to (9), $\kappa(T_{Ba})$, the profit-maximizing level of aggregate FDI. Not surprisingly, $\kappa'(T_{Ba}) < 0$. Given this definition, home and host national income equals

$$(10) \quad Y(t,t^*) = f(K - \kappa(T_{Ba}),L) + (1 - t^*)f^*_K(K^* + \kappa(T_{Ba}),L^*)\kappa(T_{Ba})$$

and

$$(11) \quad Y^*(t,t^*) = f^*(K^* + \kappa(T_{Ba}),L^*) - (1 - t^*)f^*_K(K^* + \kappa(T_{Ba}),L^*)\kappa(T_{Ba})$$

For the home country, national income equals domestic output plus repatriated after-host-tax foreign profits. For the host country, national income equals domestic output less the after-host-tax profits home investors repatriate. Thus, the nature of tax competition here is somewhat different from that seen in models where both countries try to attract inbound capital. Reflecting the tension between home and host countries, A must balance lost home production against higher repatriated returns from its outbound FDI, while B must balance increased output against decreased tax revenues from inbound FDI. In other words, the tax competition focused on in this section is between asymmetrically positioned countries, home and host, by virtue of transnational capital flows, instead of between symmetrically positioned host countries.

Consider the subgame perfect equilibria of a game in which the home country first specifies a double tax rule and then the home and host countries simultaneously set tax rates. Each choice of a double taxation rule has the potential to induce different equilibrium tax rates. The exemption subgame is easiest as it requires t=0 and allows the host country to choose the tax rate that maximizes $Y^*(0,t^*)$. Call this optimal rate t^*_e.

For both the deduction and credit subgames, notice that the host rate influences host income directly by changing the tax rate and indirectly through its effect on T_{Ba}, which in turn determines $\kappa(\cdot)$. This creates the standard tax-base versus tax-rate tradeoff. For A, its rate influences home income only through the effective rate, T_{Ba}. Unlike B, country A is only interested in the level of FDI. Differentiating (10) with respect to T_{Ba} shows

$$(12) \quad dY/dT_{Ba} = [-(1 - T_{Ba})f^*_K + (1 - t^*)f^*_K + (1-t^*)f^*_{KK}\kappa]\kappa'(T_{Ba}).$$

The first term in the brackets is the value of lost home production when κ increases. The sum of the last two terms equals the marginal repatriated profits. The rate, T_{Ba}, is never smaller than t^* and if $T_{Ba}=t^*$, home national income is strictly increasing in T_{Ba}. Therefore, if A has the ability to influence T_{Ba}, it is always optimal for A to raise T_{Ba} above t^* in order to restrict outbound capital.

Under a deduction rule, an increase in t always increases T_{Ba} and the competing trade-offs of the home and host countries define unique equilibrium tax rates that are both positive and that imply positive FDI. The credit case is surprisingly quite different. For the home country, as long as t is less than t^*, small increases in t have no effect on the effective rate. But for $t \geq t^*$, $T_{Ba} = t$. Thus, at $t = t^*$, the above-mentioned incentives for A to raise the effective tax rate kick in. For the host country, when $t^* < t$, an increase in t^* has no impact on T_{Ba} and thus it increases the transnational's host taxes by the same amount it decreases home taxes. Raising t^* up to t has the effect of raising host tax revenues without lowering its tax base. Like the home country, the host can influence the effective tax rate and hence the level of FDI only when $t^* \geq t$. To the host country, this situation looks like the exemption case. B's incentive is then to set t^* as close to t_e^* as possible. Figure 4.1 illustrates the implications of this discussion. For the host country, its best response to any home rate is to set t^* equal to the larger of t and t_e^*. The result is the best response curve $BR^*(t)$. For the home country, its best response is to set t above t^* as long as κ is positive. A's best response is the curve $BR(t^*)$. The only equilibrium under credits given these two sets of incentives results in no FDI (κ=0).

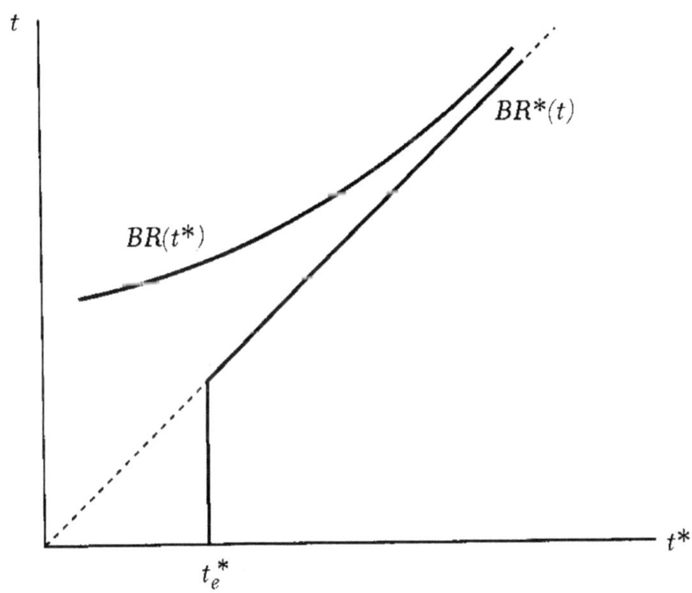

Figure 4.1 Best response curves for the home country and the host country

Comparing all three subgames, home national income is highest under a deduction rule. The analysis also reveals that the promotion of double tax rules based on static national income interests can Pareto dominate the promotion of double tax rules based on global income interests. Both observations are surprising in light of the information in Table 4.1 noting that very few countries can be characterized as deduction countries. One way to interpret the results, using the terminology of cooperative game theory, is to note that many countries use the deduction method as a 'threat point' by listing the deduction method as the one to be used in the absence of a tax treaty with the host country. In this regard, most tax treaties follow the 1997 OECD tax treaty convention of which the main provision proscribes the use of the deduction method (see also United Nations, 1980). But why would a home and host country sign a treaty that results in a Pareto inferior outcome? According to Ronald Davies (1999), the answer is related to the fact that most OECD countries experience two-way transnational capital flows and thus simultaneously face the trade-offs of both a home and a host country.[26] Now both countries must select double tax rules in an initial stage before competing in tax rates. The opposing effects a tax hike has on inbound and outbound FDI moderates incentives to raise tax rates too high. For countries with identical production technologies and endowments, proscribing the use of deductions results in a subgame perfect equilibrium in which both countries use a credit method and tax rates yield Pareto optimal capital allocations. With asymmetric countries, credit-exemption combinations can also arise in equilibrium, and equilibrium tax rates may not be Pareto preferred to those arising in the absence of a treaty. Negotiating a treaty agreeable to both countries may require some coordination of tax rates, which in turn may require some provisions for enforcement as in the literature on trade agreements. Maintaining the use of a deduction method in the event a treaty is abrogated may very well be part of effective treaty enforcement. More work needs to be done on this issue.

The results of Bond and Samuelson depend on three assumptions: inelastic domestic capital supplies (investors do not face intertemporal consumption/investment trade-offs), discriminatory taxes, and perfectly competitive output markets.[27] Relaxing the first assumption can, but need not, result in positive equilibrium FDI flows under credits. Thus, the supply of capital would need to be sufficiently elastic before a credit tax-competition equilibrium could dominate a deduction tax-competition equilibrium.

The second assumption allows the home country to tax domestic-source income and foreign-source income at different rates. Eckhard Janeba (1995) shows that with uniform tax rates (i.e. t_{Aa} and t_{Ba} must be equal to some common value t and move in tandem) and with inelastic capital and labor supplies, a higher tax rate can simultaneously yield more FDI and less domestic investment. This new trade-off has implications for the equilibrium performance of credit, deduction, and exemption rules. Using the same notation as above, let t denote the home country's tax rate on the returns from both foreign and domestic investment (t_{Aa} and t_{Ba}). The effective after-tax return from a dollar of FDI income relative to a dollar of

---

[26] For actual statistics, see OECD (1998).

[27] There may also be some interaction between trade and tax policies. For instance, Bond (1991) shows that the use of tax credits by a capital exporter can influence the tariff policies of a small capital-importing country.

domestic income can be calculated by dividing ($1\text{-}T_{Ba}$) by ($1\text{-}t$). With a credit rule, this relative effective after-tax return equals ($1\text{-}\max\{t,t^*\})/(1\text{-}t)$; with a deduction rule it equals ($1\text{-}t^*$), i.e. t serves as a pure profit tax; and with an exemption rule it equals $(1\text{-}t^*)/(1\text{-}t)$. Clearly, the home country's choice of tax rate under a deduction rule will not influence FDI flows. The same is true under a credit rule for $t > t^*$. When $t \leq t^*$, the effect of a change in t under a credit rule is identical to that under an exemption rule. In both cases, higher home tax rates encourage *more* FDI at the expense of domestic investment. For a given level of FDI, any change in domestic tax revenues is purely distributional and hence will not increase home national income. By lowering t, the home country encourages less FDI which increases home output and the return on FDI. Thus, home's optimal tax rate is zero. In equilibrium, then, there is no difference in the equilibrium levels of FDI and home and host income under the three different rules. This implies that the choice of a double taxation rule is irrelevant if domestic capital income and foreign capital income is taxed uniformly. While this seems like a common occurrence, Hines (1988) demonstrates how variations in components of a country's tax code, such as tax investment tax credits and depreciation rules, can allow a country to tax domestic and foreign income at different rates.[28]

The last assumption rules out the possibility of investment choices being made with an eye towards influencing output prices. Endowing home investors with market power in the host output market can create a new linkage between the home country's choice of a double taxation rule and host country tax incentives. In Janeba (1996), the host market is assumed to be imperfectly competitive as there is one host firm and one foreign controlled subsidiary.[29] Now a change in the home country's tax rate shifts the transnational's reaction function in a product market competition subgame and creates profit-shifting effects reminiscent of those first pointed out by James Brander and Barbara Spencer (1985). If the firm competes in quantities and the home country offers a full tax credit, this profit-shifting can support a home rate less than the host rate. In yet another imperfect competition model, Janeba (1998) analyzes a source-tax competition game with two mobile transnationals. Mobility implies that both firms always locate all their production in the lower tax country. Tax competition in this setting eliminates source taxes since small changes in one's tax rate can attract a large amount of FDI. As in the prior paper, once residence taxation and tax credits are considered, the traditional

[28] Gordon (1992) not only assumes uniform taxes in analyzing the equilibria of tax competition with a credit rule, he also endogenizes the capital supply decision of a representative agent. His analysis suggests that a pure-strategy equilibrium in tax rates may not exist. As such he adopts the Feldstein and Hartman (1979) assumption that the home country is a Stackelberg leader in tax rates and claims this assumption is descriptive of the global economy in the early post-World War II period with the United States playing the role of the dominant capital exporting country. Since the United States is now a capital importer, this model is presumably less relevant. Also, analysis under the deduction and exemption methods is not included.

[29] Unlike most models of transnational tax competition and inconsistent with standard legal definitions of controlled subsidiaries, Janeba assumes that subsidiary financing involves no parent equity.

Brander-Spencer results reemerge. Thus at a minimum, the introduction of imperfect competition can be seen to increase the sensitivity of capital and national income allocations to the choice of tax policies.

At this point it is perhaps worthwhile stepping back a moment in order to compare what we know of international tax policies with how they are described in tax competition models. Sections 2 and 3 hopefully conveyed the sense that national tax policies with respect to transnational investment are not only complex and multidimensional but that this complexity is a direct response to the many different dimensions along which a transnational can be organized both to promote higher pre-tax profits and higher post-tax profits. Moreover, the empirical evidence concerning how transnationals respond to variations in tax policy imply that the strategic linkages between the various standard components of international tax policy, e.g. double taxation rules, transfer price regulations, interest allocation rules, are important and discernible. On the other hand, the above tax competition papers, reflecting the core of the tax competition literature reasonably well, omit consideration of all but the most basic tax policy element – double taxation rules. This suggests that one of the more fruitful directions for tax competition research is to analyze the impact of the standard policy linkages on tax competition equilibria.

Only a few papers have begun to consider such issues. I will discuss two of them. One important tool transnationals have to manage income taxes on FDI not available in the above models is debt financing. Recall from section 3, Feldstein's (1995) evidence on the significance of debt acquired by the subsidiary in its host country as well as the econometric studies by Altshuler and Mintz (1995) and Froot and Hines (1995) showing that changes in U.S. interest allocation rules increased the incentive for U.S. transnationals to use subsidiary debt. One suggestion made by Feldstein (1994) is that the availability of host debt financing can reduce the incentive for a home country to tax the returns from FDI under a credit rule and hence can mitigate the harmful effects of tax competition with foreign tax credits. Davies and Gresik (2000) show that while host debt financing can improve the equilibrium performance of foreign tax credits it also improves the equilibrium performance of foreign tax deductions. From the home country's perspective a credit rule is still weakly dominated by a deduction or an exemption rule.

More important than the specific welfare ranking of double tax rules, Davies and Gresik (2003) identify several new strategic effects that arise when subsidiary financing can include both equity and debt. Because borrowing is treated as a transfer of capital from local host firms to subsidiaries of home transnationals, how home and host investors respond to a change in either government's tax rate (given any double taxation rule) will depend upon the relative factor intensities between subsidiaries and host firms. To capture the effect of capital transfers within the host country, consider the introduction of a third technology, f^s. While the production function f still represents home country production, f^* now denotes production in the host country by host investors and f^s denotes production in the host country by a subsidiary of a home transnational. If K^s denotes the amount of capital borrowed by the subsidiary from host sources, aggregate global post-tax transnational profit equals

$$(13) \quad \pi = f(K - \kappa, L) - wL + (1 - T_{Ba})(f^S(\kappa + K^S, L^S) - r^* K^S - w^* L^S)$$

where w and w^* are wage rates, r^* is the cost of borrowed host funds, and L^S is the amount of host labor employed by subsidiaries.[30] A final key assumption of the model is that the marginal cost of subsidiary borrowing increases with the subsidiary's debt-equity ratio. A simple way to capture this effect is to require the subsidiary to have at least some minimum level of collateral (i.e. equity) denoted by γ. Thus, $K^S \leq \gamma\kappa$.

For factor market equilibria in which the collateral constraint does not bind, $K^S < \gamma\kappa$, (13) implies

$$(14) \; w^* = f^*_L = f^S_L, \; r^* = f^*_K = f^S_K, \text{ and } f_K = (1 - T_{Ba}) f^S_K.$$

With a binding collateral constraint, K^S and κ are now complements, and factor market equilibria satisfy

$$(15) \quad w^* = f^*_L = f^S_L, \; r^* = f^*_K, \text{ and } f_K = (1 - T_{Ba})((1+\gamma) f^S_K - \gamma f^*_K).$$

For the simpler first case, (14) implies $d\kappa / dT_{Ba} = f_K / (1 - T_{Ba}) f_{KK} < 0$ and

$$(16) \quad \frac{dK^S}{dT_{Ba}} = \frac{-f_K k^*}{(1 - T_{Ba}) f_{KK}(k^* - k^S)}$$

where $k^S = (\kappa + K^S)/L^S$ and $k^* = (K^* - K^S)/(L^* - L^S)$ are the subsidiary and host-firm capital-labor ratios. A similar expression exists with respect to L^S. The sign of (16) depends on the difference in the factor intensities of host and subsidiary firms. This ambiguity is due to the Tadeus Rybczynski (1955) effect which states that an increase in the supply of a factor will increase output in the sector that uses the factor more intensively. In this case, an increase in T_{Ba} causes κ to fall and lower the supply of capital in the host country. If subsidiary production is more capital intensive than host production, this decrease in κ will result in lower subsidiary output and less subsidiary borrowing. Analogous results arise in the binding case as well.

Since changes in tax rates induce a Rybczynski (1955) effect, the home country can use changes in its tax rate on FDI to effectively implement V. K.

---

[30] In practice subsidiary debt is but one form of debt financing. Because current tax laws discourage parent-debt financing and because extant tax competition models ignore debt financing altogether, Davies and Gresik (2003) focus on this sole source of transnational debt.

Ramaswami's (1968) national income improving strategy of restricting home capital exports and importing host capital and labor, without changing factor prices, in a manner that does not require the physical transfer of the host capital and labor. Changes in the effective tax rate on FDI can also strengthen or weaken the borrowing constraint and endogenously shift the economic relationship between subsidiary debt and parent equity from one of substitutes to one of complements or vice versa. This too depends on a Rybczynski effect. On a technical level, the conjunction of these three effects – Rybczynski on factor market equilibria, Ramaswami and Rybczynski on the collateral constraint – introduces non-convexities in the home country's preferences over tax rates, with credits and deductions, and results in a richer set of equilibria. The fact that one can characterize these equilibria in terms of well-known international trade concepts holds out hope for our ability to integrate more features of transnational taxation into tax competition models.

The second issue involves transfer pricing between divisions of a transnational located in different countries. As noted in earlier sections, done successfully, the transnational can shift profits between jurisdictions before they are taxed by either a home or host country. And, in the case of profit shifting out of the home country, transfer pricing can transform domestic-source income eventually into foreign-source income. (Recall the advantages of doing so when the parent company has excess credits.) Both internal (managerial) and external (regulatory) factors can create scope for profit-shifting via transfer prices. The latter case will be taken up in the next section.

From an internal management perspective, home office managers are often less well informed about local host country demand or labor conditions. Transfer prices provide one way for a parent division to align the incentives of host subsidiary managers with the transnational's goal of maximizing global after-tax profits. This means that seemingly low transfer prices may imply both a tax minimization strategy as well as a managerial incentive strategy. While the first strategy works against host country objectives, the second need not. Ramy Elitzur and Mintz (1996) introduce managerial transfer pricing motives into a corporate tax competition model.[31] While the authors do not isolate the significance of the managerial motive, they are able to show that, unlike in Mintz and Tulkens (1986), when the countries set their tax rates non-cooperatively, an increase in one country's tax rate unambiguously lowers the other's tax revenues. Because tax competition with internal transfer pricing motives creates negative fiscal externalities, tax harmonization in this context will unambiguously result in lower tax rates for both countries and higher tax revenues.[32]

---

[31] At the same time, the authors abstract away from the usual double taxation issues.

[32] Sinn (1997) points out that a very important reason to promote cooperative tax policies is that presumably governments arose to deal with a variety of market failures. To the extent that tax competition strengthens the role of markets in the provision of government services, it re-emphasizes the sources of market failures.

The Role of Information in Taxing Transnationals

Transfer pricing as a response to government policies provides a good vehicle for a more detailed discussion of the role of information in taxing transnationals because it is an issue that arises precisely because transnationals have superior information about demand conditions and operating costs than do the governments with whom they interact. A central characteristic of most transfer price regulations is the arm's-length price which was introduced in section 3. This is the price at which one would expect independent parties in a competitive market to transact. In the simplest cases, an external market for the transferred good exists and governments can use data from that market to identify the appropriate arm's-length price. For example, in a recent U.S. court case (U.S. Tax Court, 1999) in which the IRS was contesting the transfer price of a semiconductor chip purchased by COMPAQ from a subsidiary, market data on semiconductor chips showed that COMPAQ's transfer price satisfied the arm's-length legal standard. When the transfer involves highly proprietary products or non-tangibles such as managerial services, U.S. and OECD regulations elicit information from the transnational under review. How governments use this information will affect the incentives transnationals have to report the requested information accurately. From the models of sections 4 and 5, we know that the specific regulations also have real effects. Because of these real effects, an arm's-length standard may not be welfare optimal for a country.

The following model will help explain normatively how an uninformed (or poorly informed) tax authority should manage the information it receives from a transnational.[33] To focus on the impact of private information, the literature has so far ignored issues related to double taxation rules and cost allocation rules. This simplification is maintained in the following discussion.

Suppose that the transnational produces an intermediate good at home and ships it to a subsidiary in a host country where it is converted into a final product and sold to host consumers. Let q denote both intermediate and final good production. The subsidiary is a monopolist in the host final good market and faces demand of $P(q)$. The intermediate good is produced at a constant marginal cost of c and sold to the subsidiary at a price ρ. The host country has two tax instruments: a profit tax, t^*, and a lump-sum subsidy, S^*. For simplicity, assume that the home income tax rate is zero but that the transnational has a preference for where it locates profits denoted by i. If i is positive, the transnational prefers to locate profits at home and if i is negative, it prefers to locate profits in the host country. This variable can be thought of as a proxy for a number of economic factors including expropriation risk, exchange rate risk, capital controls, and location of shareholders. These assumptions yield a global post-tax profit for the transnational of

$$(17) \quad \Pi = (1 - t^*)(P(q)q - \rho q + S^*) + (1 + i)(\rho - c)q .$$

---

[33] For details of this model, see Gresik and Douglas Nelson (1994) and Gresik (1999).

Thus, the first term in Π defines the after-tax profits of the subsidiary and the second term defines the parent's transfer price profits.

In regulating the transfer prices, the tax authority wishes to maximize the social welfare function

(18)
$$W = V(q) - P(q)q + t^*(P(q)q - \rho q + S^*) - S^* + \alpha^*(1 - t^*)(P(q)q - \rho q + S^*)$$

where $V(\cdot)$ denotes consumer surplus gross of revenues and α^* is the host government's welfare weight on firm profit, $0 \leq \alpha^* \leq 1$. That is, the host government is interested in maximizing a weighted sum of consumer surplus, net tax revenues, and subsidiary profit. Because an allocation in this model consists of a production level and a distribution of profits between home and host sources, in a normative analysis the regulator is assumed to have control over q, ρ, and S^*. Without the subsidy, which allows the host government to control the transnational's global profits in a non-distortionary manner, the distortions induced by regulating the transfer price would be even larger.

Using (17) to substitute S^* from (18) yields

(19) $$W = V(q) - (1+i)(1-\alpha^*)cq - (1-\alpha^*)\Pi + [(1+i)(1-\alpha^*) - 1]\rho q .$$

Notice that the coefficient on transfer price revenues, ρq, is positive only if $\alpha^* < i/(1+i)$. When transfer price revenues increase, subsidiary profits, host tax revenues and the subsidy needed for any given Π all decrease. The net social benefit from transfer price revenues is positive only when the host government puts small enough weight on subsidiary profit. In light of the linearity of W with respect to ρ, two additional constraints are imposed. First, assume that transfer price profit cannot be negative. This is consistent with what Hugh Ault and David Bradford (1990) call a 'commensurate with income standard.' It is a typical home country policy that prevents host countries from earning tax revenues from parent operations unrelated to the subsidiary's product. Second, assume that subsidiary profit cannot be negative. In reality, negative profit would require additional capitalization from the parent and increases the opportunity cost of such funds.

If the government has complete information about the transnational's costs, it can use its subsidy to extract any rents from the transnational, $\Pi=0$. If Π were driven below zero, the transnational could cease operating and guarantee itself zero profit. For $\alpha^* > i/(1+i)$, $\partial W/\partial \rho < 0$ which implies $\rho=c$. For $\alpha^* < i/(1+i)$, $\partial W/\partial \rho > 0$ which implies $\rho q = P(q) + S^*$. With (17) this implies

(20) $$\Pi = (1+i)(\rho - c)q/(1-t^*).$$

Since $\Pi=0$, this case also requires $\rho=c$. Thus, regardless of the values of α^* and i, the optimal transfer price meets an arm's-length standard.

Now suppose the government does not know c but only has probabilistic beliefs about its value. Denote these beliefs by the distribution $F(c)$ with support $[c_0,c_1]$. Again for normative purposes, it is sufficient to focus on the allocations the tax authority can realize. This can be done by having the regulator specify a value of q, ρ, and S^* for every possible value of c. That is, the regulator begins by announcing a triplet of schedules $(q(r),\rho(r),S^*(r))$ where the variable r is used instead of c to distinguish the transnational's report of its cost from its actual cost. This additional notation leads us to rewrite (17) as

$$(21) \qquad \Pi(r,c) = (1 - t^*)(P(q(r))q(r) - \rho(r)q(r) + S^*(r)) + (1 + i)(\rho(r) - c)q(r).$$

Now the transnational's objective is to choose a profit-maximizing cost report. At this point, it is convenient to invoke the Revelation Principle which allows us to restrict attention to regulations (q,ρ,S^*) for which the transnational's optimal report is truthful. Applying the Envelope Theorem then to (21) implies that $d\Pi(c,c)/dc = -(1+i)q(c)$ and that $q'(c) \le 0$. Thus, truthful reporting requires that firms reporting higher costs produce less and earn strictly lower global profits than lower cost firms. Alternatively, the first condition implies

$$(22) \qquad \Pi(c,c) = \Pi(c_1,c_1) + (1 + i)\int_{s=c}^{c_1} q(s)ds.$$

If under the regulations, the highest cost transnational earns zero profit, all other cost types will earn strictly positive profit referred to as an information rent. That is, inferior government information places an upper bound on the surplus a host country can extract from a transnational. With (20), it also means that it is optimal for a host government to allow a transfer price above actual cost when $\alpha^* < i/(1+i)$. Although the transnational is guaranteed an information rent because of its superior cost information, the host country has some discretion in how that rent is earned. When the host country does not value subsidiary profits very much, the welfare costs of having the transnational earn its rents in the form of transfer price profit are lower than the welfare costs of having the transnational earn its rents in the form of subsidiary profit.

In practice, governments do not directly set production levels for transnationals. Rather, the transnational chooses its production quantities and cost reports given the rules under which its transfer prices may be set by national authorities. What the above analysis identifies are the second-best or information-constrained allocations that might arise from any given set of policies. Completing the analysis requires the derivation of actual and credible policies that in the equilibrium of a game between the national authorities and the transnational these second-best allocations arise.

A nice example of this type of exercise is found in a paper by Petter Osmundsen, Hagen, and Schjelderup (1998). Instead of focusing on transfer pricing, the authors look at the issue of capital mobility in which the benefit of locating a transnational's investments outside a country is private information to the firm. In this case, a capital investment of K in a host country yields revenues of $R(K)$ and has economic costs of $C(K,\theta)$. θ is the firm's mobility parameter. Higher values of θ denote more profitable non-host investments and hence a higher opportunity cost of host investment. Both C_θ and $C_{K\theta}$ are taken to be positive so that a higher mobility parameter also reflects higher marginal opportunity costs of host investment. Abstracting away from double tax issues, profits from host investment are

$$(23) \qquad \pi(K,\theta) = R(K) - C(K,\theta) - T^*(\theta)$$

where $T^*(\cdot)$ equals host taxes. Because immobile (low θ) firms have lower opportunity costs of host investment (i.e. poorer non-host investment opportunities), Revelation Principle calculations similar to those above imply that $d\pi(K(\theta),\theta)/d\theta = -C_\theta(K(\theta),\theta) < 0$ and $K'(\theta) < 0$. These conditions mean less mobile firms earn higher information rents and are encouraged to invest more capital in host investments.[34] Together these conditions discourage immobile firms from claiming to be mobile.

Denote the optimal host policies by $(\hat{K}(\theta),\hat{T}^*(\theta))$. Under mild technical conditions $\hat{K}(\theta)$ will be strictly decreasing and thus invertible. Direct implementation of these policies requires the host government to ask the transnational how mobile it is and then require a firm of type θ to invest $\hat{K}(\theta)$ in capital and pay a tax of $\hat{T}^*(\theta)$. A more practical, but indirect, method of implementation would be to announce a non-linear tax schedule $\sigma^*(K)$ and to let the transnational choose its investment level. As long as $\sigma^* = (\hat{T}^* \circ \hat{K}^{-1})(K)$, a transnational with mobility type θ will choose to invest $\hat{K}(\theta)$ in capital and will pay $\hat{T}^*(\theta)$ in taxes. This equivalence has been coined the 'taxation principle' by Jean-Charles Rochet (1986). Osmundsen, Hagen and Schjelderup show that the appropriate tax policy σ^* can be written as $t^*[R(K) - \delta(K)K - e(K)]$ where $e(\cdot)$ is a tax base exemption and $\delta(\cdot)$ is a (non-linear) depreciation schedule, two common elements of most commercial tax codes.

Returning now to the regulation of transfer prices, suppose that a host country effectively implements its second-best (incentive-constrained) policies. When $\alpha^* >$

[34] These counterintuitive results arise because host investment opportunities are uncorrelated with a firm's non-host opportunities. Thus, both firms with good outside investments and poor outside investments are equally capable of generating host revenues, $R(\cdot)$. Introducing type dependent host revenues, say $R_\theta > 0$, introduces countervailing incentives. A strong enough revenue effect would reverse the information rent and investment rankings. The important contribution of this paper, however, is not the derivation of the optimal host allocation but rather the forthcoming implementation result.

$i/(1+i)$, one result will be reduced home tax revenues as the optimal host regulations eliminate transfer price profits. Although in the simple model described above the home rate was set to zero, in general profits shifted out of the host country would be subject to some home taxation. Even when $\alpha^* < i/(1+i)$ and the optimal host regulations call for positive transfer price profits, these transfer price profits could be smaller than those the transnational would generate under less than optimal host policies. In either case the home government can be expected to offer the transnational countervailing incentives that encourage the transnational to misreport its cost information to the host country, thereby creating larger rents for the firm and larger home tax revenues. Once both governments are allowed to actively regulate the transnational, a problem of 'common agency' is created. While in principle all tax competition models account for this type of interaction, the addition of private information raises a number of new and challenging theoretical problems.

Common agency models span two main dimensions. First, one can distinguish between agency models with moral hazard (unobservable actions) or adverse selection (unobservable information).[35] In this paper, I focus only on adverse selection models. Second, to use terminology introduced by Douglas Bernheim and Michael Whinston (1986b), one should also distinguish between *intrinsic* and *delegated* common agency problems. Intrinsic common agency refers to the case in which the agent's (e.g., transnational's) only options are to deal with all its principals (e.g. governments) or none of them. Delegated common agency refers to the case in which the agent can choose to deal with any subset of principals. Both possibilities are relevant to the study of transnationals and tax competition.

One important issue involves assessing the welfare implications of tax competition or transfer pricing competition in which the policies through which home and host countries compete are endogenous. For technical reasons that are beyond the scope of this paper, there are significant problems in using the Revelation Principle to conduct this type of normative common agency analysis.[36] Recently, Martimort and Stole (1999) have shown that it is possible to focus attention on competition in non-linear tax schedules when the agent's preferences are quasi-linear, a condition generally satisfied by global, after-tax transnational profits. So far, there are only a recent few papers tackling this sort of analysis.[37] Because equilibria of non-linear tax games are characterized by systems of differential equations, robust welfare results have not yet been obtained.

[35] Bernheim and Whinston (1986a, b) provide general solutions to common agency models with moral hazard, much of which (e.g. menu auctions) has been used recently to study the political economy of trade agreements (e.g. Gene Grossman and Elhanan Helpman, 1994). General analyses of common agency models with adverse selection have been provided by Jean-Jacques Laffont and Jean Tirole (1991), David Martimort (1992), Lars Stole (1992), James Peck (1996), Bond and Gresik (1997), Martimort and Stole (1997), Larry Epstein and Michael Peters (1999), and Peters (1999).

[36] The interested reader is referred to Peck (1996), Epstein and Peters (1999), Martimort and Stole (1997), Martimort and Stole (1999), and Peters (1999).

[37] See Giacomo Calzolari (2000) and Trond Olsen and Osmundsen (2000).

The alternative to a normative analysis is to exogenously set the form of the policies countries use to compete for transnational investment and tax revenues and derive the equilibrium policies. This type of positive analysis helps identify the broader tax competition issues that arise when private information is present. The remaining discussion will focus on such positive results.

Bond and Gresik (1996) consider a model similar to that in Gresik and Nelson (1994). There is a transnational that produces an intermediate good at home at constant marginal cost, c. The good is shipped to a subsidiary in a host country where it is transformed in a 1-1 ratio into a final product (at zero cost) and sold to host consumers represented by the downward sloping demand curve $P(q)$. The subsidiary is again assumed to be a monopolist in the host country so that q simultaneously denotes intermediate good and final good production. The two governments regulate the transnational by setting a unit tax on the intermediate good flow, t and t^*, and a lump sum subsidy, S and S^*. These choices are made simultaneously, after which the transnational chooses q to maximize its profits,

$$(24) \quad P(q)q - (t + t^* + c)q + S + S^* .$$

This yields an output level $Q(t+t^*+c,S+S^*)$, and an indirect profit function for the transnational, $\pi(t+t^*+c,S+S^*)$. The home country is assumed to maximize the sum of net tax revenues and weighted profit (with welfare weight α and $0 \leq \alpha \leq 1$),

$$(25) \quad W = tQ - S + \alpha\pi$$

while the host country is assumed to maximize the sum of net consumer surplus and net tax revenues,

$$(26) \quad W^* = V(Q) - P(Q)Q + t^* Q - S^*$$

as all the owners of the firm are assumed to be home residents.

With complete information, any positive production equilibrium results in efficient production, $P(Q)=c$, and no rents, $\pi=0$. The home country does not use its tax to distort the firm's production decision, $t=0$. Instead, inefficient monopoly production is eliminated by a host production subsidy, i.e. $t^* < 0$. Now suppose neither country knows the value of c and that the range of possible values is $[c_0,c_1]$. As with the above two examples, if the countries act as a single principal by cooperatively setting their taxes, the optimal policies will involve zero profit for the transnational with cost c_1 and positive profits for firms with lower values of c. In addition, the induced output level will be first-best only for the transnational with cost c_0. Output levels for firms with higher costs will be distorted downward reflecting the higher social marginal cost of production due to the presence of information rents.

What happens if the countries set their tax schedules non-cooperatively? The game now involves both countries setting tax policies, $(t(r),S(r))$ for the home country and $(t^*(r^*), S^*(r^*))$ for the host country. Given these policies the transnational then reports cost r to the home country and r^* to the host country, r and r^* need not be the same, and produces $Q(t(r)+t^*(r^*)+c, S(r)+S^*(r^*))$. Bond and Gresik (1996) derive equilibria in which $r=r^*=c$, that is, in which the transnational reports its cost truthfully to both governments. Applying the Envelope Theorem to (24), truthtelling implies

(27)
$$d\pi(t(c) + t^*(c) + c, S(c) + S^*(c))/dc = -Q(t(c) + t^*(c) + c, S(c) + S^*(c)) < 0.$$

Thus, the transnational will continue to earn an information rent in equilibrium as long as its cost is less than c_1 and the magnitude of this rent is increasing in output. This last fact means each country can limit the rents the transnational must earn or alternatively each country can increase the rents it extracts from the transnational by inducing lower firm output. This is done by setting a positive unit tax. Given the rents implied by (27), (24) also implies that

$$S + S^* = \pi - P(Q)Q + (t + t^* + c)Q. \quad (28)$$

Substituting (28) into (25) and (26) yields

$$W = P(Q)Q - (t^* + c)Q - S^* + (\alpha - 1)\pi \quad (29)$$

and

$$W^* = V(Q) - (t + c)Q + S - \pi. \quad (30)$$

The presence of each country's tax rate in the welfare function of the other identifies a negative externality associated with tax competition.[38] The existence of this externality means that equilibrium welfare levels are lower for the two governments relative to the cooperative tax-setting case. Thus, tax competition with incomplete information introduces another factor limiting the ability of countries to extract transnational rents. Surprisingly, the transnational is also made worse off due to higher equilibrium unit taxes that arise when each country raises its unit tax to extract rents without taking account of the impact on the other country.

As Stole (1992) points out, these welfare implications are sensitive to both the nature of the tax competition and the nature of the private information. Claudio Mezzetti (1997) examines the case in which the transnational's private information

[38] In general, it will also be the case that tax competition creates an information externality as changes in one country's tax schedule can alter the reporting incentives the transnational faces with the other country. Because the unit taxes are perfect substitutes in this model, such an externality does not exist.

countries, the Subpart F restrictions effectively accelerate the rate at which foreign-source earnings generate U.S. tax liabilities. With subsidiaries in both high- and low-tax countries, transnationals can use this differential treatment to their advantage by using the following 'triangular investment' strategy. Initial investments in both locations are made to equate the after-host-tax returns with the after-tax U.S. return. Once the low-tax subsidiary begins to generate earnings in excess of those needed for its new (active) investments, it invests these excess earnings in the high-tax subsidiary. The high-tax subsidiary then repatriates all of its earnings and enough of its initial equity investment (by buying back the parent's shares) to maintain after-tax rates of return. Because repatriations from this subsidiary generate excess credits, they incur no additional U.S. tax, nor do the equity repayments.[40]

This example is also intended to illustrate the fact that models of tax competition with transnationals must eventually allow for dynamic behavior if they are to have any chance of capturing the effects of issues like repatriation and the timing of investments. At the level of modeling transnational behavior, Altshuler and Grubert (1996) illustrates the importance of repatriation in a dynamic setting while Newlon (1987), Hines (1994a), and Weichenrieder (1996a) address dynamic issues caused by both deferral and the timing of investments.[41] In tax competition models, such dynamic concerns have been largely unaddressed.

References

Altshuler, Rosanne and Paolo Fulghieri. 1993. 'Incentive Effects of Foreign Tax Credits on Multinational Corporations.' *Nat. Tax J.* 47, pp. 349-361.

Altshuler, Rosanne and Harry Grubert. 1996. 'Balance Sheets, Multinational Financial Policy, and the Cost of Capital at Home and Abroad.' Mimeo, Rutgers University.

Altshuler, Rosanne and Jack Mintz. 1995. 'U.S. Interest-allocation Rules: Effects and Policy.' *Int. Tax Public Finance* 2, pp.7-35.

Altshuler, Rosanne and T. Scott Newlon. 1993. 'The Effects of U.S. Tax Policy on the Income Repatriation Patterns of U.S. Multinational Corporations,' in *Studies in International Taxation*. Alberto Giovannini, R. Glenn Hubbard, and Joel Slemrod, eds. University of Chicago Press.

Altshuler, Rosanne, T. Scott Newlon, and William Randolph. 1995. 'Do Repatriation Taxes Matter? Evidence From the Tax Returns of U.S. Multinationals,' in *The Effects of Taxation on Multinational Corporations*, Martin Feldstein, James Hines Jr., and R. Glenn Hubbard, eds. University of Chicago Press.

Arnold, Brian. 1994. General report, in Cahiers de Droit Fiscal International, *Deductibility of Interest and Other Financing Charges in Computing Income*, International Fiscal Association 79, Kluwer, Amsterdam.

Auerbach, Alan. 1979. 'The Optimal Taxation of Heterogeneous Capital.' *Quart. J. Econ.* 93, pp. 589-612.

[40] Private communication with one of the authors revealed that, at the time this paper was first written, U.S. Treasury officials were unaware of the profitability of this strategy.

[41] In addition, many of the empirical studies cited in section 3 attempt to capture the dynamic behavior of transnationals.

Ault, Hugh and David Bradford. 1990. 'Taxing International Income: An Analysis of the U.S. System and Its Economic Premises,' in *Taxation in the Global Economy*. Assaf Razin and Joel Slemrod, eds. University of Chicago Press.

Bernard, Jean-Thomas and Robert Weiner. 1990. 'Multinational Corporations, Transfer Prices, and Taxes: Evidence from the U. S. Petroleum Industry,' in *Taxation in the Global Economy*. Assaf Razin and Joel Slemrod, eds. NBER, University of Chicago Press.

Bernheim, Douglas and Michael Whinston. 1986a. 'Menu Auctions, Resource Allocation, and Economic Influence.' *Quart. J. Econ.* 101, pp.1-32.

________. 1986b. 'Common Agency.' *Econometrica* 54, pp.923-942.

Bond, Eric. 1991. 'Optimal Tax and Tariff Policies with Tax Credits.' *J. Int. Econ.* 30, pp.317-329.

Bond, Eric and Thomas Gresik. 1996. 'Regulation of Multinational Firms With Two Active Governments: A Common Agency Approach.' *J. Pub. Econ.* 59, pp.33-53.

________. 1997. 'Competition Between Asymmetrically Informed Principals.' *Econ. Theory* 10, pp.227-240.

________. 1998. 'Incentive Compatible Information Transfer Between Asymmetrically Informed Principals.' Mimeo, Pennsylvania State University.

Bond, Eric and Larry Samuelson. 1989. 'Strategic Behaviour and the Rules for International Taxation of Capital.' *Econ. J.* 99, pp.1099-1111.

Bovenberg, A. Lars and Roger Gordon. 1996. 'Why is Capital So Immobile Internationally? Possible Explanations and Implications for Capital Income Taxation.' *Amer. Econ. Rev.* 86, pp.1057-1075.

Brander, James and Barbara Spencer. 1985. 'Export Subsidies and International Market Share Rivalry.' *J. of Int. Econ.* 18, pp.83-100.

Calzolari, Giacomo. 2000. 'Incentive Regulation of Multinational Enterprises.' Mimeo, GREMAQ, Universitat Sciences Sociales de Toulouse.

Chan, K. Hung and Lynne Chow. 1997. 'An Empirical Study of Tax Audits in China on International Transfer Pricing.' *J. Acc. Econ.* 23, pp.83-112.

Collins, Julie and Douglas Shackelford. 1992. 'Foreign Tax Credit Limitations and Preferred Stock Issuances.' *J. Acc. Res.* 30, pp.103 124.

Coopers & Lybrand. 1998. *1998 International Tax Summaries*. Wiley: New York.

Copithorne, Lawrence. 1971. 'International Corporate Transfer Prices and Government Policy.' *Can. J. Econ.* 4, pp. 324-341.

Davies, Ronald. 1999. 'The OECD Model Tax Treaty: Tax Competition and Two-way Capital Flows.' Mimeo.

Davies, Ronald and Thomas Gresik. 2003. 'Tax Competition and Foreign Capital.' International Tax and Public Finance (10): 127-145.

Diamond, Peter and James Mirrlees. 1971. 'Optimal Taxation and Public Production I: Productive Efficiency.' *Amer. Econ. Rev.* 61, pp.8-27.

Diewert, W. Erwin. 1985. 'Transfer Pricing and Economic Efficiency,' in *Multinationals and Transfer Pricing*. Alan Rugman and Lorraine Eden, eds. St. Martins, New York, pp. 47-81.

Eden, Lorraine.1985. 'The Microeconomics of Transfer Pricing,' in *Multinationals and Transfer Pricing*. Alan Rugman and Lorraine Eden, eds. St. Martins, New York, pp. 13-46.

Elitzur, Ramy and Jack Mintz. 1996. 'Transfer Pricing Rules and Corporate Tax Competition.' *J. Pub. Econ.* 60, pp. 401-422.

Epstein, Larry and Michael Peters. 1999. 'A Revelation Principle For Competing Mechanisms.' *J. Econ. Theory* 88, pp. 119-160.

Feldstein, Martin. 1994. 'Taxes, Leverage, and the National Return on Outbound Foreign Direct Investment.' NBER Working Paper #4689.

________.1995. 'The Effects of Outbound Foreign Direct Investment on the Domestic Capital Stock,' in *The Effects of Taxation on Multinational Corporations*. Martin Feldstein, James Hines Jr., and R. Glenn Hubbard, eds. University of Chicago Press.

Feldstein, Martin and David Hartman. 1979. 'The Optimal Taxation of Foreign Source Investment Income.' *Quart. J. Econ.* 93, pp.613-630.

Froot, Kenneth and James Hines Jr. 1995. 'Interest Allocation Rules, Financing Patterns, and the Operations of U.S. Multinationals,' in *The Effects of Taxation on Multinational Corporations*. Martin Feldstein, James Hines Jr., and R. Glenn Hubbard, eds. University of Chicago Press.

Gordon, Roger. 1986. 'Taxation of Investment and Savings in a World Economy.' *Amer. Econ. Rev.* 76, pp.1086-1102.

________. 1992. 'Can Capital Income Taxes Survive in Open Economies?' *J. Finance* 47, pp.1159-1180.

Gordon, Roger and Jeffrey MacKie-Mason. 1995. 'Why Is There Corporate Taxation In a Small Open Economy? The Role of Transfer Pricing and Income Shifting,' in *The Effects of Taxation on Multinational Corporations*. Martin Feldstein, James Hines Jr., and R. Glenn Hubbard, eds. University of Chicago Press.

Gordon, Roger and Joel Slemrod. 1998. 'Do We Collect Any Revenue from Taxing Capital Income?' *Tax Policy and the Economy* 2, pp.89-130.

Gordon, Roger and John Wilson. 1986. 'An Examination of Multijurisdictional Corporate Income Taxation Under Formula Apportionment.' *Econometrica* 54, pp. 1357-1374.

Gresik, Thomas. 1999. 'Arm's-length Transfer Pricing and National Welfare,' in *Advances in Applied Microeconomics, volume 8, Oligopoly*. Michael Baye, ed. JAI Press.

Gresik, Thomas and Douglas Nelson. 1994. 'Incentive Compatible Regulation of a Foreign-owned Subsidiary.' *J. Int. Econ.* 36, pp. 309-331.

Grossman, Gene and Elhanan Helpman. 1994. 'Protection For Sale.' *Amer. Econ. Rev.* 84, pp.833-850.

Grubert, Harry, Timothy Goodspeed, and Deborah Swenson. 1993. 'Explaining the Low Taxable Income of Foreign-controlled Companies in the United States,' in *Studies in International Taxation*. Alberto Giovannini, R. Glenn Hubbard, and Joel Slemrod, eds. NBER, University of Chicago Press.

Grubert, Harry and John Mutti. 1991. 'Taxes, Tariffs and Transfer Pricing in Multinational Corporate Decision Making.' *Rev. Econ. Statist.*72, pp. 285-293.

Grubert, Harry and Joel Slemrod. 1998. 'The Effect of Taxes on Investment and Income Shifting to Puerto Rico.' *Rev. Econ. Statist.* 80, pp. 365-373.

Hagen, Kåre and Vesa Kanniainen. 1995. 'Optimal Taxation of Intangible Capital.' *Europ. J. Polit. Economy* 11, pp. 361-378.

Halperin, Robert and Bin Srinidhi. 1996. 'U.S. Income Tax Transfer Pricing Rules for Intangibles as Approximations of Arm's Length Pricing.' *Acc. Rev.* 71, pp. 61-80.

Hamada, Koichi. 1966. 'Strategic Aspects of Taxation of Foreign Investment Income.' *Quart. J. Econ.* 80, pp.361-375.

Harris, David. 1993. 'The Impact of U.S. Tax Law Revision on Multinational Corporations' Capital Location and Income-shifting Decisions.' *J. Acc. Res.* 31, pp.111-140.

Harris, David, Randall Morck, Joel Slemrod, and Bernard Yeung. 1993. 'Income Shifting in U.S. Multinational Corporations,' in *Studies in International Taxation*. Alberto Giovannini, R. Glenn Hubbard, and Joel Slemrod, eds. University of Chicago Press.

Harris, David and Richard Sansing. 1998. 'Distortions Caused By the Use of Arm's-length Transfer Prices.' Mimeo, Syracuse University.

Hartman, David. 1985. 'Tax Policy and Foreign Direct Investment.' *J. Pub. Econ.* 26, pp. 107-121.

Haufler, Andrea and Guttorm Schjelderup. 2000. 'Corporate Tax Systems and Cross Country Profit Shifting.' *Oxford Econ. Pap.* 52, pp. 306-325.

Hines, James Jr. 1988. 'Taxation and U.S. Multinational Investment,' in *Tax Policy and the Economy.* Lawrence Summers, ed. National Bureau of Economic Research, MIT Press.

________. 1993. 'On the Sensitivity of R&D to Delicate Tax Changes: The Behavior of U.S. Multinationals in the 1980s,' in *Studies in International Taxation.* Alberto Giovannini, R. Glenn Hubbard, and Joel Slemrod, eds. University of Chicago Press.

________. 1994a. 'Credit and Deferral as International Investment Incentives.' *J. Pub. Econ.* 55, pp. 323-347.

________. 1994b. 'No Place Like Home: Tax Incentive and the Location of R&D by American Multinationals,' in *Tax Policy and the Economy.* James Poterba ed. National Bureau of Economic Research, MIT Press.

________. 1995. 'Taxes, Technology Transfer, and the R&D Activities of Multinational Firms,' in *The Effects of Taxation on Multinational Corporations.* Martin Feldstein, James Hines Jr., and R. Glenn Hubbard, eds. University of Chicago Press.

________. 1996. 'Altered States: Taxes and the Location of Foreign Direct Investment in America.' *Amer. Econ. Rev.* 86, pp.1076-1094.

________. 1999. 'Lessons from Behavioral Responses to International Taxation.' *Nat. Tax J.* 52, pp.305-322.

Hines, James Jr. and R. Glenn Hubbard. 1990. 'Coming Home to America: Dividend Repatriations by U.S. Multinationals,' in *Taxation in the Global Economy.* Assaf Razin and Joel Slemrod, eds. University of Chicago Press.

Horst, Thomas.1971. 'Theory of the Multinational Firm: Optimal Behavior under Differing Tariff and Tax Rates.' *J. Polit. Economy* 79, pp. 1059-1072.

________. 1977. 'American Taxation of Multinational Firms.' *Amer. Econ. Rev.* 67, pp. 376-389.

Janeba, Eckhard. 1995. 'Corporate Income Tax Competition, Double Taxation Treaties, and Foreign Direct Investment.' *J. Pub. Econ.* 56, pp.311-325.

________. 1996. 'Foreign Direct Investment Under Oligopoly: Profit Shifting or Profit Capturing?' *J. Pub. Econ.* 60, pp.423-445.

________. 1998. 'Tax Competition in Imperfectly Competitive Markets.' *J. Int. Econ.* 44, pp.135-153.

Kemp, Murray. 1964. *The Pure Theory of International Trade.* Prentice-Hall, Englewood Cliffs.

Laffont, Jean-Jacques and Jean Tirole. 1991. 'Privatization and Incentives.' *J. Law, Econ., and Organ.* 7, pp.84-105.

Leechor, Chad and Jack Mintz. 1993. 'On the Taxation of Multinational Corporate Investment When the Deferral Method is Used by the Capital Exporting Country.' *J. Pub. Econ.* 51, pp.75-96.

MacDougall, George. 1960. 'The Benefits and Costs of Private Investment Abroad: A Theoretical Approach.' *Econ. Rec.*36, pp.13–35.

Madan, Vibhas. 1998. 'Endogenous Transfer Prices, Tariffs, and a Host-country Duopoly.' Mimeo, Drexel University.

Markusen, James. 1995. 'The Boundaries of Multinational Enterprises and the Theory of International Trade.' *J. Econ. Perspect.* 9, pp.169-189.

Markusen, James and Anthony Venables. 1998. 'Multinational Firms and the New Trade Theory.' *J. Int. Econ.* 46, pp.183-203.

Martimort, David. 1992. 'Multi-principaux Avec Anti-selection.' *Ann. Econ. Statist.* 28, pp.1-38.

Martimort, David and Lars Stole. 1997. 'Communication Spaces, Equilibria Sets and the Revelation Principle Under Common Agency.' Mimeo, University of Chicago.

________. 1999. 'The Revelation and Taxation Principles in Common Agency Games.' Mimeo, University of Chicago.

Mezzetti, Claudio. 1997. 'Common Agency With Horizontally Differentiated Principals.' *RAND J. Econ.* 28, pp.323-345.

Mintz, Jack and Thomas Tsiopoulos. 1994. 'The Effectiveness of Corporate Tax Incentives For Foreign Investment in the Presence of Tax Crediting.' *J. Pub. Econ.* 55, pp.233-255.

Mintz, Jack and Henry Tulkens. 1986. 'Commodity Tax Competition Between Member States of a Federation: Equilibrium and Efficiency.' *J. Pub. Econ.* 29, pp. 133-172.

________. 1996. 'Optimality Properties of Alternative Systems of Taxation of Foreign Capital Income.' *J. Pub. Econ.* 60, pp.373-399.

Musgrave, Peggy. 1969. *United States Taxation of Foreign Investment Income: Issues and Arguments*. Cambridge, MA: International Tax Program, Harvard Law School.

Mutti, John and Harry Grubert. 1998. 'The Significance of International Tax Rules for Sourcing Income: The Relationship Between Income Taxes and Trade Taxes,' in *Geography and Ownership as Bases for Economic Accounting. NBER Studies in Income and Wealth, vol. 59.* Robert Baldwin, Robert Lipsey, and J. David Richardson, eds. University of Chicago Press, pp. 259-280.

Newlon, T. Scott. 1987. 'Tax Policy and the Multinational Firm's Financial Policy and Investment Decisions.' Unpublished PhD dissertation, Princeton University.

OECD. 1995. *Transfer Pricing Guidelines for Multinational Enterprises and Tax Administrations*. OECD.

________. 1998, *International Direct Investment Statistics Yearbook, 1997*. OECD, Paris.

OECD Committee on Fiscal Affairs. 1984. *Transfer Pricing and Multinational Enterprises: Three Taxation Issues*. OECD.

________. 1997, *Model Tax Convention On Income and On Capital*. OECD, Paris.

Olsen, Trond and Petter Osmundsen. 2000. 'Common Agency With Outside Options: The Case of International Taxation of an MNE.' Mimeo, University of Bergen.

________. 2001. 'Strategic Tax Competition: Implications of National Ownership.' *J. Pub. Econ.* 81, pp. 253-277.

Osmundsen, Petter, Kåre Hagen, and Guttorm Schjelderup. 1998. 'Internationally Mobile Firms and Tax Policy.' *J. Int. Econ.* 45, pp.97-113.

Peck, James. 1996. 'Competing Mechanisms and the Revelation Principle.' Mimeo, Ohio State University.

Peters, Michael. 1999. 'Common Agency and the Revelation Principle.' Mimeo, University of Toronto.

Price Waterhouse. 1995. *Corporate Taxes: A Worldwide Summary*. Price Waterhouse World Firm Services BV, London.

Ramaswami, V. K. 1968. 'International Factor Movement and the National Advantage.' *Economica* 35, pp. 309-310.

Razin. Assaf and Efraim Sadka. 1990. 'Integration of International Capital Markets: The Size of Government and Tax Coordination,' in *Taxation in the Global Economy*. Assaf Razin and Joel Slemrod, eds. University of Chicago Press.

________. 1991. 'International Tax Competition and Gains From Tax Harmonization.' *Econ. Letters* 37, pp.66-76.

Razin, Assaf, Efraim Sadka, and Chi-Wa Yuen. 1998. 'A Pecking Order of Capital Inflows and International Tax Principles.' *J. Int. Econ.* 44, pp.45-68.

Rochet, Jean-Charles. 1986. *Le Controle Des Equations Aux Derivees Partielles Issues De La Theorie Des Incitations*. PhD thesis, Universite Paris IX.

Ross, Stephen. 1988. 'Comment on the Modigliani-Miller Propositions.' *J. Econ. Perspect.*2, pp.127-133.

Rybczynski, Tadeus. 1955. 'Factor Endowments and Relative Commodity Prices.' *Economica* 22, pp.336-341.

Schjelderup, Guttorm and Alfons Weichenrieder. 1999. 'Trade, Multinationals, and Transfer Pricing Regulation.' *Can. J. Econ.* 32, pp. 817-834.

Sinn, Hans-Werner. 1984. 'Die Bedeutung Des Accelerated Cost Recovery System Für Den Internationalen Kapitalverkehr.' *Kyklos* 37, pp.542-576.

________. 1997. 'The Selection Principle and Market Failure in Systems Competition.' *J. Pub. Econ.* 66, pp.247-274.

Stole, Lars. 1992. 'Mechanism Design Under Common Agency.' Mimeo, University of Chicago.

United Nations. 1980. 'U.N. Model Double Taxation Convention Between Developed and Developing Countries.' U.N. Document #ST/ESA/102. New York.

United Nations Conference on Trade and Development Secretariat. 1978. *Dominant Positions of Market Power of Transnational Corporations: Use of the Transfer Pricing Mechanism.* United Nations.

U.S. Department of the Treasury. 1988. 'Study of Intercompany Pricing Rules.' *Federal Register* 53 (208), pp. 43522-43581.

U.S. Department of the Treasury. 1994. 'Intercompany Transfer Pricing Regulations Under Section 482: Final Regulations.' *Federal Register* 59 (130), pp. 34971-35033.

U.S. Tax Court. 1999. 'COMPAQ vs. U.S. Commissioner.' 78 T.C.M., CCH 20.

Weichenrieder, Alfons. 1996a. 'Anti-avoidance Provisions and the Size of Foreign Direct Investment.' *Int. Tax Public Finance* 3, pp. 67-81.

Weichenrieder, Alfons. 1996b. 'Transfer Pricing, Double Taxation, and the Cost of Capital."'*Scand. J. Econ.* 98, pp. 445-452.

Wilson, G. Peter. 1993. 'The Role of Taxes in Location and Sourcing Decisions,' in *Studies in International Taxation.* Alberto Giovannini, R. Glenn Hubbard, and Joel Slemrod, eds. University of Chicago Press.

Wilson, John. 1999. 'Theories of Tax Competition.' *Nat. Tax J.* 52, pp. 269-304.

Chapter 5

Substantial Petroleum Wealth: Does Monetary Policy Regime Matter?

Torbjørn Eika and Knut Moum

Introduction

The net value of Norway's petroleum reserves per January 2004 is estimated[1] at twice the value of mainland GDP, if real petroleum prices remain at the 2003 level. This petroleum wealth is then defined as the present value of future petroleum rent, which is the revenue from petroleum extraction exceeding the normal compensation to labour and capital. The government's permanent income (theoretical real return) from this wealth is estimated to 5.3 per cent of mainland GDP. The sheer magnitude of the figures illustrates Norway's vulnerability to developments in the markets for crude oil and gas – a vulnerability that is unique in the OECD area, but also is seen in highly natural resource based developing countries.

Norway's current spending of petroleum revenues seems moderate: in 2003 the surplus on the trade balance was 17.2 per cent of mainland GDP. Excluding export of crude oil and natural gas there was a deficit of 5.9 per cent. If the resource rent part of the petroleum export is subtracted from the trade balance, there is a surplus corresponding to 2.8 per cent of mainland GDP. Based on these figures, one could argue that Norway at the moment saves more abroad than the entire resource rent, and that the vulnerability of the Norwegian economy to the development in the petroleum market is basically through possible effects on public sector spending. However, this apparent 'lack of spending' may to a large extent be a cyclical rather than a structural phenomenon. In 2003 investments in Norway were recorded at the lowest level as a percentage of GDP for the last 30 years. In the following, we will not discuss the level of structural spending of revenues from the petroleum wealth, but focus on the hypothetical but possible case where Norway would have to reduce domestic spending of petroleum income.

If the structural spending initially were in line with the permanent income from the petroleum wealth, a reduction in the petroleum income estimate would necessitate a cut in domestic spending in order to re-establish a sustainable trade balance. The ensuing adjustment of the real exchange rate could take place through

[1] Calculations based on estimates given in Ministry of Finance (2003) and Statistics Norway (2004).

a nominal currency depreciation or through lower domestic inflation, depending on the monetary regime in operation.

This chapter discusses how adjustment costs to external shocks depend on the monetary regime in operation. We argue that adjustment costs may be somewhat lower within a regime of flexible exchange rates than if monetary policy is directed at stabilising the exchange rate. The discussion focuses on the impact of changes in oil prices, but the analysis is relevant for large changes in the estimates of real wealth from all kinds of sources and also in yields on foreign investments like a petroleum fund. The analysis is carried out through simulations on a large-scale macroeconometric forecasting model.

The Working of the Economy

In approaching the question of how different monetary policy regimes may affect the readjustment to changes in the petroleum wealth, we need a simplifying representation of the important mechanisms of the economy. We employ the KVARTS model (see Eika and Magnussen, 2000, for an overview).

In the model, production and investments in the resource-based industries are mainly treated exogenously, whereas remaining private sector behaviour is endogenous. Policy variables and variables describing impulses from abroad are exogenous. The model exhibits some well-known Keynesian characteristics in the short run, as the activity level is determined by the demand side. In the longer run, however, trends in total factor productivity, the capital stock and labour supply are crucial for economic development.

The main feature of the medium term solution of the model may be represented in a diagram with the (log of the) real exchange rate (q) on the one axis and the unemployment rate (u) on the other. The qq-locus in Figure 5.1 represents price and wage formation. A low level of unemployment indicates high pressure in the labour market, which results in a high real wage and therefore a low real exchange rate. The yy-locus represents product market equilibrium, based on a simplified description of the relationship between unemployment and production. Aggregate demand increases with the size of public sector demand, real wealth and real disposable income in the household sector and activity levels abroad. If domestic prices grow faster than prices abroad, demand for Norwegian products will be reduced in both markets. An increase in the interest rate reduces domestic demand in the short and medium term. The real exchange rate is defined as the ratio between foreign and domestic prices measured in a common currency. An increase in the real exchange rate means improved competitiveness and thereby higher production and lower unemployment.

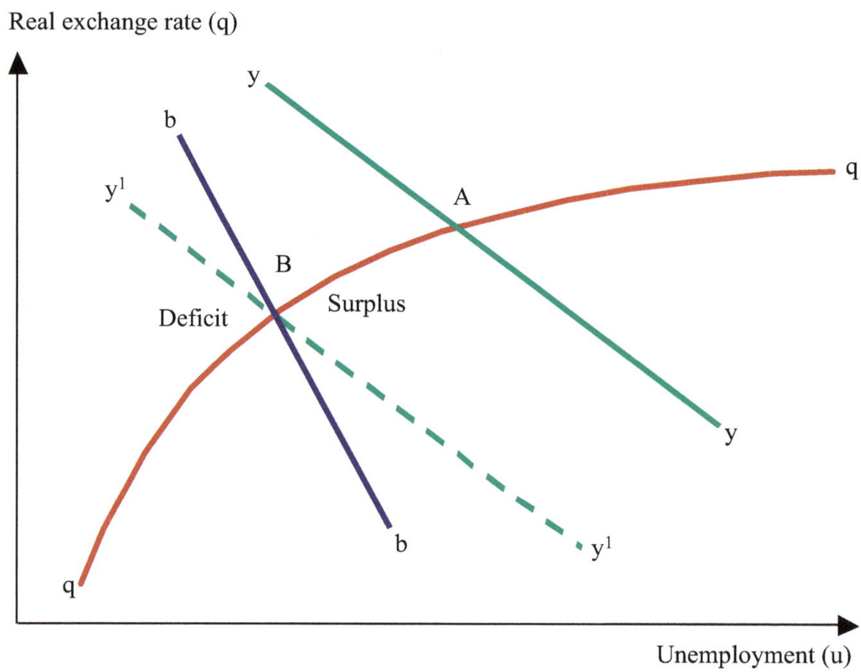

Figure 5.1 Medium term equilibrium in KVARTS

An increase in public spending shifts the yy-locus in Figure 5.1 towards southwest as competitiveness will have to deteriorate to make room for the expansion of domestic demand. From the figure we see that an expansive economic policy will result in lower unemployment and an appreciation of the real exchange rate as the economy moves from point A to point B. The relationship between a change in the unemployment rate and a change in the real exchange rate depends on the initial level of unemployment: if unemployment is high initially, the fall in unemployment will be larger relative to the change in the real exchange rate than if unemployment is low initially.

A change in the taxation of wages will shift the qq-locus. A decrease in taxes increases after-tax wages for all wage levels, and moves the qq-locus upwards: for a given level of unemployment, equilibrium nominal wages will fall, as will domestic prices. Competitiveness will improve and the real exchange rate depreciate. A reduction in taxes will also shift the yy-locus to the southwest, as household income increases.

Monetary policy in Norway was for a long time and until March 2001 aimed at keeping the exchange rate fixed or stable. In the KVARTS model the interest rate is determined by an equation estimated on historical data, and hence the equation is based on an assumption that the interest rate is set in order to stabilise the exchange rate. In the long run a stable exchange rate is accomplished if the difference between the real short term interest rate in Norway and in the euro-zone is constant. Under other monetary regimes, like the current inflation targeting regime, interest rates have to be treated exogenously in the model.

The model presentation so far may give the impression that the authorities may choose any combination of unemployment (or domestic activity) and real exchange rate through a suitable fiscal policy. However, both the real exchange rate and unemployment affect the size of the trade balance and the current account. Higher unemployment is associated with lower domestic activity thus reducing imports and improving the trade balance. In the medium run an increase in the real exchange rate will improve the trade balance – ceteris paribus. The locus of all combinations of the real exchange rate and unemployment that balances the current account may be represented by the falling line bb in the u-q diagram: west of bb the trade balance is negative, east positive.

In the short and medium term a country may run a significant deficit or surplus on the current account. In the long run, however, there will be limits to the size of a deficit or surplus and these limits will tie down economic policy. No such mechanisms are built into the model,[2] which implicitly places the responsibility of stabilising the current account on fiscal policy.

Petroleum Wealth, the Trade Balance and the Real Exchange Rate

Discussing the economic development of countries with large non-renewable natural resources, some standard macroeconomic variables should be treated with caution. In the national account, oil extraction is regarded as ordinary production, even though the value of remaining resources is reduced. A better way to look at this would be to regard the resource rent, defined as the return in excess of normal returns on labour and capital, as transformation of wealth, rather than as income. Below, we focus on the wealth transformation aspect of oil production in order to characterise a sustainable trade balance.

In the absence of transfers, the relationship for the development of a country's net foreign claims can be stated as follows:

$$(1)\quad F_t = (1+i^*)\cdot F_{t-1} + TB_t$$

In (1) F_t is the real value of net foreign claims in the end of period t, TB_t is the real value of the trade balance in period t and i^* the (constant) foreign real interest rate.

[2] There is one mechanism that works in this direction: according to the dynamics of the interest rate relationship, the real interest rate difference will increase if a current account deficit increases. This lowers domestic demand and works in the direction of improving the trade balance/current account again. Due to the equilibrium correcting form of the interest rate equation the effect will gradually disappear for any stable level of the current account. Hence, the effect can obviously not guarantee a sustainable path for the current account.

Introducing the discount factor $k = (1+i^*)^{-1}$, repeated forward substitution for F_{t+1} in (1) gives us the following expression for net foreign claims in the end of period t:

$$(2) \quad F_t = k^T \cdot F_{t+T} - \sum_{s=1}^{T} k^s \cdot TB_{t+s}$$

In (2), $\sum_{s=1}^{T} k^s \cdot TB_{t+s-1}$ is the net present value of all future trade balances up to time T. In a long term perspective it is a reasonable premise that no country will be allowed to increase its debt or should want to increase its assets relative to the size of the economy. Ruling out a long term growth rate above the real interest rate, this implies that $\lim_{T\to\infty} k^T \cdot F_{t+T} = 0$. Under this assumption (2) transforms to (3) with an infinite time horizon

$$(3) \quad F_t = -\sum_{s=1}^{\infty} k^s \cdot TB_{t+s}$$

(3) says that the present value of all future trade balance deficits should equal the present net claims. This is often referred to as a long term solvency condition. This implies restrictions on the trade balance and thereby on the current balance as well. The solvency condition does not however rule out accumulation of debt or claims in a very long (but finite) period, but such a process must be reversed in some later periods. In theory, the solvency condition does not imply any short term restrictions on a country's spending strategy at all. In practice it would be difficult for a country to finance a policy of big spending for a couple of years – in the light of the necessary period of sacrifice and saving that have to follow. In the same way it could prove politically difficult to carry out a policy of considerable 'saving' now in exchange for 'spending' later. There are costs connected to large fluctuations in economic activity and in the production structure. This indicates that economic policy should try to pick out a relatively stable development in the trade balance, from the multitudes of possible paths that are consistent with long term solvency. An example of such a stable path is given by

$$(4) \quad TB_t + i^* \cdot F_{t-1} = 0 \text{ for all t}$$

With the real trade balance deficit equal to the real return of net foreign claims, the inflation-adjusted current account stays in balance. Putting (4) in (1) gives $F_{t+1} = F_t$ and it follows that $F_{t+s} = F_t$ for all s.[3] By putting (4) in (3) we see that the solvency condition is met:

[3] In periods of a foreign inflation rate of π, this implies a nominal surplus in the current balance of $\pi \cdot F_t$ if $F_t > 0$ and a deficit of $\pi \cdot F_t$ if $F_t < 0$.

$$F_t = \sum_{s=1}^{\infty} k^s \cdot i^* \cdot F_{t+s-1}$$

$$\Updownarrow$$

$$F_t / F_{t+s-1} = i^* \cdot \sum_{s=1}^{\infty} \cdot ((1+i^*)^{-1})^s$$

$\sum_{s=1}^{\infty} \cdot ((1+i^*)^{-1})^s = (i^*)^{-1}$ and (4) implies that $F_t = F_{t+s-1}$.

A restriction such as (4) would tie up economic policy almost totally. In figure 5.1 this means an economic policy that makes the yy and the qq lines intersect through the bb-line. Business cycles and preferences for a smooth consumption path would make a strategy geared to keep (4) on a permanent basis, far from optimal. Fluctuations in the general activity level will normally induce significant fluctuations in the trade balance. In the empirical oriented literature on fundamental equilibrium exchange rates it is common to assume that the real exchange rate is in equilibrium if it is consistent with current account balance over the cycle and adjusted for structural capital movements (see for instance Wren-Lewis, 1992). In Norway's case, adjustments seem very appropriate as the capital flows connected to the petroleum wealth are of considerable magnitude. Oil prices in the area of what is observed after 1973 generates a higher return in the petroleum exploration than in other activities. The yield that exceeds normal return in this activity is known as the petroleum rent. The property right of oil reserves represents the possibility to gain this (uncertain) rent, and may thus have a wealth value. The size of the petroleum wealth depends upon the extraction profile, the net price (price less average costs) path and of course the remaining petroleum reserves. The optimal extraction path will depend on the development of the net price. As an illustrative simplification we may consider the future net prices as known and the extraction path as given. At a certain point of time the petroleum wealth may then be calculated as the present value of all future petroleum rents. If we let PR_t denote the petroleum rent in year t, we have this formal definition of the remaining petroleum wealth in the end of the year t, F^P_t:

(5) $F^P_t = \sum_{s=1}^{\infty} k^s \cdot PR_{t+s}$

The size of the petroleum wealth may be characterized by the theoretical real return on this wealth. Formally this permanent income at time t from the petroleum wealth, PI_t, is then defined as

(6) $PI_t = i^* \cdot F^P_{t-1}$

and is a concept which is useful when evaluating the sustainability of the trade balance for a petroleum economy like Norway.

The rule (4) of a balanced inflation-adjusted current account led to a path where real financial wealth was constant over time. In the presence of large petroleum wealth it therefore seems reasonable to look for a rule that keeps the sum of petroleum and financial wealth constant in real terms as the counterpart to the rule (4):

$$(7)\quad F_{s-1} + F^{P}_{s-1} = F_s + F^{P}_{s} \quad \text{for all } s \geq t$$

Equation (7) will be fulfilled if the inflation-adjusted current account equals the difference between petroleum rent and permanent income from the petroleum wealth in each period (9). To see this, let us first transform (5):

$$F^{P}_{t} = \sum_{s=1}^{\infty} k^{s} \cdot PR_{t+s}$$

$$\Updownarrow$$

$$F^{P}_{t} = k \cdot PR_{t+1} + k \cdot \sum_{s=1}^{\infty} k^{s} \cdot PR_{t+s+1}$$

$$\Updownarrow$$

$$F^{P}_{t} = k \cdot PR_{t+1} + k \cdot F^{P}_{t+1}$$

$$\Updownarrow$$

$$(8)\quad F^{P}_{t} = (1+i^{*}) \cdot F^{P}_{t-1} - PR_t$$

(8) says that petroleum wealth in the end of the present period equals the difference between the present value of the last period petroleum wealth and the petroleum rent in the present period, all in real terms. As times go by petroleum wealth is influenced by two opposite effects: It is ceteris paribus increased because all future revenues have come closer in time, and reduced due to present period extraction.

Substituting for F_s and F^{P}_{s} on the right hand side of (7) by transformations of (1) and (8) gives

$$F_{s-1} + F^{P}_{s-1} = (1+i^{*}) \cdot F_{s-1} + TB_s + (1+i^{*}) \cdot F^{P}_{s-1} - PR_s$$

$$\Updownarrow$$

$$(9)\quad i^{*} \cdot F_{s-1} + TB_s = PR_s - PI_s$$

Here we recognise the left hand side as the inflation-adjusted current account for period s, while the right hand side is the difference between the petroleum rent and the permanent income from the petroleum wealth for the same period. (9) may be rewritten as

$$(10)\quad -(TB_s - PR_s) = i^{*} \cdot (F_{s-1} + F^{P}_{s-1})$$

which says that total real wealth (defined as the sum of real financial wealth and real resource wealth) will be constant if the trade balance deficit corrected for petroleum rent equals the permanent income from total wealth.

As long as the petroleum rent exceeds the permanent income from the petroleum wealth (PR_s-PI_s>0) and rule (9) is followed, a country is converting petroleum wealth to financial wealth. The part of the surplus of the current account that has its counterpart in such conversion of wealth does not signal any underlying imbalance and should therefore not be taken as a token of any need to realign the real exchange rate.

The life cycle of petroleum extraction may be divided into three periods:

- a period of extensive investments and increasing extraction
- a period of relatively stable extraction and falling investments
- a long period of falling extraction and low level of investments

This scenario is of course based on assumptions of a reasonable development in net oil prices and no substantial shifts in the discovery of new resources. Ignoring fluctuations in the oil prices, one would expect the following underlying path in the current account: early in the first period a current account deficit is obvious as investments are high and production low, due to a substantial time lag between investment and extraction. Then one would expect a long period of increasing current account surpluses in line with growing extraction and, after a while, reduced investments. Finally, when the bulk of the resource wealth has been transformed to financial wealth, current account surpluses will diminish or even be replaced by a deficit (if not only the yield but also the wealth is gradually spent).

Only if $TB_s + i^* \cdot F_{s-1}$ diverges from $PR_s - PI_s$ after adjusting for cyclical fluctuations will the presence of resource wealth indicate a need for a change in the real exchange rate. If the adjusted current account surplus is less than the difference between petroleum rent and permanent income from the petroleum wealth ($TB_s + i^* \cdot F_{s-1} < PR_s - PI_s$), total wealth (defined as financial and petroleum wealth) is reduced. This may indicate a need for a tighter economic policy and a real depreciation of the currency in the medium term. Correspondingly a current account surplus exceeding the difference between petroleum rent and permanent income from the petroleum wealth ($TB_s + i^* \cdot F_{s-1} > PR_s - PI_s$) will imply an increase in total wealth and thus indicate the need for a medium term real appreciation. If there is constant return to scale in the long run, the real exchange rate and the sectoral composition of production should be independent of the spending of the resource rent. The KVARTS model does however not exhibit constant return in the medium term.

The permanent income from the petroleum wealth is uncertain and the estimates may be revised as new information becomes available on future petroleum prices, costs, the level of extraction and the real interest rate. We have learned that the oil price is subject to considerable short and long term fluctuations (see Figure 5.2). Assume that a set of base estimates for future petroleum rent and the permanent income from the petroleum wealth has been constructed, conditioned on a specific time path for net oil prices and extraction. A temporary deviation between the actual and the expected path of oil prices will influence both petroleum rent and the permanent income from the petroleum wealth. The petroleum rent will deviate from the base estimate as long as the price deviation persists. The permanent income from the petroleum wealth will also be altered as long as the income changes are not compensated by an opposite deviation in the oil

Adjustments to Changes in the Petroleum Wealth: The Case of Norway

The relatively large size of Norway's income from the petroleum sector may in some situations give rise to substantial needs for readjustment in the economy. A spending path in line with permanent income from the petroleum wealth would necessitate a substantial readjustment of domestic spending in order to re-establish a sustainable trade balance if the income estimates were substantially adjusted down. This kind of adjustment may at first glance look less relevant today. Since 1990 the government's net cash flow from petroleum activities has been channelled into the State Petroleum Fund. The oil-adjusted budget deficit has been financed by the fund, and for several years no asset build up took place. However, more than four years with high oil prices and peaking oil production have changed this. The petroleum fund is now of considerable magnitude. As a consequence, a new budgetary rule was introduced in 2001. The rule limits spending of petroleum revenues as measured by the structural non-oil budget deficit to the expected return on the fund. As long as this rule is followed, a change in present or expected oil price will not necessitate any change in present spending, since this prudent spending strategy puts no emphasis on expected future income. Spending in excess of the rule (as in fact was the case in 2003 and also characterises the 2004 budget) can make the economy vulnerable to oil price changes. It is more interesting perhaps that the new spending strategy is sensitive to the general development in financial markets, and especially to a change in the estimate for the expected real return in financial markets. A downward revision of the expected real return estimate would generate a similar need for readjustments as a downward revision of the petroleum wealth with a permanent income spending strategy. Consideration of how the monetary regime influences the cost of readjustments may therefore still be relevant.

In this section we take a closer look at how the monetary regime may affect the process of adjustment to changes in the petroleum wealth (or the permanent return on a mature petroleum fund) by simulations on the macro econometric model KVARTS. As a starting point we focus on a situation where petroleum wealth is reduced due to a downward adjustment in the expected future oil price.

Let us assume that the authorities have fixed the relevant policy parameters given a particular level of petroleum wealth (including the fund) and specific paths for all exogenous variables. We assume that policy is fixed as if there were no uncertainty to the level of petroleum wealth and that the actual outcome is as expected. The model then produces time-paths for all endogenous variables and we assume the setting of the policy instruments to be consistent with these developments. When spending is in line with equation (10) the oil corrected real trade balance will be constant over time. The base line is constructed in such a way that there are no significant business cycles – the unemployment rate is stable at about 3.5 per cent.

The base line scenario is compared with the two alternative simulations based on some common assumptions: from a certain point of time (t_1), the authorities change their expectations of the level/path of the petroleum wealth. As a simplifying assumption, this change is assumed to originate from a change in the expected net oil prices in a period *after* the simulation period. We want to focus on the mechanisms and the consequences of adjusting the spending path and do not want to mix it up with the direct effects of a change in the oil price (including corresponding changes in world markets, etc.). Also in this case the policy instruments are set (from time t_1) as if there were no uncertainty. Since there is no forward looking behaviour in the model, the base line and the alternative simulations are identical up to time t_1 but differ after that. Economic policy in the alternative simulations is designed in such a way that the sum of financial and petroleum wealth is constant over time, except at time t_1. At t_1 the petroleum wealth is revised downward and from this point of time the sum of the two wealth components is permanently lower than in the base run.

Since the Norwegian government receives about 90 per cent of the petroleum rent, economic policy has to readjust to restore a balanced situation. If nothing is done the trade balance corrected for petroleum rent – the left hand side in equation (10) – will remain equal to its base line value, while the permanent income from the sum of the two wealth components – the right hand side of equation (10) – is reduced. Continued spending at base line level will then result in a gradual reduction of the sum of the two wealth components from t_1 and onwards. A tighter economic policy that reduces the petroleum rent adjusted trade balance is required. The total trade balance will also be influenced by any changes in current petroleum rent. With our simplifying assumption, the petroleum rent is unaffected throughout the simulation period and thus the required change in the total trade balance is the same as in the petroleum adjusted one.

A balanced development is defined as a path where total wealth is constant. Equation (10) shows that the required increase in the trade balance surplus is constant in real terms from t_1 and in all periods up to t_2. The corrected trade balance has to improve by the same amount in all future periods. The required change is identical to the change in the permanent income from the petroleum wealth measured at t_1. Compared to base line levels, however, the current account surplus will have to increase over time, as the improvement in the trade balance will deposit increased financial wealth and thus increased financial yield. The forced build up of financial wealth compared to the base line, corresponds to the gradual decrease in the petroleum wealth component of total wealth, compared to the base line. As time moves towards t_2 the period of lower actual incomes is coming closer and the effects of discounting is consequently reduced. After t_2 the total trade balance surplus will be lower/higher than in the base line depending on whether the decrease in petroleum rent in a specific period is higher/lower than the initial decrease in the permanent income from the petroleum rent measured at t_1.

In the simulations the necessary improvement in the trade balance is obtained by tightening fiscal policy, as illustrated by the shift of the product market equilibrium curve from yy to y'y' in Figure 5.3. Such a change in policy may be carried out in many different ways. We have chosen to simulate the tightening as a reduction in public investments in construction. In our simulations the readjustments are carried out so that the required improvement in the trade balance is attained immediately. In practice, one would probably have done the tightening more gradually, but being more realistic at this point will make the simulations more complicated without any substantial gains.

The permanent yearly improvement in the trade balance relative to the base line corresponds in the simulations to the international purchasing power of NOK 4 billion in 1995 value. The simulation is done from the first quarter of 1998 and ends in 2010 (t_2 is later than 2010).

The simulations are carried out in the context of two alternative monetary policy regimes. Either the regime is aimed at keeping the nominal exchange rate or the inflation rate stable. In both regimes we assume that the Bank of Norway is capable of setting the signal rates in such a way that the goal of the regime is achieved. We disregard any direct links between petroleum wealth on the one hand and the nominal exchange rate, the interest rate or any other variables in the economy on the other. In the simulations, all changes in the interest rate can therefore be considered part of the monetary policy response to a tighter fiscal policy.

In the first simulation, monetary policy is aimed at stabilising the nominal exchange rate. This is made operational by keeping the exchange rate at the base line value. The isolated effect of the policy readjustment spurred by the fall in petroleum wealth is a reduction in domestic demand and consequently a reduction in wages and prices. According to the model, the difference between the short term Norwegian and foreign real interest rate must be kept at the base line level to stabilise the exchange rate in the long term. This is achieved by changing the nominal interest rate by the same amount as the change in the rate of inflation relative to the base line.

In the second simulation, monetary policy is aimed at stabilising inflation. We assume that inflation in the base run is equal to the target. The isolated effect of the contractive policy prompted by the fall in petroleum wealth is a reduction in prices and inflation relative to the reference path. The central bank immediately adjusts the interest rates to neutralise this effect. In the short term, the exchange rate must move to deliver the desired result. We assume that the participants in the foreign exchange rate recognise this and that they understand that the real exchange rate has to depreciate in order to reach a new equilibrium, as illustrated in figure 5.3. Due to this fact, an increase in the domestic interest rate can be consistent with uncovered interest parity and a gradual depreciation, without any initial jump in the nominal exchange rate. Since expectations are not explicit in the model, we construct a relatively crude interest/exchange rate path iteratively, based on an assumption on ex post uncovered interest rate parity.

The Tables 5.1 and 5.2 present some results from the simulations reported as differences from the base line for selected years and for the 13-year period 1998 to 2010 as averages. The Figures 5.4 to 5.11 show the path of the deviations from the base line for some main variables.

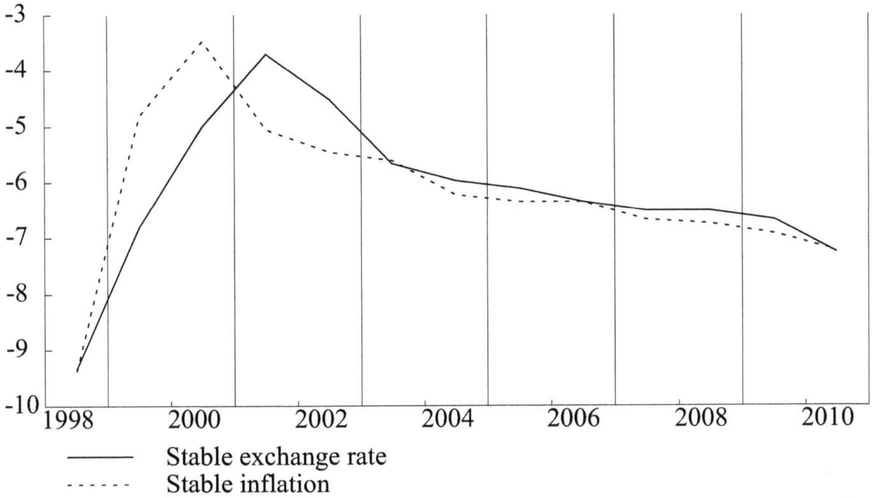

Figure 5.4 Required change in public investments. Bn 1995-NOK

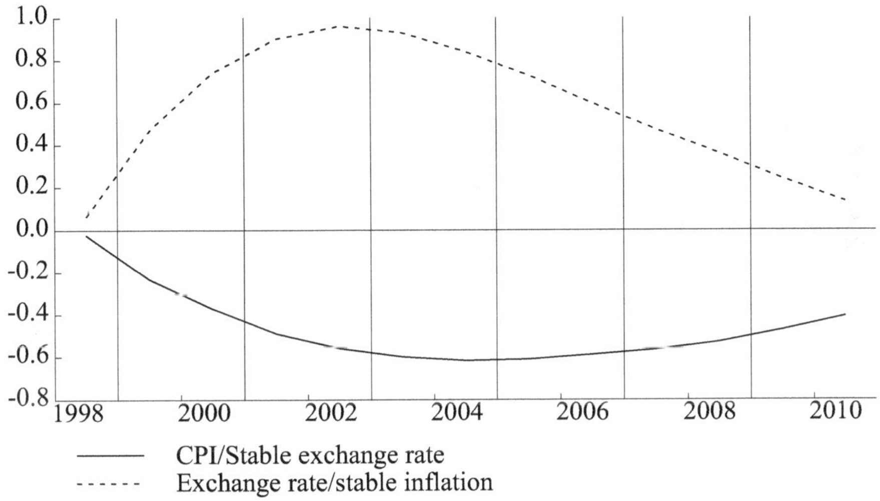

Figure 5.5 Effects on the NOK/EUR exchange rate and CPI. Per cent

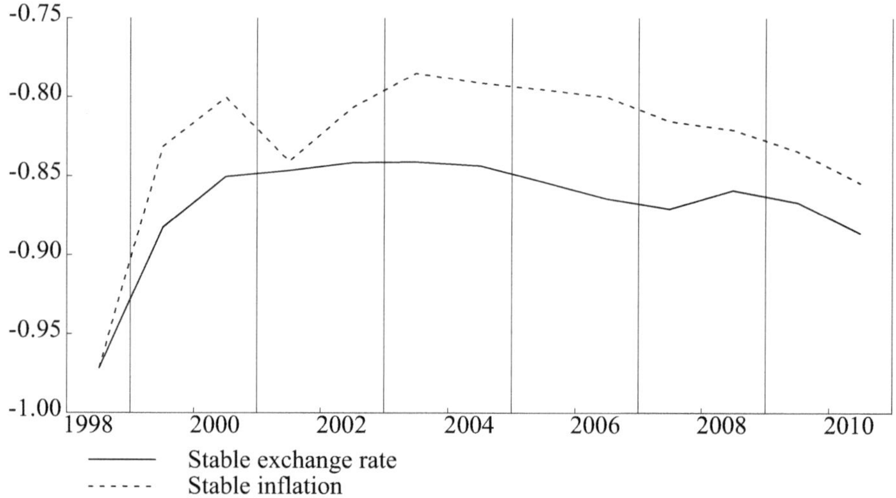

Figure 5.6 Effects on the GDP. Mainland Norway. Per cent

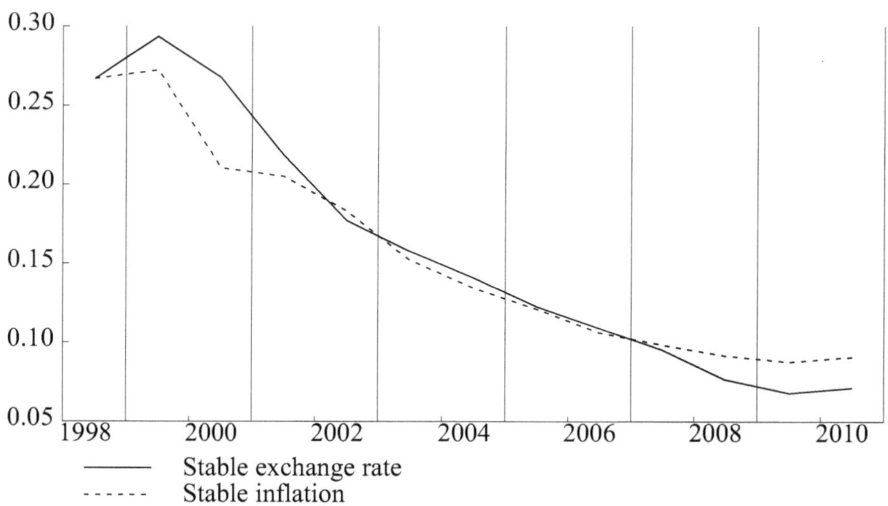

Figure 5.7 Effects on the rate of unemployment. Percentage point

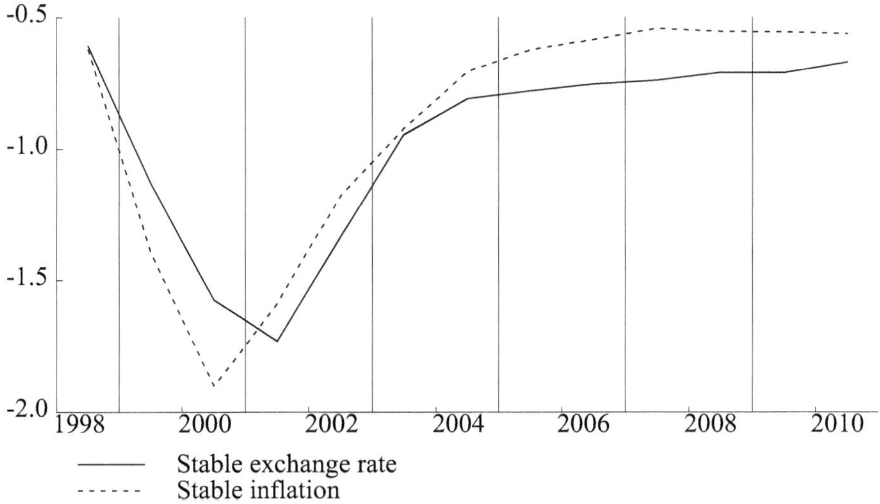

Figure 5.8 Effects on private investments in fixed capital. Per cent

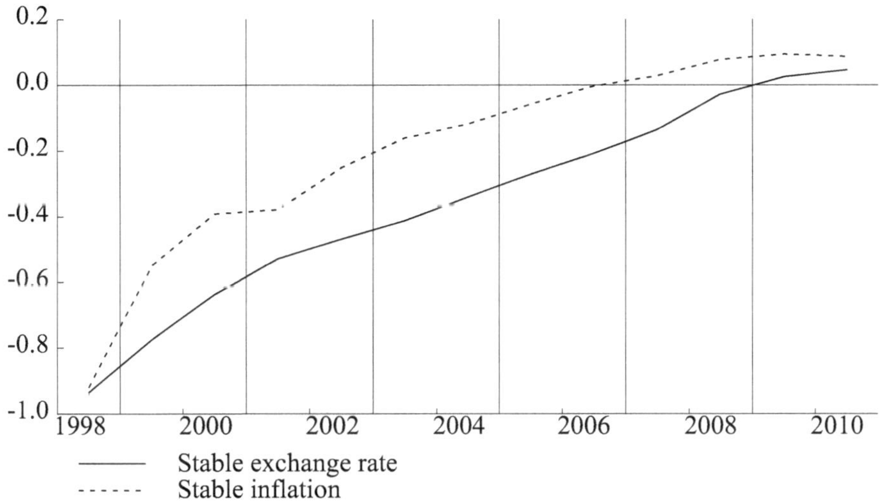

Figure 5.9 Effects on the value added in the manufacturing industries. Per cent

explain the different reaction in household demand in the two regimes, and thereby the difference between the fiscal policy response to an expected fall in future petroleum revenue. In the inflation-targeting regime monetary policy reinforces the effects of the fiscal policy tightening by increasing real interest rates and boosting competitiveness through a weakening of the domestic currency. In contrast, an unaltered real interest rate and no direct improvement in cost competitiveness imply that no similar amplifying effect is present in the fixed exchange rate regime.

To achieve the desired improvement in the trade balance, public investments have to decrease again on a year-by-year basis after three to four years. There are several reasons for this: the reduction in domestic demand has a negative effect on overall economic activity and thus lessens the need for real capital in the private sector compared to the base line. The adjustment process to the new desired level of capital stock calls for a period of substantial reductions in investments compared to the base line. After most of the adjustments to the new and lower capital level are completed, the effects on private investments become much smaller. Consequently, public investment must again shoulder a larger part of the necessary adjustment of total demand.

Table 5.1 Effects of fiscal policy tightening[1] with fixed exchange rate. Deviation from base line in per cent unless otherwise indicated

	1998	1999	2000	2001	2002	2010	1998-2010
Private consumption	-0.36	-0.57	-0.75	-0.98	-0.98	-0.76	-0.80
Mainland investments	-6.72	-5.70	-5.13	-4.52	-4.41	-3.77	-4.53
Public sector	-33.25	-20.65	-14.46	-10.24	-12.07	-13.45	-15.36
Housing	-0.46	-1.86	-4.90	-6.97	-4.94	-1.37	-2.73
Business sector	-1.23	-1.95	-1.62	-1.14	-0.82	-0.62	-0.90
Mainland GDP	-0.97	-0.88	-0.85	-0.85	-0.84	-0.89	-0.87
Manufacturing	-0.93	-0.77	-0.64	-0.53	-0.47	0.05	-0.36
Employed persons	-0.39	-0.57	-0.55	-0.48	-0.40	-0.16	-0.33
Labour force	-0.08	-0.22	-0.23	-0.22	-0.19	-0.08	-0.14
Unemployment rate (percentage point)	0.27	0.29	0.27	0.22	0.18	0.07	0.16
Unit labour cost	0.12	-0.55	-0.90	-1.01	-1.03	-0.76	-0.86
Wages per hour	-0.23	-0.63	-0.97	-1.15	-1.26	-1.25	-1.18
Consumer price index	-0.03	-0.23	-0.37	-0.49	-0.56	-0.41	-0.47
Money market rate (percentage point)	-0.15	-0.18	-0.10	-0.10	-0.05	0.06	-0.03

[1] Giving a permanent improvement in the trade balance (compared to the base line) corresponding to the international purchasing power of NOK 4 billion in 1995.

The effects of the improvement in cost competitiveness on the trade balance become smaller in the long run: the policy tightening leads to a rapid increase in unemployment. However, some people react to the increase in unemployment by withdrawing from the labour market. This gradual reduction in labour supply partly counteracts the negative impact on unemployment from lower demand for labour, and delays the improvement in cost competitiveness. The fall in the stock of real capital compared to the base line reduces labour productivity. This partially offsets the fall in labour demand due to lower production and also points in the direction of a smaller increase in unemployment and thus in cost competitiveness over time.

The direct, short term effect of higher interest rates on the overall price level is positive. The CPI goes up due to higher housing rents and higher costs of inventory in the retail sector. After two to three years the interest rate effect on the CPI changes from positive to negative as a result of a lower pressure in the economy. According to the model, a permanent increase in the rate of unemployment will not affect wage *growth* in the long run. In line with most other studies of wage formation in Norway, the model links the real wage *level* to the rate of unemployment. This comes in addition to the previous mentioned effects of shrinking increase in unemployment. All these are factors which lower the effects on inflation in the fixed exchange rate regime and on wage growth in both regimes over time. In the inflation-targeting regime the inflation impulses that need to be neutralised are also reduced after a while and thus the necessary reduction in the value of the NOK becomes smaller.

Table 5.2 Effects of fiscal policy tightening[1] with inflation/price level targeting. Deviation from base line in per cent unless otherwise indicated

	1998	1999	2000	2001	2002	2010	1998-2010
Private consumption	-0.37	-0.86	-0.94	-0.87	-0.88	-0.66	-0.78
Mainland investments	-6.76	-4.84	-4.59	-5.20	-4.79	-3.64	-4.45
Public sector	-33.38	-14.61	-10.05	-13.98	-14.58	-13.37	-15.22
Housing	-0.52	-3.55	-6.88	-6.33	-4.31	-0.93	-2.67
Business sector	-1.24	-1.95	-1.57	-1.07	-0.74	-0.65	-0.85
Mainland GDP	-0.97	-0.83	-0.80	-0.84	-0.81	-0.85	-0.83
Manufacturing	-0.92	-0.55	-0.39	-0.38	-0.25	0.09	-0.20
Employed persons	-0.39	-0.54	-0.47	-0.44	-0.40	-0.19	-0.32
Labour force	-0.09	-0.22	-0.21	-0.19	-0.18	-0.08	-0.13
Unemployment rate (percentage point)	0.27	0.27	0.21	0.21	0.18	0.09	0.16
Unit labour cost, foreign currency	0.06	-0.92	-1.17	-1.28	-1.33	-0.39	-0.86
Wages per hour	-0.22	-0.52	-0.56	-0.58	-0.59	-0.70	-0.60
Exchange rate	0.07	0.47	0.74	0.90	0.96	0.13	0.57
Money market rate (percentage point)	0.06	0.40	0.27	0.16	0.06	-0.10	0.01

[1] Giving a permanent improvement in the trade balance (compared to the base line) corresponding to the international purchasing power of NOK 4 billion in 1995.

Conclusion

Except for the two alternative monetary target variables, the *differences* between the effects of a fiscal tightening in the two regimes are in general quite small relative to the size of the effects. In years two to five, however, the discrepancies are more pronounced. In the second and third year, the necessary tightening of fiscal policy is much smaller in the inflation-targeting regime than in the fixed exchange rate regime, since monetary policy contributes to a reduction in household demand in the former, but not in the latter. In the next two years these demand effects are reversed, and as an average over the four-year period, the differences are small.

Looking at the entire simulation period as a whole, the differences between the two regimes may be summed up as follows: within the inflation-targeting regime, the improvement in the trade balance through reduced public demand is accomplished with a slightly smaller reduction in activity levels, private investments and manufacturing production than within the fixed exchange rate regime. But as we have already stated, the differences are small relative to the size of the effects. The main source of the differences is the much quicker improvement in cost competitiveness under inflation targeting, since monetary policy within this regime supports the change in the fiscal policy stance. As a consequence, a smaller part of the improvement in the trade balance needs to be brought about by a reduction in domestic demand, production may be kept on a somewhat higher level and there is some more room for consumption and investments.

The simulations also give a good approximation of the effects of an increase in petroleum wealth which makes it possible to sustain an equally *larger* non-oil trade deficit. In spite of some non-linearities in the model, one will come close to the calculated effects by changing the signs of the various results of the present simulations. If preferences go in the direction of highest possible consumption, private investments, level of activity and manufacturing production, the conclusions about which of the two regimes is the most advantageous have to change. An alternative may be to rank the two monetary policy regimes according to the size of the necessary fiscal policy response, when a readjustment of national spending is called for. By this criterion, smaller fiscal impulses in the second and third year of readjustment may be taken as support for an inflation-targeting regime.

Within an inflation-targeting regime, a fiscal policy adjustment will, in the short and medium term, be supported by changes in the interest rate as well as in the exchange rate, if the working of the foreign exchange market is as described in the present paper. In a fixed exchange rate regime, monetary policy would be close to neutral, judged by the experience from the previous Norwegian fixed exchange rate regime. Income effects from changes in the nominal interest rates would, however, slightly counteract the effects of changes in fiscal policy, necessitating a somewhat stronger fiscal response. Adjustment to changes in the petroleum wealth may in principle be brought about by a shift in the real exchange rate or by changes in domestic demand. In an inflation-targeting regime a larger part of these adjustments are accomplished through changes in the real exchange rate and private demand and less through shifts in public demand.

These conclusions rest strongly on some key assumptions about the implementation of monetary policy and the working of the foreign exchange market. The interpretation of inflation targeting as price *level* targeting makes it easy to solve the model. The isolated effect of a tighter fiscal policy is to bring inflation down in the short and medium term. To immediately counteract this effect by monetary policy, the exchange rate must depreciate, the interest rate must increase, or both. However, if the target of the central bank is inflation some years ahead, these conclusions may change.

If the central bank has to counteract a tight fiscal policy by stimulating aggregate demand, the two policy measures will counteract each other and the effectiveness of the policy instruments will be low. A crucial point is to what extent the inflation effect from lower public demand is counteracted directly by the exchange rate or indirectly through lagged demand effects brought about by changes in interest rates. In general one goes for a setting where fiscal and monetary policy mutually support each other in bringing the economy back to a sustainable long term path.

References

Bowitz, E. and T. Eika (1989), 'KVARTS - 86. A Quarterly Macroeconomic Model. Formal Structure and Empirical Characteristics', Reports 89/2, Statistics Norway

Eika T. and K.A. Magnussen (2000), 'Did Norway Gain from the 1979-1985 Oil Price Shock?', *Economic Modelling* 17, 107-137.

Eika, T. and K. Moum (1999), 'Stabilising Activity or Exchange Rate: The Role of the Monetary Policy in the Norwegian Oil Economy' (in Norwegian). Reports 99/23, Statistics Norway.

Ministry of Finance (2003), 'National Budget 2004', (in Norwegian). White paper nr. 1 2003-2004.

Statistics Norway (2004), 'Economic Survey 2003', (in Norwegian), Økonomiske analyser 1/2004.

Wren-Lewis, S. (1992), 'On the Analytical Foundations of the Fundamental Equilibrium Exchange Rate', in C.P. Hargreaves (ed.), *Macroeconomic Modelling of the Long Run*, Aldershot: Edward Elgar, 75-91.

Chapter 6

Saving Petroleum Wealth: Tales of Three Jurisdictions

Rögnvaldur Hannesson

Non-renewable resources like oil and natural gas are a form of wealth. In contrast to renewable resources like fish and forests, or productive investments like production equipment or money in the bank, non-renewable resource wealth is by definition unproductive; it does not grow in the ground. It is comparable to forms of wealth such as jewelry or works of art. The 'supply' of a Rembrandt painting is given and certainly not augmentable; for some reason copies will not do no matter how good they are.

Nevertheless, the value of a non-renewable natural resource deposit lying idle in the ground is not necessarily immutable. The same is indeed true of a Rembrandt painting. The value of a resource deposit may change over time, due to two and sometimes offsetting processes. First, technological progress affects the value of resources as objects of direct consumption or inputs into the production process. Earth coal (in contrast to charcoal) was not particularly valuable until a way had been found to use it to make iron and steel and, perhaps even more importantly, the steam engine had been invented. And petroleum was not particularly valuable until ways had been found to use oil instead of coal as a source of energy. Future innovations in energy production are likely to reduce the price of oil, just as the increasing use of oil put pressure on the price of coal and brought economic depression on the coal mining areas of Europe.

Secondly, as more is dug out of a particular non-renewable resource, less will remain. This, all else equal, will lead to a rising price of the resource over time. As shown in a famous article by Harold Hotelling (1931), an owner of a mineral deposit would not leave any of it in the ground unless he got a return from his waiting equal to the return on digging up the mineral and investing the money in financial markets or whatever gives the highest return. Return on mineral lying in the ground can only come from a rising net price of the mineral, either through a rising market price or a falling cost of extraction. In this sense, a non-renewable natural resource is not unproductive; its value can rise over time because of its growing scarcity, despite the fact that it does not grow in a physical sense.

The Hotelling paradigm does not seem particularly helpful, however, for those who seek to preserve the value of their mineral wealth. Looking at mineral prices in a historical perspective of, say, a hundred years, they seem to have fallen in most cases rather than increased in real terms. This does not rule out the possibility that the net prices of minerals have increased in accordance with the Hotelling Rule; this could have happened because of a falling cost of extraction, but this seems unlikely. One possible reason why mineral prices have not developed in accordance with the Hotelling Rule is that the total supply of non-renewable resources such as oil and minerals is not known. The known reserves that are worthwhile to extract depend on economic circumstances in two ways; first, finding resource deposits costs money, and, second, what is worthwhile to extract depends on prices and costs, due to variable grades and ease of access to different resource deposits. It appears that mineral companies regard natural resource deposits as a producible commodity which they need a certain inventory of, but they will not spend more money on finding such deposits than necessary. The record shows that the inventory of such resources, oil included, has grown roughly at the same rate as production.

There are reasons, therefore, to believe that it would not be a particularly good 'investment' for owners of mineral deposits to keep them in the ground. Due to the non-increasing real price and the risk of technological obsolescence, they might be better advised to dig out their deposits as quickly as possible. Needless to say, if everybody did so it might be as devastating as when a crowd in a discotheque runs for the exit when someone cries 'fire', but the fact that production and discovery of new deposits need to be stretched over time for cost reasons mitigates against that. The point is that in order to obtain the highest possible return on the wealth it must be transformed into other and more productive forms of wealth.

Maximization of returns aside, transformation of non-renewable natural resource wealth into some other form of wealth is imperative if the wealth is to be preserved, let alone augmented. Yet this very simple and elementary point tends to be overlooked in popular debate in resource-rich jurisdictions where management of resource wealth is an issue. Revenues from oil extraction are, misleadingly, referred to as income. But while ordinary income can be spent without affecting a person's wealth, the same is certainly not true of 'income' from mineral extraction. Only after such resource wealth has been transformed into some form of productive wealth can we really talk about income, the income being the return we would be able to get on the new and productive wealth. In order to ensure a sustainable income from resource wealth we thus need to save and invest the 'income' we get as we dig the resource out of the ground. But should it all be saved?

Optimal Savings of Mineral Revenues

There is a choice of alternative settings for discussing the optimal savings rate for mineral revenues. One is macroeconomic, where one looks at the optimal savings rate for an economy, regarding mineral rents as one of many sources of savings. In that context, the presence of mineral rents eases the burden of accumulating production capital and speeds up the rate with which it approaches its optimal value (Hannesson, 2000a). Here we shall use the investment fund perspective, partly because we shall in this chapter take a closer look at three cases where investment funds have been used as vehicles for transforming oil wealth, and partly because the investment fund approach is not a bad approximation to optimal accumulation of capital for a small, open economy which is well integrated into a larger economy, as is true of the three jurisdictions we shall look at.

Suppose the real rate of interest is constant and equal to r. The value of a given non-renewable natural resource deposit is equal to the discounted value of all future rents (revenues less costs of extraction). Call this W. Productive wealth of an equal amount would yield a rate of return r and could provide an even stream of income equal to rW per unit of time. By saving an appropriate share of the rent from the resource extraction it would be possible to turn the unproductive resource wealth into productive wealth. Let the rent per unit of time be constant and denoted by R and denote the savings rate by s. Suppose the rent flow lasts for T years. At the end of the extraction period we must have accumulated a fund equal to W, the resource wealth we started with. Thereafter our fund would yield an income rW per unit of time in perpetuity. Hence

$$W = \int_0^T sRe^{r(T-t)}dt = sR\left(e^{rT} - 1\right)/r$$

The initial resource wealth is, by definition

$$W = \int_0^T Re^{-rt}dt = R\left(1 - e^{-rT}\right)/r$$

From these two expressions we can calculate the necessary savings rate:

$$s = \frac{1 - e^{-rT}}{e^{rT} - 1}$$

As shown in Figure 6.1, s becomes smaller as the extraction period T gets longer. What happens is that we would get leveraged by the return on the money that we had already invested in our fund. The money invested in the beginning of the extraction period will have grown considerably at the end of the extraction period if T is large. As we might expect, s tends to zero as T tends to infinity; if the resource lasts for ever we will not need to invest anything. And if T is very short we will have to invest most of it (by applying L'Hôpital's Rule, we can see that s tends to unity as T approaches zero and zero if T approaches infinity). Figure 6.1 shows how s depends on the length of the extraction period and the rate of return. The higher the rate of return, the less needs to be saved (the more leverage we get from what has already been invested). For a time horizon of 50 years we only need to save and invest about eight per cent of the revenue if the rate of return is five per cent, and less than one per cent if the rate of return is ten per cent.

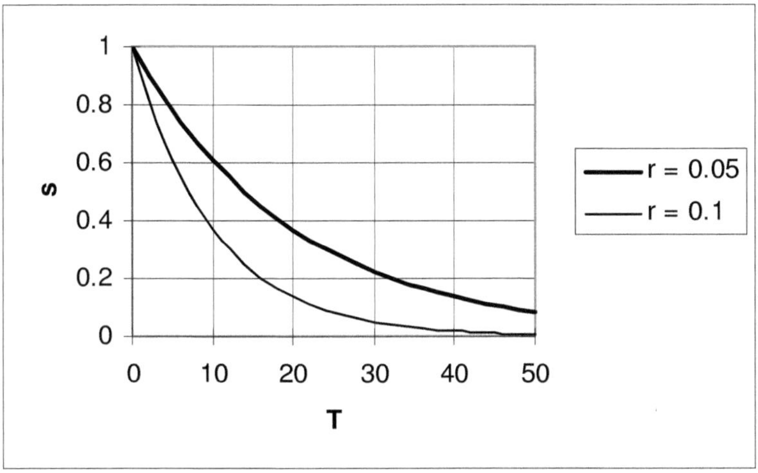

Figure 6.1 Optimal savings rate (*s*) for mineral rents as a function of the length of the extraction period (*T*), for two different rates of interest (*r*)

Another point we may note is that the amount we need to invest is equal to the difference between the rent (*R*) and the return on the wealth (*rW*). Using the equations above we get the following expression for the amount we need to invest at each point in time.

$$sR = \frac{rW}{e^{rT} - 1} = \frac{rW\left(1 - e^{rT} + e^{rT}\right)}{e^{rT} - 1} = R - rW$$

In other words, we can at each point in time consume an amount equal to the return on the mineral wealth, also known as the 'permanent income'. This is the consumption which the mineral wealth can sustain indefinitely, but it is, of course, sustainable only if we consume no more than the permanent income and invest the rest of the rent flow. This principle is of general validity and does not depend on the assumption that the revenue flow is constant. Consider, for example, the case when the revenue falls at the rate *k*. Then the initial resource wealth is

$$W = \int_0^T R_0 e^{-(k+r)t} dt = R_0\left(1 - e^{-(k+r)T}\right)/(k+r)$$

where R_0 is the initial revenue flow. The sustainable consumption from this wealth is rW, so the amount invested at each point in time is $R_0e^{-kt} - rW$. Hence the investment fund at the end of the extraction period will have grown to

$$\int_0^T \left[R_0 e^{-kt} - rW\right] e^{r(T-t)} dt = \frac{R_0}{k+r} e^{rT}\left[1 - e^{-(k+r)T}\right] - W\left(e^{rT} - 1\right) = W$$

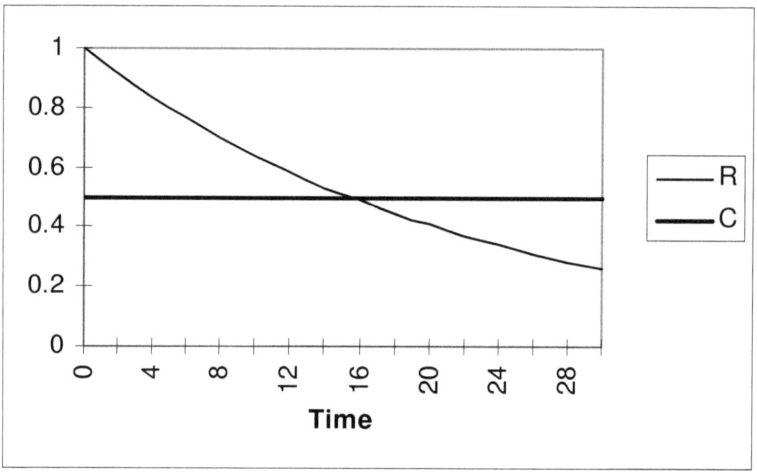

Figure 6.2 Time profile of rent (*R*) and sustainable consumption (*C*) of a mineral resource, with k = 0.045, r = 0.05, and T = 30

Figure 6.2 shows the rent and consumption profile for given parameters. About half way through the extraction period the rent has fallen to a level equal to the sustainable consumption. The investment will thus be largest to begin with, and the investment phase will be followed by a period where some of the rent saved is consumed until enough is left at the end of the extraction period to sustain the even consumption $C = rW$ indefinitely. It is, of course, possible to construct different and perhaps more realistic rent profiles, such as one where the rent flow is small or negative to begin with, due to high initial costs of investment, and falls thereafter. In such a case one would borrow against the future; there would be a phase of disinvestment, followed by a period of investment, and a third phase of disinvestment again, leaving just enough to sustain a permanent, even consumption.

Implicit in this is that an even consumption is more desirable than uneven consumption. There are equity arguments in favor of smoothing consumption over time, both within and across generations. One can modify this approach to allow for a growing population. For example, if we want to maintain a given wealth per capita (W/N) for a population (N) that grows at a constant rate g, both W and N

would have to grow at the same rate. Consuming a fraction c of the wealth, the rate of growth in wealth would be $r - c$. Setting this equal to the rate of population growth, we find that the permanent income per capita (the amount we could consume per capita without reducing the wealth per capita) would be $(r - g)W/N$. Further modifications would be necessary to account for uncertainty. These points will not be elaborated here; suffice it to say that the simple principles discussed above are encountered in various guises in the more complicated settings (see, for example, Brekke, 1997).

There are several jurisdictions around the world where mineral wealth is a substantial component of national wealth. Preservation of this wealth requires that it be transformed to other forms of wealth, as already discussed. Different jurisdictions have taken different approaches in this regard, with a variable degree of success. Here we shall look at three jurisdictions, Alberta, Alaska, and Norway, and how they have fared in this regard. All of the three contain petroleum deposits which yield a substantial rent. The governments of all three appropriate a substantial share of these rents through taxation, royalties, or participation in the extraction of oil and gas. The power to preserve, or to waste, the national or provincial petroleum wealth therefore lies squarely in the hands of the governments of these jurisdictions. How have they wielded this power?

All three jurisdictions have chosen to transform some of their petroleum wealth through investment funds. The Alberta Heritage Savings Trust Fund and the Alaska Permanent Fund were both set up in 1976. The Norwegian Petroleum Fund was set up in 1990, but it took about five years before it acquired any significance. The institutional set-ups and the track records of these funds are quite different, and important lessons can be learned with respect to what arrangements best facilitate preservation of non-renewable resource wealth. In the following we discuss these three funds separately, and conclude this chapter with a section on what lessons can be learned from the three funds.

The Alaska Permanent Fund

In the late 1960s the state of Alaska suddenly became rich through the discovery of oil on the northern coast of the state. The extraction licenses were allocated through competitive bidding which brought the state a windfall income amounting to several annual state budgets. Not all of this income was well spent; some development projects initiated by the state government were expensive flops.

Partly as a result of this experience, there was a strong sentiment in the state for limiting the power of the state legislature to spend the oil money. This gave rise to the idea that a portion of the state revenue from oil should be set aside in a separate fund out of reach of the legislature. This required an amendment of the state constitution, which forbade the use of dedicated funds. Hence the Alaska Permanent Fund was set up by a constitutional amendment, requiring both a qualified majority in the state legislature and a referendum.

As the name indicates, the Permanent Fund is meant to be permanent. The principal of the fund cannot be withdrawn, except by a constitutional amendment.

This is certainly in accordance with the principle of wealth transformation; mineral wealth in the ground is permanent but of no use until it is extracted, and technological development could make it obsolete. Financial wealth is permanent if care is taken only to spend the return on the wealth and not the principal. The constitution, however, safeguards only the nominal value of the principal of the Permanent Fund. The state legislature has the power of deciding how the income of the fund is spent and chose early on to distribute the earnings of the fund to the residents of the state through a 'dividend program', by which every person gets an equal share of the income of the fund. About half of the fund income is handed out to the residents of the state in this way. The rest goes to inflation proofing, and whatever is left is at the legislature's disposal. So far the legislature has decided to add this residual to the fund's principal.

The Permanent Fund automatically gets 25 per cent of all royalties on oil production in the state. This does not, however, mean that 25 per cent of the state revenues from oil are invested in the fund. The state also gets revenues from severance taxes and tax dispute settlements. The required deposits to the Permanent Fund probably amount to 10-15 per cent of the state's total income from oil. The fund has nevertheless grown more rapidly than these required deposits would have permitted. The main sources of the fund's principal are three, required deposits, inflation proofing, and special appropriations by the state, about one-third from each. In November 2003 the fund was worth about $26 billion, which is about $40,000 for each inhabitant of Alaska.

The Permanent Fund is an institution separate from the state government and legislature, with its own governing board. The fund's money is invested in blue chip bonds and company stock, both US and foreign, and some in real estate.[1] Very little is invested in Alaska. The fund has earned a return well above its target of five per cent in real terms; the average return over the last 20 years is about ten per cent per year in nominal terms. The income of the fund has grown handsomely over the years; Figure 6.3 shows the actual and projected oil revenues of the state of Alaska and the investment income of the fund. One could hardly have designed a more pedagogical illustration of how a non-renewable resource wealth can be turned into a permanent, renewable financial wealth capable of providing a permanent income.

---

[1] Information on the investment portfolio, as well as on other aspects of the fund, is available on its website (www.apfc.org).

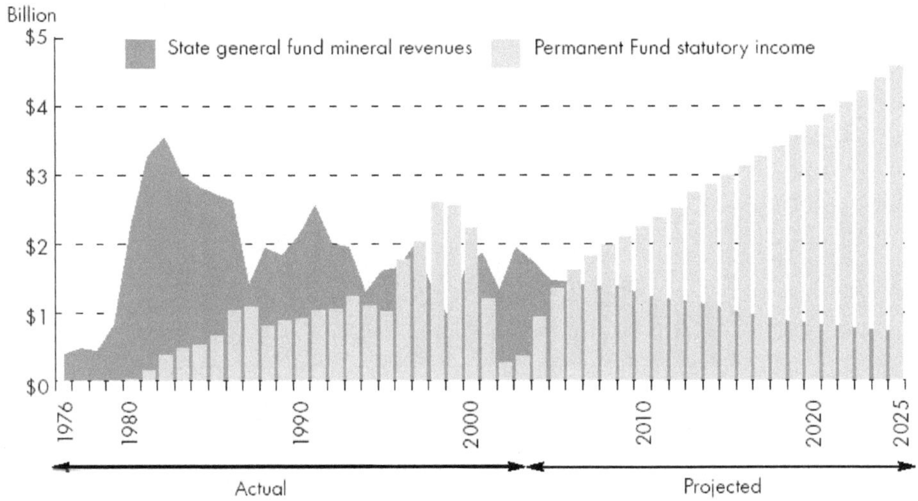

Figure 6.3 Oil revenues of the state of Alaska General Fund (i.e. excluding the Permanent Fund) and earnings of the Permanent Fund

Source: Alaska Permanent Fund website (www.apfc.org).

The dividend program is certainly one of the most interesting aspects of the Permanent Fund and probably the key to its success. The dividend is calculated with a formula that roughly amounts to allocating one-half of the average earnings over the last five years to dividends. The dividend per person has grown handsomely over the years, from $386 in 1983 (except for an accumulated dividend of $1000 in 1982, owing to litigation over the dividend program) to a peak of $1964 in 2000, but has fallen after that because of the worldwide decline in stock markets. Figure 6.4 shows the development of the dividend.

One of the purposes of the dividend program was to provide a safeguard against spendthrift legislators. Substantial dividends could be expected to be popular. Since the dividends depend critically on the size of the fund and how well it is managed, people could be expected to rally around the fund and oppose any attempt to use it for other purposes. Experience so far confirms this. In 1999 it was proposed to use a part of the return on the fund for covering the chronic deficit on the state budget. The proposal was defeated by an overwhelming majority in a state-wide referendum in September 1999. It is worthwhile to note that the safeguard against legislators 'raiding' the fund was provided by none other than the legislators themselves, as the dividend program was established by statutory law. Apparently the legislators of Alaska have chosen to set up mechanisms that tie their hands when it comes to a portion of the oil money, something akin to an independent central bank that can pursue the monetary policy it deems appropriate no matter what the majority of legislators might find convenient.

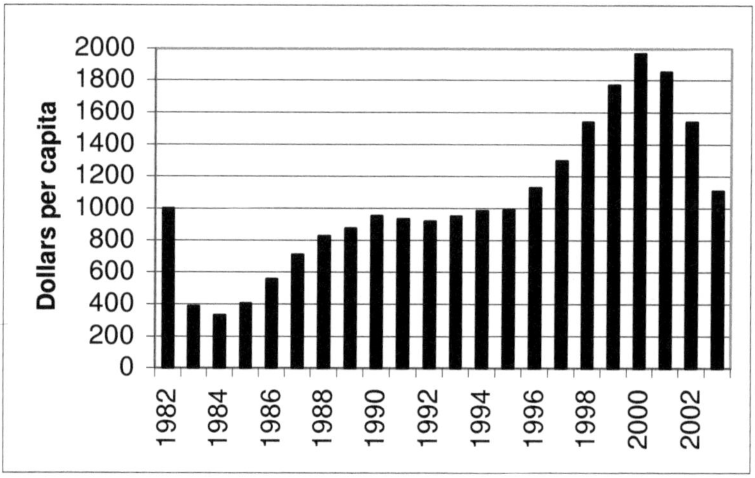

Figure 6.4 The dividends from the Alaska Permanent Fund Dividend Program

Source: Alaska Permanent Fund website (www.apfc.org).

The proposal to use some of the return on the Permanent Fund to cover deficits in the state finances points to a weakness in the mechanism that Alaska has chosen to ensure that some of the oil money is saved. Little will be accomplished in terms of savings if the state accumulates wealth on one account and debt on another. The real savings of any government can never be anything other than the surplus on its consolidated budget. Constitutional rules such as those governing the savings of Alaska's oil money may therefore accomplish less than they appear to do at first glance. The state budget of Alaska has been in the red for ten of the last twelve fiscal years.[2] The deficit has been covered from reserves accumulated from tax dispute settlements with the oil companies. The real savings of the state have therefore been considerably less than the build-up of the Permanent Fund. These budgetary reserves are expected to become exhausted in a few years, so new ways will therefore have to be found to cover the deficit. Given that Alaska can neither print its own money nor borrow to cover its ordinary expenses, both of which are doubtful propositions anyway, there are only three avenues open, reduce the expenditure, raise taxes, or use the return on the Permanent Fund. Expenditures have been reduced drastically over the years, and the last option appears to have been closed by the referendum in 1999. The tax option remains; the state income tax was abolished in 1980, when the oil revenues were at their highest, and the state has no sales tax.

---

2 Alaska's Fiscal Crossroads: A Discussion. Office of Management and Budget, 14 March, 2003.

The Alberta Heritage Fund

The set-up of the Alberta Heritage Fund is quite different from the Alaska Permanent Fund. The fund is not a separate institution at an arm's length from the provincial government and legislature; it is managed by the government of Alberta and overseen by the legislature. Originally its goals were diffuse. While wealth preservation and saving for future generations is a prominent goal of the Alaska Permanent Fund, the Alberta Heritage Fund was often referred to by legislators as 'saving for a rainy day'. Saving for a rainy day is not the same as wealth preservation; a rainy day fund could be depleted when the rainy day comes and it rains enough whereas a fund that preserves wealth is permanent and independent of shifting economic prospects.

Initially, 30 per cent of the province's oil and gas revenues were set aside in the Heritage Fund. In the early 1980s this was reduced to 15 per cent, and after the fall in oil prices in 1986 the deposits into the fund came to a halt and have not since been resumed. This was logical enough; after 1986 the province began to accumulate debt, and no real savings would have been accomplished if oil and gas money had been put into the fund unless there had been a corresponding surplus on the provincial budget. Despite the mounting provincial debt the fund was kept more or less intact, but its real value was eroded by inflation. In the beginning the return on the fund was added to its principal, but later it was used to finance the province's expenditures, which certainly was logical enough after the provincial budget turned into the red.

The investment policy of the Heritage Fund has been quite different from the Alaska Permanent Fund. The Alaska Permanent Fund has a clear investment policy; secure a high real financial return for the long term. To this end it invests in blue chip securities and company stocks. The Alberta Heritage Fund used to have a multitude of goals; some of its money was invested in financial markets, but some was lent to other Canadian provinces at concessionary rates, and some was used for 'province building'. Some of the province building consisted of investments with intangible returns such as grants to education and research, and public parks. This investment may well have provided good value for money, but no assessment seems to have been done on this. Some investments in province building were, however, in undertakings that, if worthwhile, would have yielded a return comparable to other investments and were indeed expected to do so. This usually did not happen, however. Ventures that were supposed to yield a competitive return did not, or even lost money. Loans to crown corporations that were supposed to pay the going rate of interest often did so with subsidies from the provincial government.

Over the years the existence of the Heritage Fund was increasingly called into question. It was no longer used as a vehicle for saving the oil and gas wealth and it did not represent any net wealth of the province, as the provincial debt came to exceed the assets of the fund. To many it seemed sensible to liquidate the fund and pay off some of the debt. In the mid-1990s a province-wide debate was initiated on the future of the Heritage Fund. In the end it was decided to keep the fund and turn it into an investment fund similar to the Alaska Permanent Fund. By early 2003 the value of the fund was Can$11.7 billion, or about Can$4,000 for each inhabitant of Alberta. This is less than one-tenth of the Alaska Permanent Fund in per capita terms.

At about the same time as it was decided to restructure the Heritage Fund, the government of Alberta also began to pay off the debt of the province. Without this it would probably not have made much sense to keep the Heritage Fund. Alberta's net debt disappeared in 1999 and the province has moved into a net surplus of financial assets; the remaining gross debt was Can$4.8 billion by early 2003, far below the value of the Heritage Fund. Recently there have been proposals to revive the role of the Heritage Fund as a vehicle for transforming the province's oil and gas wealth into renewable wealth. The Canadian Taxpayers' Federation initiated a study of the feasibility of building up the fund to a level which would make it possible to eliminate the personal income tax in the province and replace it with the earnings of the fund (Wen, 2001). The study indicates that investing 10-20 per cent of the province's oil and gas revenues in the fund would be sufficient to accomplish this. The time it would take to build a fund that could replace the income tax depends on a variety of factors; the level of oil and gas prices, the growth of the province's expenditures, and much else. The Alberta provincial government has not adopted this plan, however. Instead a new regime for spending the petroleum revenues has been put in place, limiting the use of revenues to Can$3.5 billion per year. Any surplus is put into a new fund, The Alberta Sustainability Fund. This is a stabilization, or a 'rainy day' fund; when petroleum revenues drop below Can$3.5 billion per year, the gap can be bridged by withdrawing money from the fund.[3]

The Norwegian Petroleum Fund

Due to the oil price rises in the 1970s, the Norwegian oil and gas fields in the North Sea became immensely profitable. The Norwegian petroleum tax code was quickly amended in the wake of the two oil price hikes, in order to cream off a substantial share of the oil rent. It has been estimated that the Norwegian government captures about 80 per cent of the oil rent. Not all of this is due to taxes; the government is a sleeping partner in many extraction licenses, paying its share of the costs and getting its share of the profit.

Figure 6.5 shows the government net cash flow from oil and gas extraction. This has waxed and waned since oil extraction began in the 1970s. In the early 1980s, when oil prices were high and a number of high-yield fields had come on stream, the revenues from oil and gas were 10-20 per cent of the total government revenue. In the late 1980s they fell almost to zero, due to low oil prices and the government's share of the development costs of the fields in which it held shares. Lately the oil and gas revenues have exceeded 20 per cent of government revenue.

---

[3] On this and other recent development in Alberta, see budget documents available at the website of the Ministry of Finance (www.finance.gov.ab.ca).

As is to be expected, the petroleum incomes have been the subject of much analysis and public debate. The wealth management perspective was long curiously absent from this debate, which tended to revolve around how much money the Norwegian economy could absorb. The idea of putting some of the money aside in a special fund was put forward in the early 1980s, but the fund was mainly conceived as a buffer useful for evening out fluctuations in revenues and deferring the use of money which the economy could not immediately absorb without running into problems of inflation and structural changes difficult to reverse. This kind of fund was proposed in a report to the Norwegian parliament in 1983, but the Norwegian Petroleum Fund was not established until 1990. No money was deposited into the fund, however, until 1995. There were several reasons for this. The oil revenues of the state were hard hit by the fall in oil prices in 1986 (see Figure 6.5). Soon after that the Norwegian economy went into a severe recession, and much of the oil money was used to balance the government budget. Lastly the government had large expenses to pay for its share of investments in the extraction licenses. In the mid-1990s things started looking up; economic recovery was well under way, the government's cash flow from oil turned sharply upwards, and oil prices recovered.

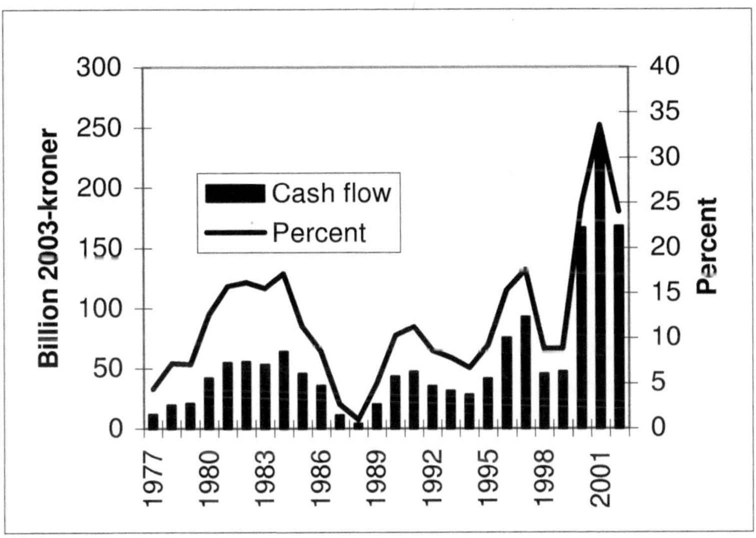

Figure 6.5 The Norwegian government's net cash flow from petroleum, in 2003-kroner and as share of total government income

Sources: Department of Oil and Energy, Fact Sheet; Statistics Norway, Yearbook of Statistics.

In the beginning there was no explicit rule determining the amount of money to be invested in the fund; the savings are simply the surplus on the government budget in any particular year and thus the outcome of the government's fiscal policy in general. This is logical enough, as the real government savings will never be anything other than the surplus on the consolidated government budget. Whether the absence of any explicit savings rule is a good idea is another issue, and as it turns out, the Norwegian government found it necessary to formulate such a rule in 2000. This savings rule is based on a real rate of return of four per cent on the money invested in the Petroleum Fund. The fund is invested in foreign assets on financial markets worldwide, which in the long term is expected to yield a real rate of return of four per cent per year.[4] The rule is not binding in any sense, it is a guideline to be combined with prudence and good judgment. The Ministry of Finance calculates a structural budget deficit exclusive of oil revenues, and it is this structural deficit which is meant to be equal to the expected four per cent return on the Petroleum Fund. The structural deficit corrects for the ups and downs in the business cycle. In recession years the actual deficit will be greater than the structural deficit, and more of the oil money will be used than a blind application of the savings rule would dictate.

It may be noted that the said savings rule is much more strict than the permanent income rule discussed above. According to the permanent income rule, one could use four per cent of the entire petroleum wealth per year, provided the four per cent is the expected real rate of return on financial investments. The savings rule only takes into account the wealth that has already been invested in the Petroleum Fund and ignores the reserves in the ground. Precaution could be advanced as a reason for this; oil prices are notoriously volatile, and following the savings guidelines would amount to using only the return on the petroleum wealth that has been extracted and invested. This is, however, an extremely conservative attitude; even if oil prices are volatile it is highly unlikely that the reserves still in the ground will one day suddenly become worthless. There are, however, better arguments to support the savings guidelines. One is that the use of as much money as the permanent income amounts to would expose the Norwegian economy to strong inflationary tendencies and kill off a good portion of the export and import-competing industries. Another is that the Norwegian government, like many other governments in Western Europe, faces enormous retirement liabilities in the not too distant future because of an underfunded retirement system and a major increase in the number of retirees relative to people of working age. Even with the best of luck and strict adherence to the savings guidelines, the Petroleum Fund would probably not suffice to fund these liabilities.

What is the experience thus far? Since the mid-1990s the government has indeed managed to save a good portion of its net cash flow from oil and gas. Table 6.1 shows some key figures pertaining to the petroleum wealth of the government of Norway and its management since investment in the Petroleum Fund began in earnest. The first row shows the government petroleum wealth embedded in oil and gas reserves at the beginning of each year. This is defined as the present value of

---

[4] The fund is managed by the Bank of Norway, and information on the fund can be obtained from its website (www.norges-bank.no).

the expected net cash flow at a four per cent real rate of interest. This figure is rather stable, being based on price forecasts which envisage prices moving relatively quickly from their present high or low level to a stable, 'normal' level.[5]

Table 6.1 Some key figures on government petroleum income and wealth in Norway. Billion NOK

	1998	1999	2000	2001	2002	2003
1. Gov't petroleum wealth in oil and gas reserves	1890	1800	1710	1870	2100	2000
2. Gov't Petroleum Fund per January 1	115	169	221	387	619	666
3. Permanent income per capita	68.2	66.9	65.7	76.7	92.4	90.6
4. Gov't cash flow from petroleum	45.0	44.6	161.4	243.2	169.2	172.8
5. Return on Petroleum Fund	6.2	7.3	10.9	17.2	22.3	24.0
6. Warranted savings, perm. income rule (4+5-3)	-17.0	-15.0	106.6	183.7	99.1	106.2
7. Warranted savings, guidelines (4+5-4% of 2)	46.6	45.1	163.5	244.9	166.7	170.2
8. Actual savings	33.8	39.9	164.3	258.8	149.6	162.0
9. Structural budget deficit		19.8	18.9	21.6	27.6	30.7
10. Four per cent of Petroleum Fund		6.7	8.8	15.5	24.8	26.6

Sources: National Budget, various years

The second row shows the value of the Petroleum Fund at the beginning of each year. The sum of the first two rows is the total government petroleum wealth. The third row shows the permanent income of this wealth adjusted for population growth [$(r - g)W$; cf. supra], where the rate of return is set at four per cent and the population growth rate at 0.6 per cent, which is close to the annual average growth rate of the population in Norway since 1990. Row four shows the revenue from oil and gas extraction accruing to the government due to taxes and equity interest. Row five shows the return on the Petroleum Fund, and so the sum of rows four and five is the government revenue due to its petroleum wealth.

Row six shows what the savings of petroleum revenues would be if an amount equal to the permanent income, adjusted for population growth, on the petroleum wealth were used. Row seven shows what the savings would be according to the savings guidelines, using only an amount equal to four per cent of the value of the Petroleum Fund. Row eight shows the actual savings.

---

[5] The oil price predictions are published in the National Budget each year.

shareholders regularly. In countries where corruption in public life is rampant, which is not the case in any of the three jurisdictions considered here, it would be correspondingly worse to put money into the hands of politicians.

Second, in order to secure that non-renewable resource wealth be successfully made permanent through an investment fund, it is necessary, in democratic societies at any rate, that people get a perceptible benefit from the fund. This is what has been successfully achieved with the dividend program in Alaska. In Alberta there was no such program, and the general public in Alberta appears to have taken relatively little interest in the Heritage Fund. A dividend program as in Alaska is, of course, not the only possible way of benefiting people at large. In Alberta there is currently a discussion whether the Heritage Fund should be built up to a level that would make it possible to abolish the personal income tax to the province. This ought to be popular among taxpayers. In Norway there is currently a discussion about turning the Petroleum Fund into a retirement fund. Such a fund ought to be popular among those who are in or close to retirement but not only that; provision of retirement benefits in a non-funded system such as the Norwegian one must come from those who pay taxes, so even the working generation should see some benefit in turning the Petroleum Fund into a retirement fund providing tax relief through capital income from abroad.

These last comments raise further questions on the incentive effects of alternative schemes for distributing the return on a permanent petroleum fund. What is really the point of handing out money to the people of Alaska when their state finances show an unsustainable deficit? The only solution to that problem, assuming that the state has come to the end of the road as regards cutting expenditures, is either to use the return on the Permanent Fund or introduce an income tax or a sales tax or both. What, then, would be the point of raising taxes and keeping the dividend program simultaneously? First, taxes are paid in proportion to income and expenditure, so different individuals benefit differently from the absence of taxes versus the dividend program. Since the dividend program distributes an equal sum to each individual and is directly related to the Permanent Fund, it probably provides stronger incentives for maintaining the fund than using its income to keep taxes low or absent. Secondly, using taxes versus return on an investment fund to pay for public expenditures has different effects on the efficiency of the economy. Taxes reduce efficiency through reducing the incentives to invest and to work while using the return on a fund invested out of state has no such effects. On the other hand, the pain caused by taxes is the only effective budget constraint on elected politicians. It can be argued that they would overexpand the public sector if they had access to easy money from investment funds or resource rents.

A further question, and a very fundamental one, that arises with respect to saving oil wealth in an investment fund is whether the general public will respond by reducing its own savings by an equal amount. This is similar to the problem we discussed in relation to earmarking a certain share of oil revenues to an investment fund no matter what; if the government runs an offsetting deficit on its general budget, no real savings will, of course, be accomplished. If dividends are handed out or taxes are reduced through public investment funds the individuals in the economy will become correspondingly richer, and their capacity to spend will grow in tandem. If, as is now suggested by some in Alberta, future taxes will disappear when an investment fund has been built up, the expected lifetime income of an Albertan will rise by the present value of those tax savings and he or she could spend that amount, implying that the real savings for the Alberta economy due to the build-up of the Heritage Fund would be small or maybe zero. A similar argument could be made for a privately funded retirement scheme; if that were to be funded instead by a public investment fund, the need for the individual to save for his or her own retirement would disappear. In the present Norwegian context this is of limited interest, however, since the Norwegian pension system is of the pay-as-you-go variety. Whether the consumers of the real world behave in this super-rational way is another issue; there are reasons to expect that savings decisions are only partly and perhaps not at all governed by a calculation of expected lifetime income, using all evidence available in the public domain at a point in time. The effect of the three funds on the savings decisions in the three jurisdictions is a question that begs to be researched, as little seems to have been done on this. One study of the effect of the Heritage Fund on savings in Alberta concludes that there has been no effect (Hoffman, 1995).

Yet a further question that comes up when considering the possibility of small, open jurisdictions to preserve their resource wealth by way of investment funds concerns to what extent this would be diluted by immigration into the jurisdiction. All the three jurisdictions considered here are open to other jurisdictions, Alaska and Alberta by being parts of federal states, and as for Norway, there is now free movement of labor vis-á-vis the European Union and even considerable immigration from other parts of the world. It is possible, and indeed quite likely, that immigrants will be drawn to jurisdictions that are more wealthy than others. The populations of Alaska and Alberta have grown more than the average of American states versus Canadian provinces, but whether this is due to the existence of their investment funds is another issue; the economies of both are dynamic and offer good opportunities. In Norway net immigration rose sharply in the mid-1990s, which coincides with the build-up of the Petroleum Fund, but more importantly these were boom years for the Norwegian economy; net immigration to Norway turned positive around 1970 and has shown some response to the business cycle. It may be noted in this context that the original proposal for the dividend program in Alaska envisaged differentiating the dividend according to the length of residency in the state, but this was challenged by recent immigrants to the state and ultimately struck down by the Supreme Court of the United States. Using the investment fund as a retirement fund would to some extent accomplish the same thing, i.e. rewarding those who have a long residency in the jurisdiction.

References

Auty, R.M. and R.F. Mikesell (1998), *Sustainable Development in Mineral Economies*. Clarendon Press, Oxford.

Brekke, K.A. (1997), 'Hicksian Income from Resource Extraction in an Open Economy'. *Land Economics*, Vol. 73, pp. 516 – 527.

Gelb, A. and associates (1988), *Oil Windfalls: Blessing or Curse?* Oxford University Press, New York.

Goldsmith, S. (1998), 'From Oil to Assets: Managing Alaska's New Wealth'. *Fiscal Policy Papers*, Institute of Social Policy and Economic Research, University of Alaska, Anchorage, No. 10.

—— (1999), 'Safe Landing: Charting a Flight Path Through the Clouds'. *Fiscal Policy Papers*, Institute of Social Policy and Economic Research, University of Alaska, Anchorage, No. 12.

Hannesson, R. (2000a), 'Resource Windfalls: How to Use Them'. *OPEC Review*, Vol. 24, pp. 195 – 209.

—— (2000b), *Investing for Sustainability: The Management of Mineral Wealth*. Kluwer, Boston.

Hoffman, M.D. (1995), *The Economic Impact of the Alberta Heritage Savings Trust Fund on the Consumption-Savings Decision of Albertans*. Master of Arts Thesis. University of Alberta.

Hotelling, H. (1931), 'The Economics of Exhaustible Resources'. *Journal of Political Economy*, Vol. 39, pp. 137 – 175.

Karl, T.L. (1997), *The Paradox of Plenty*. University of California Press, Berkeley.

Mumey, G. and J. Ostermann (1990), 'Alberta Heritage Fund: Measuring Value and Achievement'. *Canadian Public Policy*, Vol. 16, pp. 29 – 50.

NOU (1983), 'Petroleumsvirksomhetens framtid' (The Future of the Petroleum Activity). *Norges offentlige utredninger* (NOU) 1983:27.

Stauffer, T.R. (1988), 'Oil Rich: Spend or Save? How Oil Countries Have Handled the Windfall', *in* Wealth Management, A Comparison of the Alaska Permanent Fund and Other Oil-Generated Savings Accounts Around the World. *Alaska Permanent Fund, The Trustee Papers*, No. 2, Juneau.

Warrack, A.A. and R.R. Keddie (undated), *Alberta Heritage Fund vs. Alaska Permanent Fund: A Comparative Analysis*. Faculty of Business, University of Alberta, Edmonton (available at www.apfc.org).

Wen, J-F. (2001), 'Eliminating Alberta's Personal Income Tax'. *Department of Economics, University of Calgary*, February 2001.

Chapter 7

Petroleum Policy and Prospects in the UK Continental Shelf

Alex Kemp and Linda Stephen

Key Features of Recent Trends

The UK Continental Shelf (UKCS) is frequently described as a mature petroleum province. This term is used somewhat loosely but is often taken to imply a situation with characteristics including (a) falling average size of discovery and development, (b) declining production, (c) failure to replace depletion by new additions to reserves, and (d) declining exploration interest. Some of these characteristics do apply to the UKCS. Thus official estimates of remaining known reserves (proven plus probable plus possible) have been falling for some years. For oil they were just over 2 billion tonnes in 1997 and 1.35 billion tonnes at the end of 2002. For natural gas the known reserves were 1,960 billion cubic metres in 1996 and 1,330 billion cubic metres at the end of 2002.[1] Total hydrocarbon production peaked in 1999 at 250 million tonnes of oil equivalent and has been falling at an average rate of just over three per cent per year since then to 220 million tonnes of oil equivalent in 2003. The long-term trends in production are shown in Figure 7.1.

The average size of discovery and new field development has fallen dramatically since the peak levels of around 600 million barrels of oil equivalent (mmboe) in the first half of the 1970s. In recent years the average size has been around 34 mmboe. This average conceals substantial likely variations. The most likely size is less than the average, reflecting the lognormal distribution generally associated with reserves in a petroleum province. There are also occasional very large discoveries. Thus, as recently as 2001, the Buzzard field with estimated recoverable reserves in the range 450-550 mmbbls was discovered. A further feature is that the average size has not fallen significantly over the last decade.

---

1 See UK Department of Trade and Industry (DTI), (2003), *UK Energy in Brief*, July, London.

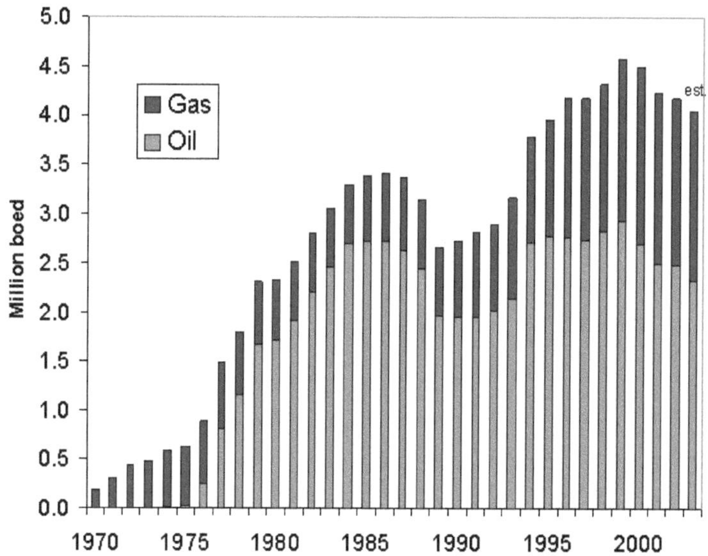

Figure 7.1 UKCS oil and gas production 1975-2003

The exploration and appraisal (E and A) effort has fallen sharply over the last few years. The trend in the numbers of wells drilled by category is shown in Figure 7.2. The exploration effort has fallen dramatically since its peak in 1990 and has been especially low since 1999. The average number of pure exploration wells drilled in the period 1999-2003 has been 21. Throughout this period oil prices have been relatively high. It is also noteworthy that appraisal activity which historically accounted for far less wells than exploration has recently become relatively more important, and since 1999 has accounted for more wells than pure exploration. Nevertheless, the total E and A effort has fallen substantially.

The inevitable result has been a major reduction in the number of discoveries. Using the DTI definition of significant discovery[2] the average annual number in the period 1990-2003 has been 11 significant discoveries. But in the period 1990-1997 the average was 14.5 such discoveries, while from 1998 to 2003 it has been only 6.3 discoveries.

The exploration success rate (significant discovery) has actually increased in recent years. For many years it was in the range 20 per cent-25 per cent, but dipped below 20 per cent for some years in the early-mid 1990s. Since 1999, however, it has averaged over 30 per cent. This has coincided with the period of low effort. The conventional explanation is that the reduced effort has been concentrated on low-risk prospects. Hence the comparatively high success rate. There are probably several reasons for the reduced exploration effort, including the relatively small size of expected discovery, the opportunities for larger discoveries in other parts of

[2] At least 1,000 b/d of oil or 15,000,000 cf/d of gas from a test well.

the world, and the comparatively high costs (per boe) in the UKCS resulting from a combination of the difficult operating environment and the relatively small sizes of fields.

The so-called maturity of the UKCS has brought with it some advantages. A major one is the presence of a large infrastructure which can be employed to facilitate the development of further fields and encourage exploration. The infrastructure includes pipelines and processing facilities on platforms and at terminals. For gas, access to the Transco national transmission system (NTS) is available at many terminals. Third party tariffing arrangements are very common for pipeline transportation, and often for processing at offshore platforms and at terminals. Tariffs are determined by individual negotiations. For some years a voluntary Code of Practice has applied whereby indicative tariffs for pipeline and processing with available capacity are published by the asset owners. Tariff terms offered should be on a non-discriminatory basis. At the time of writing the operation of the Code of Practice is being revised with a view to enhancing the transparency of terms and the introduction of a dispute resolution procedure with the DTI undertaking the role of arbitrator.

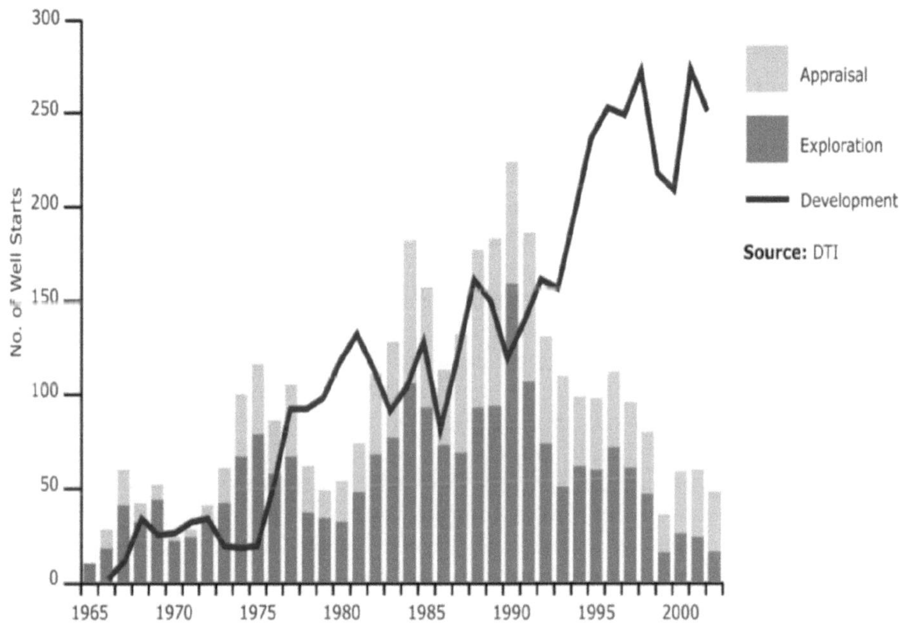

Figure 7.2 UKCS drilling activity 1965-2002

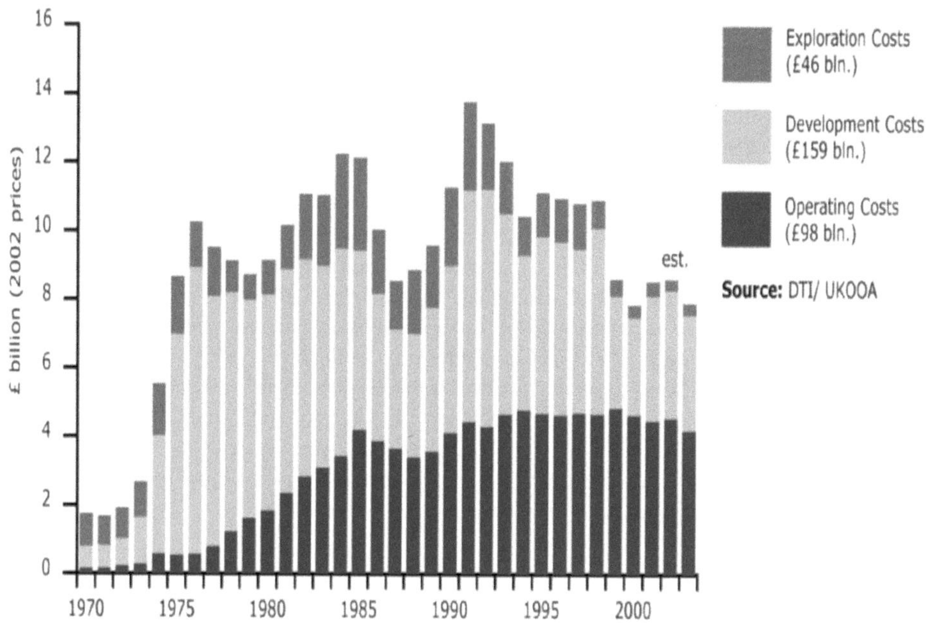

Figure 7.3 UK North Sea expenditures (2002 prices) 1970-2003

Source: DTI/UKOOA.

Trends in investment expenditure provide another indication of the health of the industry. The historical behaviour is shown in Figure 7.3. The phenomenal growth in field development expenditures in the period from 1974 to the early 1980s reflected the investment in the very large fields discovered in the early 1970s. In recent years field investment has fallen as well as outlays on E and A activities. To some extent this may have reflected the cost reductions initiated in the 1980s, especially following the oil price collapse in 1986, and pursued with increased vigour in the 1990s. This was through the Cost Reduction Initiative for the New Era (CRINE). While the CRINE initiative reduced costs of all types of projects the *net* effect on total expenditures by the industry is a more complex issue. The reduction in *unit costs* has enabled more projects to go ahead than otherwise would have been the case. The developments in the West of Scotland region are examples of projects which have been facilitated by the cost reducing initiatives.[3] The data on field investment expenditures are better seen in conjunction with those on drilling of development wells. These increased rapidly in the 1990s (Figure 7.2) but a worrying recent feature has been the reduction in numbers from 282 in 2001 to 235 in 2003.

3 For a detailed analysis of this issue see A.G. Kemp and B. MacDonald, (1995), 'Cost Savings and Activity Levels in the UKCS: a Positive Sum Game', *Energy Policy*, Vol. 23, No. 1, pp. 71-83.

Such reductions have taken place despite the prevalence of relatively high oil prices. This raises the perspective of the various financial flows from the whole activity. The key aggregates are shown in Figure 7.4. The industry experienced a negative net cash flow in the early 1990s but in the last few years, when oil prices have been relatively high, the gross income and net cash flows have both been quite strong.

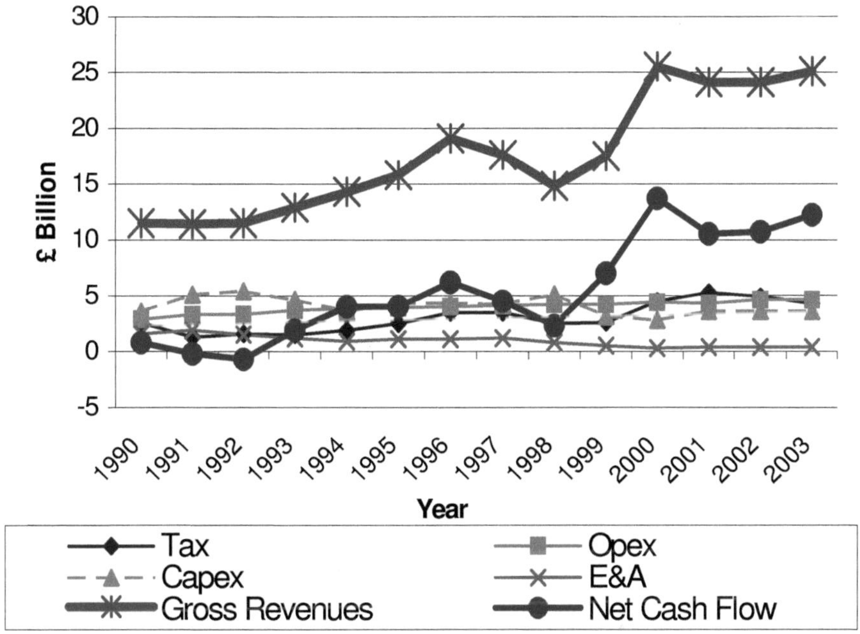

Figure 7.4 Financial flows from UKCS activities

Source: DTI.

The current concern is that, despite this healthy cash flow, production is falling. Some further insights into the behaviour of production can be obtained by examining the profiles of the individual fields. When data for all the fields sanctioned by 2002 were subjected to statistical analysis it was found that the production decline rates were strongly related to the vintage of their initial development.[4] In Figure 7.5 the mean decline rates according to vintage of initial development are shown. The decline is measured from the year of peak production. The exercise was conducted for dry gas fields separately from oil and gas/condensate ones, but the results were not noticeably different. The increase in

[4] For a detailed discussion see A.G. Kemp and A.S. Kasim (2002), 'An Analysis of Production Decline Rates in the UK Continental Shelf (UKCS)', *North Sea Study Occasional Paper* No. 87, University of Aberdeen, Department of Economics, June.

the decline rate with the proximity of the field vintage is noticeable. It was also found that there was a statistically significant relationship between the decline rate and (a) the size of fields, and (b) the presence of incremental investments, as well as the vintage of development. Logistic curves generally produced the best fits to the decline rates.

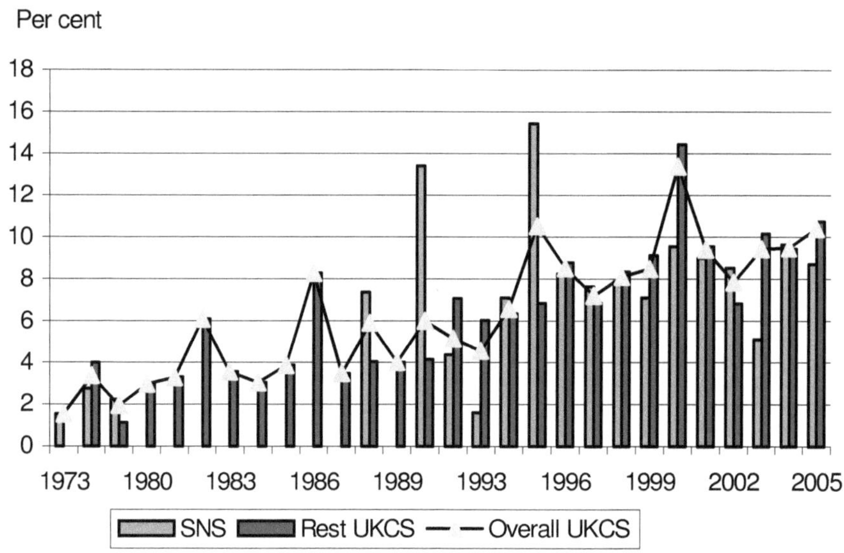

Figure 7.5 Annual mean decline rates by year of decline commencement and field location

Methodology and Assumptions for Making Projections

In spite of the indications of maturity discussed above there is still much remaining potential from the UKCS. Reputable estimates of remaining recoverable reserves are large. The DTI estimates that while around 33 mmboe have been produced to date, remaining recoverable reserves (including as yet undiscovered) could well be 28.5 bn boe.[5] The DTI also estimates that the maximum remaining potential could be as high as 47 bn boe, though clearly the probability of this being achieved may not be high. The UK Offshore Operators Association has recently estimated that remaining recoverable reserves are in the range 23.5-31.6 bn boe.[6] The issue is thus not the availability of physical oil and gas in place, but the problems of their economic exploitation.

5 See. P. Haile (2004), 'Opportunities, Initiatives, Regulations and Licensing in the UK', paper presented to conference on North Sea: Acquisition, Divestiture and Development, organised by Center for Business Intelligence, Houston, 26/27 February.

6 UKOOA (2004).

Projections of activity levels may be made by various methods including financial simulation and econometric techniques.[7] In this study the projections of production and expenditures have been made through the use of financial simulation modelling, including the use of the Monte Carlo technique, informed by a large, recently updated field database validated by the relevant operators. The field database incorporates key, best estimate information on production, and investment, operating and decommissioning expenditures. These refer to 270 sanctioned fields, 135 incremental projects relating to these fields, 43 probable fields, and 40 possible fields. The latter three categories are as yet unsanctioned but are currently being examined for development. An additional database contains 199 fields defined as being in the category of technical reserves. Summary data on the reserves (oil/gas) and block location are available. They are not currently being examined for development by licensees.

Monte Carlo modelling was employed to estimate the possible numbers of new discoveries in the period to 2030. The modelling incorporated assumptions based on recent trends relating to exploration effort, success rates, and sizes and types (oil, gas, condensate) of discovery. A moving average of the behaviour of these variables over the past five years was calculated separately for six areas of the UKCS [Southern North Sea (SNS), Central North Sea (CNS), Moray Firth (MF), Northern North Sea (NNS), West of Scotland (WOS), and Irish Sea (IS)], and the results employed for use in the Monte Carlo analysis. Because of the very limited data for WOS and IS over the five-year period judgemental assumptions on success rates and average sizes of discoveries were made for the modelling.

It is postulated that the exploration effort depends substantially on a combination of (a) the expected success rate, (b) the likely size of discovery, and (c) oil/gas prices. In the present study three future oil/gas price scenarios were employed as follows:

Table 7.1 Future oil and gas price scenarios

	Oil Price (real) $/bbl	Gas Price (real) Pence/therm
High	25	24
Medium	20	18
Low	15	14

The postulated numbers of annual exploration wells for the whole of the UKCS are as follows:

[7] For recent examples of econometric techniques see A.G. Kemp and A.S. Kasim (2003), 'An Econometric Model of Oil and Gas Exploration, Development and Production in the UK Continental Shelf', The *Energy Journal*, Vol. 24, No. 2, April, and A.G. Kemp and A.S. Kasim (2003), 'Forecasting Activity Levels in the UK Continental Shelf', The Role of Perceptions, *Energy Economics*, Vol. 25, No. 6, November.

Table 7.2 Exploration wells

	2004	2018	2028
High	35	23	15
Medium	25	16	10
Low	15	9	5

The annual numbers are modelled to decline in a generally linear fashion over the period.

It is postulated that success rates depend substantially on a combination of (a) recent experience, and (b) size of the effort. It is further suggested that higher effort is associated with more discoveries but with lower success rates compared to reduced levels of effort. This reflects the view that low levels of effort will be concentrated on the lowest risk prospects, and thus that higher effort involves the acceptance of higher risk. For the UKCS as a whole 3 success rates were postulated as follows:

Table 7.3 Success rates. Per cent

Medium effort/Medium success rate	= 25
High effort/Low success rate	= 20
Low effort/High success rate	= 30

It is assumed that technological progress will maintain these success rates.

The mean sizes of discoveries made in the period 1997-2003 inclusive for each of the six regions were calculated. It was then assumed that the mean size of discovery would decrease in line with this historic experience. Such decline rates are quite modest. For 2004 the average size of discovery for the whole of the UKCS is 34 million barrels of oil equivalent (mmboe). For purposes of the Monte Carlo modelling of new discoveries the Standard Deviation (SD) was set at 50 per cent of the mean value. In line with historic experience the size distribution of discoveries was taken to be lognormal.

Using the above information the Monte Carlo technique was employed to project discoveries in the six regions to 2028. For the period the total numbers of discoveries for the whole of the UKCS were are follows:

Table 7.4 Total number of discoveries to 2028

High effort/low success rate	=133
Medium effort/medium success rate	=115
Low Effort/High Success Rate	= 77

For each region the average development costs (per boe) of fields sanctioned since the late 1990s and those in the probable and possible categories were calculated. Using these as the mean values, the Monte Carlo technique was employed to calculate the development costs of new discoveries. A normal distribution with a

SD = 20 per cent of the mean value was employed. For the whole of the UKCS the average development costs on this basis were \$4.33/boe. Annual operating costs were modelled as a percentage of accumulated development costs. This percentage was taken to increase as the size of field was reduced reflecting the presence of economies of scale.

With respect to fields in the category of technical reserves it was recognised that many have remained undeveloped for a long time. Accordingly, it was assumed that their average development costs would be \$1/boe higher than for new discoveries for each of the regions. For purposes of Monte Carlo modelling a normal distribution of the recoverable reserves for each field with a SD = 50 per cent of the mean was assumed. With respect to development costs the distribution was assumed to be normal with a SD = 20 per cent of the mean value.

The annual numbers of new field developments were assumed to be constrained by the capacity of the industry. The ceilings were assumed to be linked to the oil/gas price scenarios with maxima of 25, 20 and 15 respectively under the high, medium and low price cases. These constraints do *not* apply to incremental projects which are additional to new field developments.

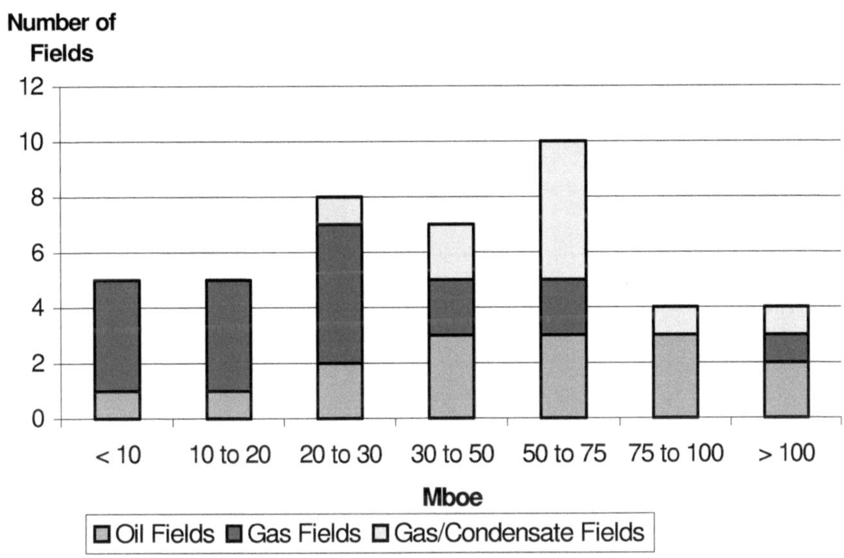

Figure 7.6 Probable fields \$20/bbl, 18p/therm. Hurdle rate 10 per cent

A noteworthy feature of the 135 incremental projects in the database validated by operators is the expectation that the great majority will be executed over the three years from 2004. It is virtually certain that in the medium and longer term many further incremental projects will be designed and executed. They are just not yet at the serious planning stage. Such projects can be expected not only on currently sanctioned fields but also on those presently classified as in the categories of probable, possible, technical reserves, and future discoveries.

Accordingly, estimates were made of the potential extra incremental projects from all these sources. Examination of the numbers of such projects and their key characteristics (reserves and costs) being examined by operators over the past four years indicated a decline rate in the volumes. On the basis of this, and from a base of the information of the key characteristics of the 135 projects in the late 2003 database, it was felt that every four years, with a decline rate reflecting historic experience, further portfolios of incremental projects could reasonably be expected. As noted above such future projects would be spread over *all* categories of host fields.

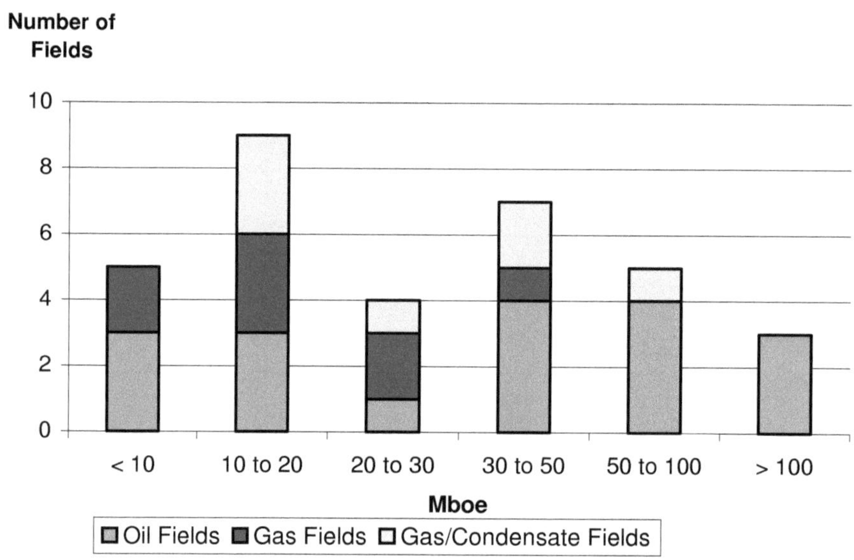

Figure 7.7 Possible fields $20/bbl, 18p/therm. Hurdle rate 10 per cent

The financial modelling incorporates a threshold or hurdle rate, field economic cut-off, and the full details of the current petroleum tax system. The base case emphasised has a post-tax threshold rate of return of 10 per cent in real terms. An important assumption is that adequate infrastructure will be available to facilitate the development of the future incremental projects.

The potential contributions of discovered fields and current incremental projects to future activity levels are shown in Figures 7.6-7.9 under the $20, 18p price scenario. Under this scenario the 43 probable fields pass the economic threshold. The mean development costs are $3.3/boe and the mean lifetime operating costs $2.56/boe. Mean total costs (including decommissioning) are $6.13/boe with 68 per cent being in the range $3.54/boe-$10.1/boe. Under the $20,

18p scenario 33 of the 40 possible fields proceed. The mean development cost is \$3.2/boe and the mean lifetime operating cost is \$1.68/boe. The mean total costs are \$5.34/boe with 68 per cent being in the range \$3.11/boe-\$6.96/boe, and 95 per cent in the range \$2.40/boe-\$11.81/boe. Under the \$20, 18p scenario 121 of the 135 incremental projects proceed. Mean development costs are \$4.4/boe, and mean lifetime operating costs \$1.43/boe. Mean total costs are \$5.89/boe, with 68 per cent being in the range \$2.89/boe-\$9.35/boe, and 95 per cent in the range \$0.85/boe-\$14.99/boe. Under the \$20, 18p scenario 175 of the 199 fields in the technical reserves category proceed. The mean size is 20 mmboe, though the most likely size is much lower.

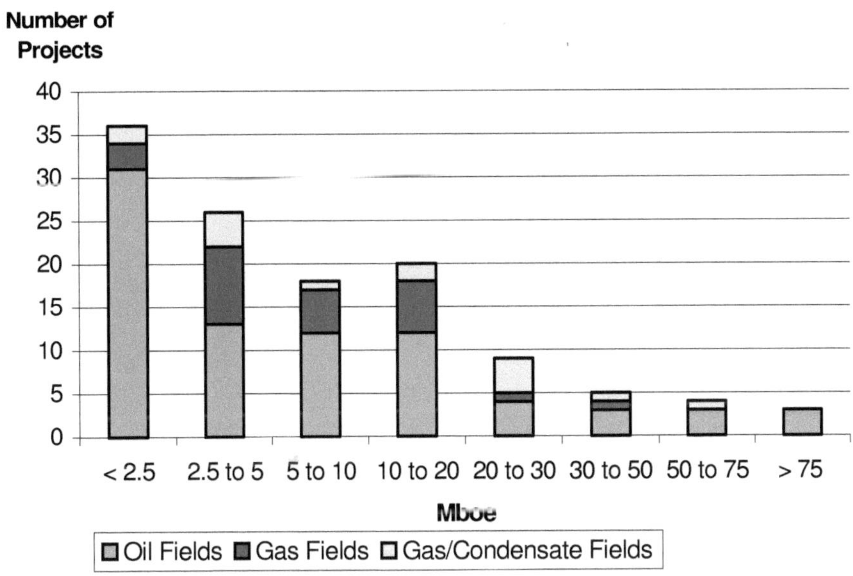

Figure 7.8 Current incremental projects \$20/bbl, 18p/therm. Hurdle rate 10 per cent

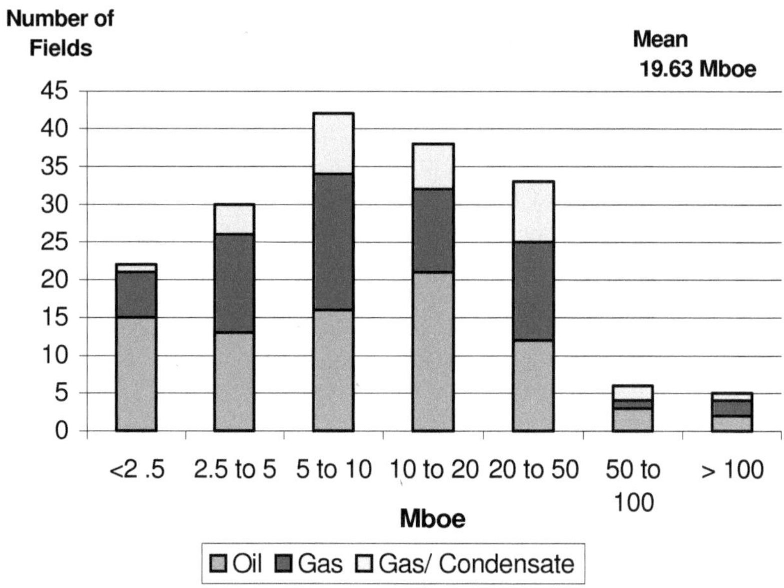

Figure 7.9 Technical reserve fields $20/bbl and 18p/therm. Hurdle rate 10 per cent

Production

Potential oil production (excluding NGLs) under the $20, 18p scenario is shown in Figure 7.10. A key feature is the fairly fast decline from sanctioned fields, especially over the period to 2010. In the later part of the period the pace of decline moderates, but the level in 2020 from this category of field is just 100,000 b/d. Incremental projects currently being examined make a substantial contribution to the moderation of the decline rate over the next few years. Fields in the probable category dramatically change the whole profile for a few years from 2007 onwards. A very substantial contribution comes from one field, Buzzard, which, at the time of the database construction, was still in the probable category.

Other features of the results are the major long-term contributions made by fields in the technical reserves category and by future incremental projects (related to all categories of fields). Total production in 2020 is around 1 mmb/d of which technical reserves contribute around 350,000 b/d. Their combined contribution is substantially greater than that from new discoveries (excluding incremental projects on these). The contribution from this category of field is fairly modest due to a combination of the relatively small number of discoveries and their small average size.

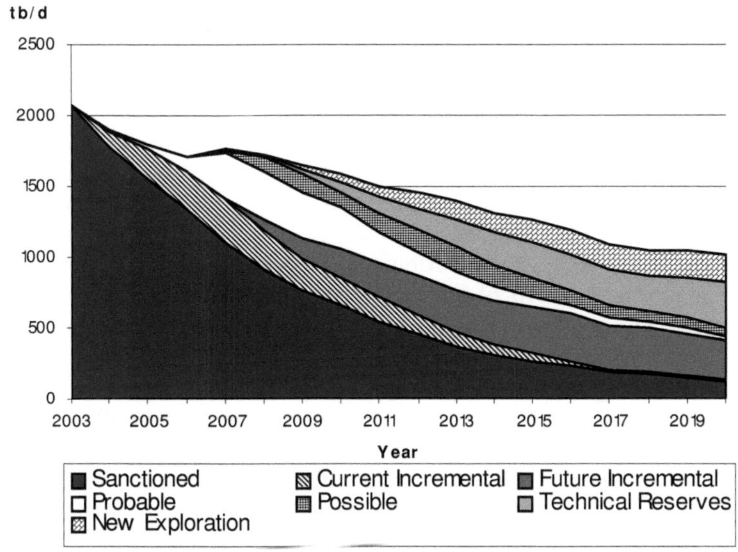

Figure 7.10 Potential oil production $20/bbl and 18p/therm. Hurdle rate 10 per cent

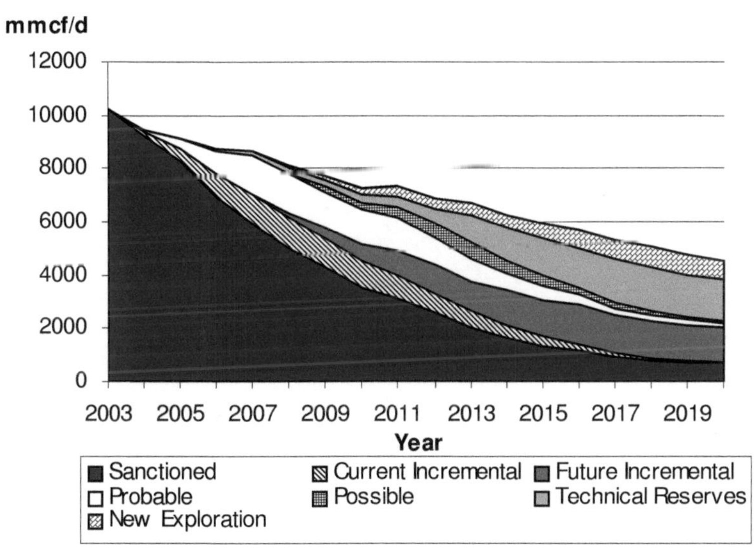

Figure 7.11 Potential gas production $20/bbl and 18p/therm. Hurdle rate 10 per cent

In Figure 7.11 prospective production of natural gas (excluding NGLs) is shown. The decline rate in total output is broadly similar to that for oil. Production from the sanctioned fields falls at a fairly brisk pace. Up to 2010 this category of field accounts for 50 per cent or more of total output. Currently planned incremental projects substantially moderate the decline rate in the period 2006-2010. The development of probable fields makes an even bigger contribution in the period 2006-2012. Beyond 2012 technical reserves and further incremental projects become increasingly important. By 2020 each of these categories accounts for over 35 per cent of total output. The contribution of new discoveries remains moderate reflecting the modest numbers of finds and their relatively small size.

In Figure 7.12 prospective total hydrocarbon production (including NGLs) is shown under the $20, 18p scenario. The decline rate is seen to be fairly brisk until 2006 after which it is moderated for a few years. The large Buzzard field plays a significant role here. In 2010 the target of three mmboe/d set by PILOT (the joint government/industry body established to promote activity) is just achieved. It is noteworthy, however, that this is dependent on a significant contribution from future incremental projects, and smaller contributions from both new discoveries and the development of some fields in the technical reserves category. By 2020 total production is around 1.9 mmboe/d at which date technical reserves and future incremental projects constitute a high proportion of the total. In that year each of these categories provides more output than new discoveries.

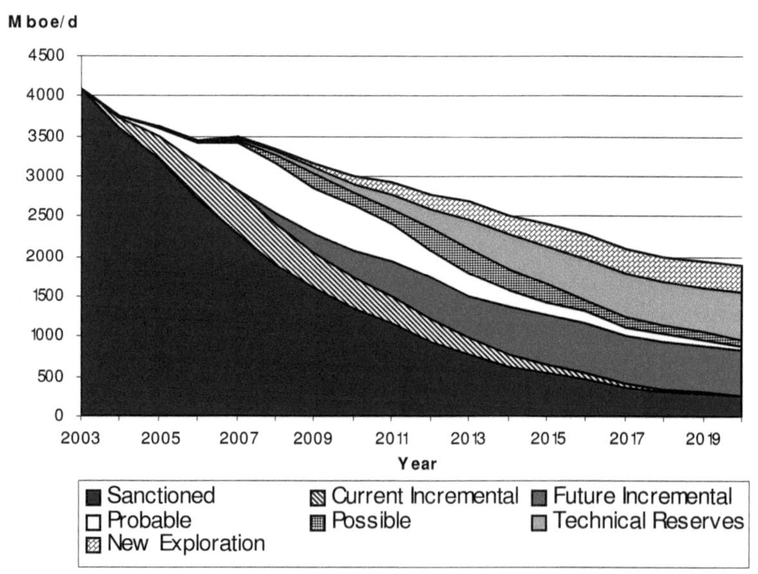

Figure 7.12 Potential total hydrocarbon production $20/bbl and 18p/therm. Hurdle rate 10 per cent

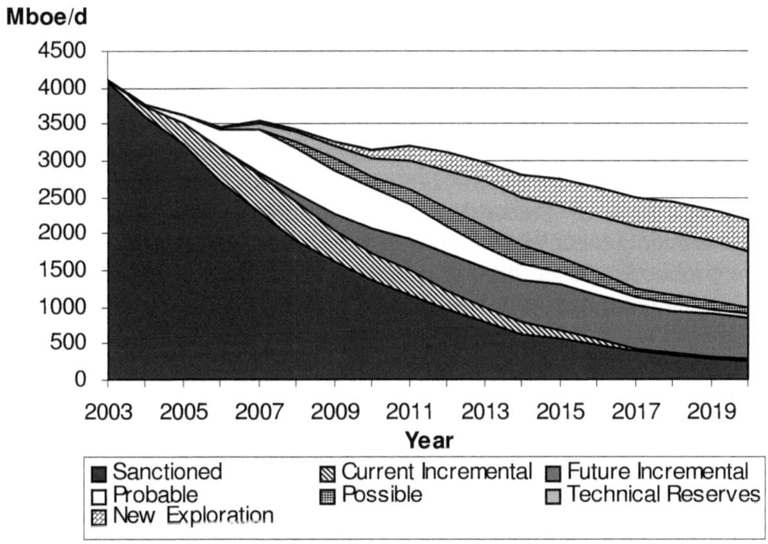

Figure 7.13 Potential total hydrocarbon production $25/bbl and 24p/therm. Hurdle rate 10 per cent

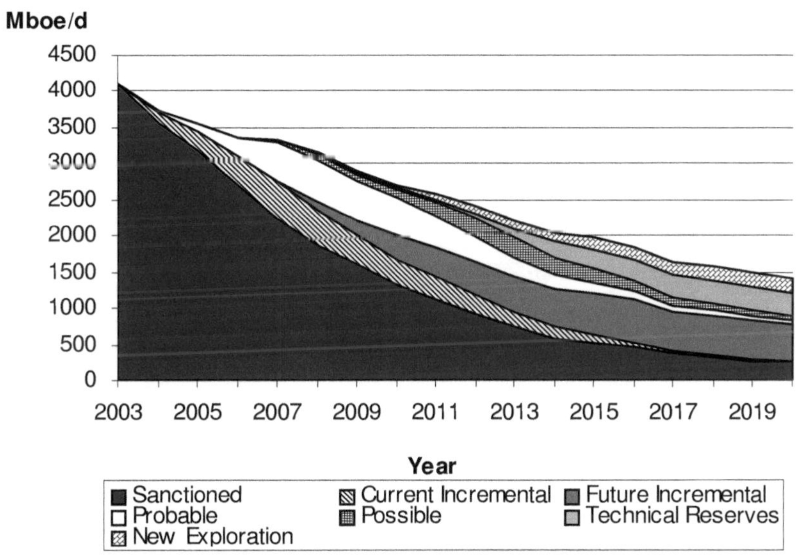

Figure 7.14 Potential total hydrocarbon production $15/bbl and 14p/therm. Hurdle rate 10 per cent

In the longer term there is considerable price sensitivity regarding the behaviour of operating expenditures. Under the high price scenario they remain over £3.7 billion annually (2004 prices) until 2011. They decline gradually thereafter but still exceed £3 billion as late as 2019. On the other hand, under the low price scenario they fall continuously at a brisk pace. In 2010 they are £3 billion and in 2020 £1.5 billion (2004 prices). The main sources of the variations are the much larger number of fields in the technical reserves category developed under the high price, and, to a lesser extent, the development of more new discoveries under the same price case.

Current Policy Issues

The production projections discussed above will not be obtained without a major effort by all key stakeholders – government, operators, and contractors. Government policy encompasses tax and licensing issues. With respect to tax, major changes took place in 2002 when the Supplementary Charge to corporation tax was introduced at 10 per cent resulting in the combined rate increasing to 40 per cent. At the same time capital allowances for field development were increased from 25 per cent declining balance to 100 per cent first year. A further measure abolished royalties from January 2003. Petroleum Revenue Tax (PRT) is payable at 50 per cent on fields developed prior to 16 March 1993. The top marginal rate is now 70 per cent on such fields.

The system is now entirely profit-related. In fact, for investors in a tax-paying position, the system is essentially a cash flow tax. Incremental projects on mature fields obtain relief against PRT for the great majority of their costs on 100 per cent first-year basis. While a net cash flow tax is well known in the literature its practical implementation is fairly unique. A key feature in terms of investment incentives emanates from the fact that the post-tax rate of return is equal to the pre-tax rate. (This excludes the effect of debt finance. It is noteworthy that loan interest is disallowed for the Supplementary Charge). At typical discount rates post-tax net present values (NPVs) are lower than pre-tax ones. Similarly, where investors are faced with the need to rank projects and employ the (NPV/I) ratio for such purposes, the post-tax values are very far below those for the pre-tax position.

As can be seen from Figure 7.8 the great majority of the incremental projects currently being examined are quite small. A significant proportion are subject to PRT. A representative selection of these projects was chosen and examined in relation to a host field where the uplift, volume and safeguard allowances have all been fully utilised (Mother field x). The sizes of the projects range from 2 mmbbls (A) to 50 mmbbls (G), with four being under 10 mmbbls. Their pre-tax and post-tax NPVs at 10 per cent real discount rate are shown in Figure 7.17 under the $20 price. The values are all positive, but for the small projects the wealth generated to the investor is very small. There may be doubts about whether they will be acceptable. It should be stressed again that the great majority of projects are very small.

Currently a joint government-industry initiative is examining the blockages to further investment in 'brownfield' projects and the issue of tax reliefs on PRT-paying fields will certainly arise. A range of PRT reliefs such as (a) uplift allowance for incremental investments, (b) extra volume allowance, and (c) rate reduction are obvious candidates for consideration. The government, having recently abolished royalties on mature fields, will require much convincing that reliefs are necessary. Even if a willingness to give reliefs was conceded the government will require to be satisfied on several counts. There is concern about the extent of any deadweight loss, meaning the loss of tax revenues as a result of giving relief for projects which would have gone ahead in the absence of the relief. The government will want to know what extra activity is generated and how the tax revenues received compare to the deadweight loss. To estimate the extra activity is by no means easy. There are several unknowns, including principally the aggregate number of potential new projects, but also their size and unit costs. There are also the more conventional uncertainties regarding the behaviour of oil and gas prices, and the investment threshold rates employed by investors.

The implementation of allowances for incremental projects also raises practical problems. A PRT rate reduction would improve the cash flow to the investor, but would also produce significant deadweight loss to the Treasury. An extra uplift on incremental capital expenditure would represent a targeted relief: the relief would not be available unless the expenditure were undertaken. But, given the tax changes of 2002, the result would be that the post-tax rate of return would exceed the pre-tax rate. To reduce the size of this difference any extra uplift could be spread over a number of years. This happens in Norway where the uplift totals 30 per cent but is now to be spread over four years. It is applicable to incremental projects. In the UK if an uplift of 25 per cent were spread over five years the result is a modest increase in the NPV. Typically the post-tax NPVs will remain far below pre-tax levels. This is probably the more important result with respect to this issue.

An uplift allowance by its nature favours capital intensive projects. The great majority of incremental projects are heavily orientated towards drilling and thus would clearly benefit from the allowance. Projects which are not capital intensive would include some EOR schemes such as injection of polymers over a long period. Clearly they would benefit to a lesser extent.

The other obvious allowance would be based on incremental volumes. There would be no question of the post-tax rate of return exceeding the pre-tax rate with this type of relief. The concept of volume allowance is well known in the PRT mechanism. The fixed amount feature was introduced to provide relatively more help to small fields. It suffers from the fact that its value varies inversely with the price of oil and gas. It is thus regressive in its impact with respect to price variations. Alternative variations include an allowance set at £x per boe. The absolute value of this would not change with the price of oil. It becomes relatively more valuable the lower the price. The concept has been employed in Nigeria for many years. Additional progressivity is built into the system in that country, at the expense of added complexity, by making the size of the allowance vary inversely with the oil price.

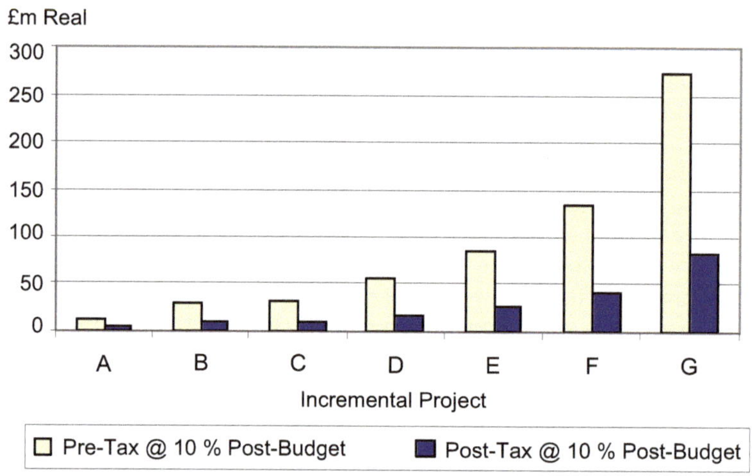

Figure 7.17 Mother field X incremental NPV @ 10 per cent. Post-budget tax system, oil price $20/bbl

From the viewpoint of government any extra volume allowance would raise the issue of deadweight loss discussed above. A further practical problem would be the need to identify the incremental volumes to be attributed to the new projects. This will sometimes be straightforward as, for example, in the case of a discrete satellite development. But in many other cases the distinction between base and incremental volumes may not be easily made. There may also be other practical problems where, for example, a field has several small incremental projects. There is then the possibility of a proliferation of incremental allowances with consequential added complexity. Such problems are not insoluble, however, though judgements would inevitably have to be made.

The possible role of tax incentives in enhancing exploration was examined in detail in the summer of 2003 by a joint government-industry working party. Various devices were considered including principally uplift on E and A expenditures but also others such as removal of the Supplementary Charge on new discoveries. There was general agreement that the full cycle rate of return under oil prices of $20 was modest,[8] and that tax reliefs of the types noted above could enhance them. The effect of an E and A uplift of 25 per cent on the volume of activity, while difficult to estimate, was generally acknowledged to be modest. An uplift of 50 per cent would have a stronger effect. Removal of the Supplementary Charge could have an effect intermediate between the smaller and larger uplift. An

8 See, for example, A.G. Kemp and L. Stephen (2002), 'The Impact of the 2002 Tax Changes on the UKCS', *North Sea Study Occasional* Paper No. 89, University of Aberdeen, Department of Economics, August. The full cycle expected rate of return on exploration undertaken in the period 1995-2001 was found to be around 10 per cent. For future exploration the return could be lower because of smaller field sizes.

uplift of 25 per cent was consistent with the R & D credit already widely available to British industry. Higher levels required very special justification, would involve a much larger deadweight loss, and might be incompatible with the European Community rules regarding state aids.

The eventual decision was not to introduce a general relief, but to propose an Expenditure Supplement for E and A for investors who did not have tax cover for their allowances. Such investors have been disadvantaged compared to existing players with tax cover. They will now be allowed to carry forward their eligible but unused E and A allowances with compound interest at six per cent for a total period of up to six years. Conceptually this type of allowance is soundly based. It deals appropriately with the variable times likely to be experienced between E and A expenditures and the receipt of taxable income. The interest rate is parsimonious, reflecting a risk-free situation. The cost of capital for E and A activities is certainly very much higher. The effect on the E and A effort will be modest. The increase in the full cycle rate of return is small. The government has for some time been encouraging new entrants into the UKCS. The new allowance will give a positive signal effect to potential new investors.

The changes made in 2002 led to an anomaly with respect to the taxation of tariff income. On infrastructure systems subject to PRT tariff income became subject to tax at 70 per cent, while on systems not subject to PRT the rate is 40 per cent. This distorts competition among systems for new tariff business. The issue of the level of tariffs has been a subject of much debate for many years. In the debate in 2003 it was argued by the industry that, if PRT were removed, and the economic benefit were passed on to users, the reduction in tariffs on new contracts could lead to increased activity in terms of further new field developments and exploration.

The majority of new field developments in the UKCS employ existing infrastructure and third party payments on average constitute more than 50 per cent of lifetime operating costs for the fields in question. The present authors found[9] that, under a $20, 18p price scenario and reduction in tariffs on new contracts of 20 per cent, cumulative extra gas production to 2020 could amount to over 120 billion cubic metres and extra oil production to around 500 million barrels. Further, in the period to 2020 there could be a net increase in tax revenues in the range £500 million - £1 billion (at 2002 prices) depending on the assumptions of the modelling. In the short-term there is a deadweight cost to the Treasury from the tax concession, but in the longterm the extra activity produces net increases.

The tax relief became effective in January 2004. The implementation of the measure necessitates reallocation of costs between those which are eligible for PRT relief and those which are ineligible. The most important reallocation applies to operating costs. The greater the reallocation of costs from eligible to ineligible for PRT purposes the lower is the net economic benefit to the asset owner from the tax relief. Thus, while the tax rate is nominally reduced by 42 per cent, the net

9 For full details see AG Kemp and L Stephen (2003), 'UK Oil and Gas Production Prospects, the Optimal Utilisation of UKCS Infrastructure, and the 2003 Budget Tax Changes', *North Sea Study Occasional Paper* No. 90, University of Aberdeen, Department of Economics, April.

benefit will be less depending on the extent of cost reallocation. According to the Oil Taxation Act the allocation of costs in the current circumstances should be done on a 'just and reasonable' basis. This term can be interpreted in different ways. Currently there is some uncertainty surrounding the practical measurement of the net economic benefit from the tax relief. This is complicating negotiations between asset owners and users.

The overall position with respect to tariffs is currently the subject of review by the government. The terms and conditions of access to infrastructure have been the subject of individual negotiations between asset owners and prospective users. The government has the right to set tariffs at the request of aggrieved users, but to date this right has not been employed. For some years a voluntary Code of Practice has been in operation whereby asset owners publish indicative tariffs and agree to consider requests for services on a non-discriminatory basis. In practice negotiations between potential user and asset owner are often protracted. The latter have generally attempted to set tariffs at as high levels as they feel the market for the services will permit. In practice this is determined by the cost of alternative transportation and processing facilities. There is thus the possibility of a local monopoly situation. Historically, the likelihood of such local monopolies were much higher than they are now due to the growth of the number of pipelines with ullage available. With oil offshore tanker loading is also generally an alternative, though environmental and other operational problems can reduce the acceptability of this method. This option is, of course, not generally available for gas.

Third party users often feel aggrieved that, after undertaking the costs and risks of discovering and developing a field, a possibly large share of the expected economic rent is in effect transferred to an asset owner who has not had to bear these costs and risks. This view is particularly felt by users in the situation where the infrastructure costs have been incurred and recovered some time in the past.

Free market economists argue that much of the above is irrelevant.[10] If some of the economic rent is transferred from the field developer to the asset owner but there are no other consequences, then, from a national viewpoint, there should be no further legitimate concern. This overlooks a number of pertinent issues. If offers of transportation services are made at tariffs which just undercut the costs of the alternative the field investor may prefer to build his own pipeline rather than pay tariffs to a competitor. If the differential costs are modest the field investor may feel that the advantages of fuller control of operations and the prospect of becoming a recipient of tariff income in the longer term confer net advantages to the construction of his own infrastructure.

There are several cases where this has happened in the UKCS. From the national viewpoint there is merit in ensuring that the oil and gas is produced at lowest resource cost to the nation. A proliferation of pipelines with large ullage available may not be consistent with this objective. From the Treasury's viewpoint it can mean that tax revenues from the UKCS are not maximised. Expenditure on

---

10 An example is P. Stevens, 'Pipeline Regulation and the North Sea Infrastructure', in G. McKerron and P. Pearson (eds.), (1996), *The UK Energy Experience: a Model or a Warning?*, Imperial College Press, London.

pipelines is, of course, allowed as a deduction for tax purposes. This was obviously a major consideration when PRT as well as corporation tax were applicable, with consequential tax relief at extremely high rates. There can thus sometimes be a divergence between the private and national interest. In recognition of this the DTI has powers to prevent the unnecessary proliferation of pipelines, but for some time has not employed this power with vigour.

The DTI has been actively promoting the introduction of new players into the UKCS. The presence of a large, developed infrastructure is an obvious attraction. At least some new players from the USA have found the position with respect to access and tariffs less congenial than in the Gulf of Mexico. Recently the DTI has been taking the lead role in revising the Code of Practice. Key issues from the government's perspective include enhanced transparency of terms and dispute resolution. With respect to the first issue the DTI wishes that actual terms for contracts are published (rather than indicative ones which some users find not particularly helpful). In the event of a difference between potential users and asset owners on terms the DTI proposes that it resolves the dispute. In making a determination it would prefer to make the tariffs cost-related, but take into account the investment risks incurred by the asset owner. The government has other weapons at its disposal in the event of a satisfactory voluntary Code of Practice not being procured. The section of the Competition Act 1998 dealing with abuse of a dominant position could be invoked. In that event the tariff would be set by the competition authorities.

There is, of course, the alternative of full-scale regulation. This already occurs in the Norwegian sector with respect to gas where tariffs are set in accordance with a formula based on rate of return. A separate state-owned company, Gassco, operates the system and ensures that regulations concerning access are observed. The UK is unlikely to proceed down this fully regulated route. The government is more likely to persevere with modifications to the voluntary code in the manner described above.

A further major policy initiative in the UK relates to fallow blocks. The issue is not new but has recently assumed more urgency with the decline in the E and A effort and the perceived lack of access to interesting acreage expressed by new players. Most acreage available for licensing now relates to territory relinquished from previous rounds. Thus, in the current 22nd Round over 1,000 blocks were offered, representing nearly all the acreage available, apart from areas in the Atlantic where there is no current investor interest. The great majority of the blocks have been relinquished from earlier rounds. There is clearly a shortage of interesting fresh acreage.

The issue of fallow acreage was highlighted by Brindex (the Association of British Independent Oil Exploration Companies) as long ago as 1988. The Association produced evidence[11] that, of all the acreage awarded in Licence Rounds 1-4 (covering 1964-1972), 26 per cent (covering 12,300 sq. km.) had either

---

[11] For full details see 'Memorandum Submitted by the Association of British Independent Oil Exploration Companies (Brindex)' in House of Commons Energy Committee, (1988), *The United Kingdom Independent Oil Sector, Memoranda*, HC382, March 1988.

never been drilled or was undrilled over the preceding ten years. This represented 50 per cent more than the total acreage awarded in the recently concluded 10th Round.

The government acknowledged the problem and made it clear that, in considering awards in future rounds, work performance in earlier rounds, including the incidence of fallow acreage, would be taken into account. From the 11th Round onwards the licence regulations relating to the length of the second period were changed. Prior to then this period had been 30 years. From the 11th Round onwards it became 12 years with an option of another 18 years if a field development had either been undertaken or was in prospect.

The measures did not resolve the issue which has become more acute in recent years with the increased lack of free prospective acreage and the perceived need to attract more new players into the UKCS to sustain the exploration and development efforts. The exhortations by the DTI culminated in an agreement with the industry made under the PILOT umbrella.[12] This agreement covers several other topical licence issues as well as fallow bocks/discoveries, including data release, pre-emption rights, financial security for decommissioning and codes of practice to enhance the efficiency of supply chain management and asset transactions. All of these issues had been identified as requiring attention with the general aim of facilitating enhanced activity whether by existing licensees or new ones.

The key features of the new provisions for fallow blocks are as follows. They are defined as those blocks which are out of their initial term and have had no drilling for four years or no other significant activity for two years. Such blocks are then put into two categories after discussions between the DTI and licensee. In the first category are those where the parties agree that actual or proposed activity is satisfactory. Progress is regularly reviewed. For blocks in the second category where there is inactivity the licensee is given a period of up to one year either to start activity, trade the block, or relinquish it. For fallow discoveries there is a broadly similar process. On discoveries where work is under way there are regular reviews. On those where no work is being undertaken the licensee is given up to two years to proceed with work, trade the asset, or relinquish it.

The process is now in progress. In January 2004, details of 151 fallow blocks and 83 fallow discoveries were published by the DTI. The result of this initiative should certainly be some increase in both exploration and development activity. Of course, the more promising blocks and discoveries continue to be held by the existing licensees. The DTI initiative will have spurred them on to initiate work, however, because of the danger of losing the assets.

A further recent initiative by the DTI has been the introduction of Promote Licences in the recent 21st Round. These are designed to encourage the participation of players who have ideas which they can investigate at relatively low capital outlay. For a two-year period the licensee undertakes to work up prospects and, if necessary, attract funding and commitments for the subsequent two-year

---

[12] For full details see PILOT (2002), *Progressing Partnership: the Work of the Progressing Partnership Work Group*, March.

stage when 'significant activity' on the block is expected. During the first period the normal licence fee is discounted by 90 per cent. As many as 34 Promote licensees received awards in the recent 21st Round. This innovative idea should lead to a worthwhile increase in activity in the medium term.

Conclusions

The UKCS is now conventionally described as a maturing petroleum province. Over 33 billion boe have been produced since exploration commenced in late 1964. Reputable estimates of remaining recoverable reserves indicate that there is the resource potential to permit the production of as much again. But much of the remaining reserves are located in small accumulations which make their economic development more challenging. Another relevant development has been the increasing tendency for the major investors to screen their potential investments in the UKCS against their worldwide opportunities. This factor and the decline in likely size of discovery has led to a substantial reduction in E and A activity in recent years. Aggregate production of hydrocarbons peaked in 1999 and has been declining at an average rate of over three per cent per year since then. For some years additions to total reserves have not kept pace with depletion of the stock.

Based on past trends and future prices of $20, 18p in real terms total production of hydrocarbons could fall from around 4.15 mmboe/d in 2003 to 3 mmboe/d in 2010 and 1.9 mmboe/d in 2020. There is a considerable price sensitivity to the longer term outcomes. But, given the economically more difficult nature of the remaining prospects, much effort will be required by all stakeholders to achieve these production levels.

The DTI is well aware of the prospects and the need to implement licensing and other measures to facilitate continuing high levels of activity. The range of measures includes principally the fallow blocks/discovery initiative, and the revisions to the infrastructure Code of Practice. Others relate to pre-emption rights of licensees, financial security arrangements for decommissioning, data release arrangements, and codes of practice for enhancing the efficiency of the operation of the supply chains and asset transactions. Together, if pursued with vigour, these initiatives should bear fruit in the medium term. The operators, old and new, can be expected to respond to any worthwhile incentives. In this area the role of the Treasury is also important, particularly with respect to the encouragement of incremental investments in mature fields where tax incentives can play a significant role.

References

Department of Trade and Industry (DTI), (annual), *The Development of the Oil and Gas Reserves of the United Kingdom*, London.

Department of Trade and Industry (DTI), (2004), 'Fifth Fallow Assets Release', *www.og.dti.gov.uk/Ukpromote/fallow_assets.htm*, London, January.

Department of Trade and Industry (DTI), (quarterly), *Energy Trends*, London.

Kemp, A.G., and Kasim, A.S., (2003), 'A Regional Model of Oil and Gas Exploration in the UKCS', *North Sea Study Occasional Paper* No. 92, University of Aberdeen, November.

Kemp, A.G. and Stephen, L., (2003), 'The Economics of Field Cluster Developments in the UKCS' in L.C. Hunt (ed), *Energy in a Competitive Market: Essay in Honour of Colin Robinson*, Edward Elgar, Chapter 8.

Kemp, A.G. and Stephen, L., (2004), 'A Reassessment of Potential Production from and Expenditures in the UKCS', *North Sea Study Occasional Paper* No. 93, University of Aberdeen, March.

3i (2004), *The Prospects for North Sea Oil and Gas*, Aberdeen, April.

UKOOA, (2004), *UK Offshore Operators' Association Limited 2003 Activity Survey*, London, January.

Watkins, G.C., (2000), 'Characteristics of North Sea Oil Reserve Appreciation', *North Sea Study Occasional* Paper No. 80, University of Aberdeen, December.

Chapter 8

The Petroleum Tax System Revisited

Nina Bjerkedal and Torgeir Johnsen

Introduction

Petroleum exploitation or other non-renewable resource industries in general give rise to pure economic rents. Due to limited supply the return on the resource may be extraordinarily high after accounting for all costs. This is the justification for having a separate fiscal regime for the petroleum sector.[1] A further justification lies in the fact that the resources are owned by the State and therefore should benefit the society as a whole.

The Norwegian petroleum tax system is an important vehicle in sharing the returns in the sector between the companies and the State. But the tax system does not work alone in the task of providing income to the State from the sector. Also, state ownership, directly through the SDFI (State Direct Financial Interest) and indirectly through company ownership, plays an important role in channelling sector revenues to the State. A stated objective in Norwegian petroleum policy is to maximise the State's income from the sector. Income that is not used to finance current expenditures in the State Budget is set aside in the Government Petroleum Fund. A large share of the State's petroleum income is now being transferred to the Fund, and the Fund is building fast. The Petroleum Fund thus serves to transform petroleum wealth into financial wealth. In the National Budget 2004 the Petroleum Fund is estimated at about 995 billion NOK at the end of 2004. This amounts to about 62 per cent of total GDP for Norway. The petroleum wealth, or the net value of petroleum reserves still 'in the ground', was estimated at 2100 billion NOK in the Revised National Budget 2004. The state's share of the petroleum wealth was estimated at about 90 per cent of the total petroleum wealth.

Remaining resources on the Norwegian Continental Shelf are still large. Out of total expected resources of 12.9 billion standard cubic metres of oil equivalents (Sm^3 o.e.), 29 per cent have already been produced. Another 45 per cent are resources in producing fields, contingent resources and improved oil recovery projects (IOR). The remaining 26 per cent are undiscovered resources.

Several new development projects are currently under consideration. An overwhelming number of them are profitable at quite low oil prices. Prospects for a

[1] Throughout this chapter the petroleum sector refers to upstream, offshore petroleum exploration and production and pipeline transportation on the Norwegian Continental Shelf.

continued long and profitable production period make it important to care about the workings of the petroleum tax system.

Background

In the spring of 1999 oil prices were at a record low, hitting the 10-dollar mark for a period in February. There was general concern in the industry that low prices and diminished profitability could endanger new field developments and reduce interest in further exploration activities on the Norwegian Continental Shelf (NCS).

In response to industry concerns, the authorities put in place several measures to improve the overall conditions on the Shelf. Royalty was tapered off for the fields that were still liable to royalty payments, the carbon dioxide tax was reduced and changes were made in the licensing policy. The Parliament, in its treatment of the Revised National Budget for 1999, also asked the government to look into the petroleum tax system. As a response to this, the government established the Petroleum Tax Commission in October 1999.

The Tax Commission delivered its report in June 2000 and in May 2001 the government proposed amendments to the petroleum tax system and the Parliament approved the amendments in June 2001.

The Mandate of the Commission

Petroleum taxes amount to a large share of total taxes in Norway. In 2000 petroleum taxes made up some 16 per cent of total tax proceeds. The mandate given to the Commission therefore pointed at the revenue aspect of the petroleum tax system as an important consideration when evaluating the system. The main focus in the mandate was on how a tax system should be designed in order to secure an appropriate share of income to the State while at the same time interfering as little as possible with sound business and resource management. The mandate also asked four specific questions. These were:

- What is the impact of the petroleum tax system on company decisions? Is the system neutral?
- What are the effects on investments outside the Norwegian Continental Shelf of the allocation rule for financial costs between the offshore tax regime and the ordinary tax regime?
- May the individual rulings on tax conditions for transfers of licences be replaced by general tax rules?
- Does the tax system create barriers to entry for new companies?

The Petroleum Tax System

Income from petroleum exploration and production and pipeline transportation is taxed separately from other sources of income at the company level. The system allows full consolidation of income and costs pertaining to all interests and licences held offshore. Thus, there is no 'ring fence' around fields.

Net petroleum income is taxed at the corporate tax rate of 28 per cent and at an additional rate, the special tax rate, of 50 per cent. The calculation of the tax bases for the two taxes follow the General Tax Act applicable to all businesses in Norway, but certain special rules for the petroleum sector are contained in the Petroleum Tax Act. The tax creditor for both taxes is the federal government. A simplified description of the petroleum tax system is the following:

Gross income (valued at norm prices)
- Operating costs (including CO_2-tax, royalty and area fee)
- Capital depreciation
- Financial costs (limited by the rule of thin capitalisation)
= Ordinary income taxed at 28 per cent
- Uplift (additional deduction based on investments)
= Income taxed at 50 per cent.

A special feature in the petroleum taxation is the system of norm prices for oil, i.a. administratively fixed tax reference prices. Consequently, there is no need for the tax authorities to determine if each individual crude sale is between independent parties. Since vertical integration between producers and buyers of crude oil is extensive in the oil business, the norm price system represents a major simplification for the tax authorities. The Ministry of Oil and Energy has authorised a special Petroleum Price Board to set norm prices. Norm prices are required by law to correspond to the price that oil could have been traded at between independent parties in a free market. As until June 2001, gas produced on the Norwegian Continental Shelf was sold jointly through the Gas Negotiating Committee (GFU) to buyers in the UK and on the continent. These sales were accepted as arm's length transactions and have not been subject to tax reference prices.

A linear depreciation schedule applies to production installations and pipelines. The annual depreciation rate is $16\frac{2}{3}$ per cent, starting from the year the investment was incurred, lasting for six years altogether.

The special tax is only payable for that part of the net income which exceeds an uplift. The uplift is an extra depreciation and the purpose of the uplift is to secure that the special tax is only levied on extraordinary returns and not on normal returns. The uplift is five per cent yearly for six years of the cost price of assets depreciated according to the six-year rule. An oil company may accordingly deduct a total of $21\frac{2}{3}$ per cent of the investment costs per year for six years. If the tax base is negative, the excess uplift may be carried forward.

In the petroleum tax system in place before 2002 a company's total net financial costs were divided between the petroleum sector and other activities in proportion to net non-financial income in the two tax jurisdictions. Net financial costs that are allocated to the Shelf are deductible against the 78 per cent rate, but only against the 28 per cent tax if allocated to other activities. A 'thin capitalisation rule' limits the amount of interest deductions that are admissible in the petroleum sector. According to this rule the maximum amount of net financial costs that can be deducted in the petroleum tax bases corresponds to a debt ratio of 80 per cent calculated on the basis of the company's full balance sheet at year end.

In the petroleum tax system in place before 2002 nominal deficits could be carried forward for 15 years or – by application – even longer. Half of deficits occurring in activities in mainland Norway are deductible against the corporate tax base for petroleum income.

Sale and purchase of licences on the Norwegian Continental Shelf are subject to individual rulings on tax treatment according to section 10 in the Petroleum Tax Act. The purpose of section 10 is to avoid tax incentives or disincentives for transfers and negative or positive revenue effects for the State. Consequently, the Ministry of Finance sets special tax rules for each licence sale in order to neutralise different tax effects of the transfer for the seller and buyer, where necessary. The method is administratively burdensome, but has made possible transfers of licence shares that would otherwise have been prohibited by tax considerations.

Contrary to many other petroleum taxation regimes, the Norwegian system is almost solely based upon net income taxation. The royalty is not formally a part of the taxation regime, but is part of concessional requirements. Royalty has not been claimed for fields developed after 1986, and is now being phased out also for the few, older fields that still pay the royalty.

Theoretical Basis for the Commission's Analysis and Suggestions

General Framework

The Commission's discussions and proposals lean heavily on academic work on neutral taxation by Boadway and Bruce (1984) and Fane (1987).

The concept of neutrality can only be meaningfully applied with reference to behavioural assumptions underlying decisions. The Commission's analysis is based on the neo-classical theory of the firm. The theory postulates profit-maximising firms, and this behaviour leads – albeit only under idealized conditions – to efficiency. A neutral tax does not distort the firms' decisions as compared to the situation without the tax. To the extent that the tax is not neutral, investment and operating decisions are affected, and the distortions arising impose real costs on the economy.

Pure rents arising from exploitation of non-renewable resources represent an extra surplus not required to motivate economic behaviour, and could therefore, in this theoretical framework, be taxed away without distorting resource allocation. In practice, however, governments do not try to extract all pure rents through taxation. Rather, governments impose an additional taxation aimed at extracting a fairly large share of the surplus. One obvious reason for not aiming at close to a 100 per cent[2] tax of pure rents is that there is no way in practice to identify a tax base that is perfectly neutral.

When tax rates are high, any deviation from neutrality gives a strong inducement to distort decisions. Furthermore, a standard result in welfare theory tells us that the costs on the economy due to distortionary taxes increase over-proportionally with the tax rate. Therefore, a neutral tax is an ideal and especially important when tax rates are high.

Net income taxation at high tax rates may imply an increased danger for erosion of the tax base through tax avoidance and tax evasion. High tax rates could motivate taxpayers to shift tax bases into tax jurisdictions with lower rates through transfer pricing or real transfers. Real transfers could be allocation of cost activities, like R&D or testing, to jurisdictions with high marginal tax rates. While the costs are fully deducted in the tax base of the high tax country, the benefits may accrue to several provinces. Since true costs discovery is more difficult than income assessment, there could be a case for relying on gross income taxation for some part of the tax revenue. However, gross taxation would impose real costs by distorting decisions, most noticeably by lowering investments, including hampering enhanced recovery projects and tail production in producing fields. The Commission did not find reason to believe that the tax authorities' monitoring of the companies' costs is not sufficiently effective. Therefore, the Commission advocated a taxation system for the petroleum sector that relies solely on net income taxation.

There are other ways of extracting rents than by way of taxation. The Commission pointed to State participation and auctioning of licences. For several reasons these possibilities were not deemed to be realistic as full alternatives to taxation of realised net income, but were seen as adequate supplements by the Commission.

Neutrality and the Corporate Tax

Given that the Commission views a neutral tax as an ideal, it is necessary to consider if the corporate tax poses a problem with respect to neutral investment decisions.

A neutral tax in the strict, traditional sense (a tax on pure economic rents) does not lower the internal rate of return on a marginal investment (the normal return), while a well-defined corporate tax lowers the internal rate of return on a marginal investment by the tax rate. Thus it may seem that a consequence of corporate taxation is that certain investments that are profitable before tax are left unprofitable with the tax, and may therefore not be undertaken.

In an open economy, however, the required rate of return after tax is determined in international capital markets. Assuming these markets are not

---

[2] A 100 percent tax would amount to the same as a development and operating contract between the firm and the government with unlimited cost coverage.

influenced noticeably by the tax in Norway, and that the marginal investor is subject to capital taxation on alternative investments in line with the corporate tax, the corporate tax will not restrict the level of investment.[3] While the first condition seems plausible, there may be more doubt about the effective taxation of alternative investments for investors. Although the Norwegian investor is taxable for capital income arising from the business sector and financial assets, the same may not hold true for relevant international investors.

Nevertheless, the Commission has taken the view that the corporate tax, even though it is not neutral in the strict, traditional sense, should be part of the petroleum taxation system. Hence, efficiency vis-à-vis other sectors is achieved. A consequence of the opposite view would be that normal returns in the petroleum sector would be exempt from tax that is applicable to other sectors, and that investments could be undertaken in this sector that did not meet the required return before tax in other sectors in Norway. Furthermore, assuming that the additional tax in the petroleum sector is neutral, levying the corporate tax will prevent incentives to transfer close-to-marginal projects into the petroleum sector.

Proper Tax Bases

First, we look at proper tax bases individually for a corporate tax and a rent collecting tax. Using the two taxes together raises specific design issues which we return to later.

The corporate tax in Norway resembles that of other countries. It taxes equity income at the source and acts as a withholding mechanism against income accruing to foreign shareholders and against earnings accruing to domestic shareholders which would not be immediately taxable at the personal level. The special tax, however, is a rent collecting tax and should apply only to extraordinary returns, that is, returns above normal.

In order to obtain neutral taxation a general requirement for both tax bases is that all current costs employed to generate income from petroleum exploitation are deducted at their full opportunity cost.

The tax base of the corporate tax should define true equity income and should therefore also deduct all capital costs except the cost of equity financing. Depreciation for tax purposes should be the realised economic depreciation. If so, the corporate tax will tax normal returns to equity capital, as well as extraordinary returns, at the rate of the corporate tax. The part of normal returns that accrues to debt financing (interest) is taxed at the receiving end.

The tax base for the special tax (the rent collecting tax) should correspond to the base of the corporate tax. In addition, the full opportunity cost of equity finance should be deducted. This tax base represents pure profits in each period. The

[3] Even though the corporate tax does not affect the level of investments, it lowers the amount of domestic savings. Therefore, it is not a strictly neutral tax and creates a welfare loss to society. Furthermore, the corporate tax causes a bias against risky investments, which is treated in the following.

present value of pure profits in all future periods is the net value of the resource. A *pure profits tax* is therefore a tax on the value of the resource.

There are alternatives to a pure profits tax that are equivalent in present value terms. They differ in terms of timing of deductions and consequently in the timing of tax proceeds. One such tax is the *cash flow tax*. In this case expenditures on capital assets are deducted immediately when they are incurred instead of deductions over time for depreciation and financing costs. There is a whole class of taxes that preserves the neutrality property of the cash flow tax. All that is needed for preserving neutrality is that the present value of deductions is maintained compared with a cash flow tax.[4] The depreciation schedule for tax purposes may be chosen arbitrarily, provided that an additional deduction is granted. This deduction is the opportunity cost of capital multiplied with the tax-written-down value of depreciable assets. The purpose of this deduction is to give financial compensation for the postponement in depreciation compared to immediate write off. The relevant financial compensation (cost of capital) is the one that represents the risk characteristics of the deductions.

The special tax may, as an alternative, deduct actual costs of debt financing. In this case the financial compensation pertains solely to the share of tax-written-down asset values that is not debt financed.

Tax Treatment of Income Risk. Consequences for Risk Characteristics of Deferred Tax Reductions

Another requirement for a neutral tax is that it must have full loss offset and thus symmetric treatment of income and losses. Current losses should be refunded (at the tax rate) by the government or carried forward with interest using the relevant cost of capital. In this way any *income risk* faced by the company is shared with the government, and the tax system will not affect the incentives to invest in income-risky versus risk-free assets.

With full loss offset the taxpayer is able to deduct the cost of income risk from its taxable income. The cost of risk is deductible because the government shares the full variability in income by providing refunds or their equivalents for tax losses. If full loss offset is allowed the appropriate cost of finance to be multiplied with the tax-written-down values of assets is the risk-free rate of return. The reason is that the risk is already deducted. If a risk premium were added in the cost of capital, risks would in effect be deducted twice. Another way to look at this is to observe that an immediate write-off given up for later deductions is a risk-free investment if the tax system offers full loss offset, and should earn the risk-free rate.

Allowing a tax shelter for the special tax consisting of only a risk-free return on remaining capital seems at odds with the common saying that the special tax should allow deductions for a normal rate of return and only tax extraordinary returns. The problem is that under uncertainty it is not so clear what is meant by a

4 The result depends critically on the assumption that the tax rate does not change over the relevant time period as pointed out by Sandmo (1979).

normal rate of return. The theory shows, however, that the risk characteristics of the cash flow of deductions define 'normal returns'. A risk-free cash flow of deductions makes the relevant cost of capital the risk-free rate.

Likewise, the relevant opportunity cost of capital to be applied for losses carried forward, is the risk-free interest rate. With full loss offset the taxpayer is certain to obtain the deduction at some point in time. Giving up an immediate loss refund from the government for a certain deduction later is a risk-free investment and should earn the risk-free interest rate. If the interest earned on the postponement is not taxed, the after-tax rate is the one to be used.

Hence, the tax system should allow deferred deductions compared to a cash flow tax, both investment and loss deductions, to be compensated using the after-tax risk-free rate.

Tax Treatment of Capital Risk

The corporate tax base generally allows depreciation of capital assets on book value according to a predetermined schedule defined by expected economic depreciation. A neutral tax on equity income, however, requires deductions for actual (ex post) economic depreciation. Therefore, the taxpayer bears the full risk of revaluation of capital assets and the risk that the asset wears at a different pace than determined ex ante. There is no deduction for this *capital risk* in the corporate tax base, and this tax therefore discriminates against investments in capital risky assets.[5] It is the mistiming of realisation of income under the tax that causes a bias against capital risky investments.[6] The inability of the corporate tax to share in an investment's capital risk is unavoidable as long as depreciation allowances are predetermined. Given this, the combined taxation should aim at not aggravating the unavoidable effects imposed by corporate taxation.

Any neutral pure profits tax (including the cash flow tax and its equivalent alternatives), however, allow for the deduction of capital risks. Clearly, the cash flow tax deducts all capital risk when capital costs are expensed immediately. In other variations of the rent tax the rate of depreciation is inconsequential since the present value of the depreciation and cost of finance deductions always equals the initial expenditure. In economic and risk terms this amounts to the same as immediate deduction of investments.

Structuring the Two Taxes

The combination of two taxes raises specific design issues. In order for the two properly defined taxes to be neutral in combination, the corporate tax should be

---

5 Tax laws usually offer extraordinary deductions, however, in the case of total loss or physical damage. There may also be some counter-effect due to shareholder taxation. Fluctuations in the value of real assets will normally be reflected in the share prices. Through sale and repurchase the shareholder may realise a capital gains loss for tax purposes.

6 Bulow and Summers (1984).

deducted in the special tax base.[7] Otherwise, the tax on 'normal returns' would be taxed again by the special tax. Hence, the special tax should treat the corporate tax as an expense like any other expense. The effect of a neutral special tax is to let the government share in the project less the corporate tax.

In the Norwegian petroleum taxation the two taxes are separate and none is deductible in the base of the other. The Commission felt that redesigning the structure of taxes would introduce large formal changes and was undesirable. The Commission therefore proposed something which is formally different, but which results in the same tax payments. The two taxes are left separate and the rate of the special tax is lower compared to a case where the corporate tax is deductible. The tax on 'normal returns' is deducted by increasing the rate of interest from the after-tax to the before-tax rate.[8]

Income risk neutrality requires that each tax has full loss offset. Loss positions should therefore be refunded at the tax rates or carried forward with interest. Furthermore, companies should be able to realise the tax value of any loss position if it goes permanently out of business.

Capital risk is not shared by the corporate tax. The effect of two taxes, with ideal properties as described above, is to counteract the taxpayers' over-proportional capital risk bearing. When the corporate tax is too high because of too low depreciation, deducting the too high corporate tax on 'normal returns' will produce a too low special tax and vice versa. In this way some capital risk is effectively transferred to the government. The result is that companies carry less capital risk in petroleum projects than in comparable investments subject only to corporate tax.

The Commission's Evaluation of the System In Place Before 2002

The Commission set out to evaluate the taxation system in the light of the requirements for a neutral tax. As we have seen, the conditions for perfectly neutral taxes may be very strict and are unattainable for a number of different reasons, among others because realised depreciation will differ from the depreciation schedule for tax purposes and because it is impossible for taxation authorities always to be able to reveal true income, and especially true costs.

An important part of the Commission's evaluation was concerned with how the tax system impinges on the incentives to investment. For this purpose the

---

7 Actually, it would work the other way around as well, if one were free to set a specific corporate tax rate for this sector.

8 Let X be realised economic result in the period, K the value of capital at the beginning of the period, r the risk free rate, t the corporate tax rate and s* the special tax rate. The special tax, S, may now be written:

$$S = (X - Kr(1-t) - Xt)s*$$

which is easily shown to be equivalent to:

$$S = (X - Kr)s$$

when $s = (1-t)s*$

Commission applied the framework developed by Hall and Jorgensen (1967) and put to use by, amongst others, King and Fullerton (1984). The starting point is an investment that is just acceptable for the company after tax. This is the so-called marginal investment. By working through the tax system one calculates the rate of return on the investment *before* tax.[9] If investment-based deductions are very large, the calculations will show that an investment that is unprofitable before tax may become profitable after tax. If deductions are too small the tax system will work to discourage profitable investments. The previous section discusses how deductions must be set in order for the tax system to be neutral. The required rate of the marginal investment in a neutral tax system with corporate taxation will be grossed up by one minus the corporate rate to arrive at the before-tax rate of return. There will be no effect of the special tax on the return on the marginal investment.

The system in place allows for depreciation and interest deduction in both tax bases and uplift in the special tax base. The Commission shows that the combined effect of depreciation, uplift and interest deductions exceeds deductions in a neutral tax system. Investments that are clearly unprofitable before tax become profitable after tax. The result pertains to companies in a tax paying position and also assumes a maximum of debt financing.

Hence, the generous tax treatment of investments may lead to investments that are not profitable on a pre-tax basis. In practice, probably all field developments on the Norwegian Shelf have been expected to be profitable, before tax as well as after tax. But the generous tax treatment may skew investment decisions within a project. The tax system stimulates the use of too much capital in any project.

Below we discuss in more detail the most important deviations from the conditions for neutrality that the Commission suggested to correct.

Depreciation

One was the depreciation scheme for tax purposes for production and pipeline assets of six years linear including the year of acquisition. Depreciation at this rate is clearly too fast for the great majority of these assets. The effect of lenient depreciation allowances is that the taxation of normal returns by the corporate tax is incomplete. This may lead to the undertaking of investments in the petroleum sector that are less profitable before tax than would be acceptable for comparable investments in other sectors.

---

9 Often the effective rate of taxation is computed, defined as the difference between the before and after rates of return divided by the after (or before) tax rate of return.

Allocation Rule for Net Financial Costs

Another was the allocation rule for net financial costs. Net financial costs were allocated according to net non-financial income in the two tax jurisdictions. The allocation rule for interest expenses placed a too large share of total interest payments in the petroleum tax regime where they are deducted against the high marginal tax rate of 78 per cent. This means that costs that were not related to petroleum activities could be deducted in the petroleum tax bases.

There are two main reasons for this. One is that activities outside the Shelf are not expected to yield the same high return as in the petroleum sector. High yields in the petroleum sector attract a disproportionally large share of the interest payments. The other reason lies in the fact that oil companies may be parent companies for subsidiaries in any industry in any country. Some oil companies have financed subsidiaries heartily with equity, which in turn has been financed by debt in the parent oil company. According to the 'thin capitalisation rule' the oil companies' capacity for debt with interest deductions against petroleum taxes increases by 80 per cent of the book value of any company asset. Any income from the subsidiaries in the form of dividends (which in fact rarely occurs) are not included in the allocation rule, but could at most be taxable in the ordinary tax jurisdiction at the 28 per cent rate.

The result is to decrease petroleum taxes and stimulate oil companies operating on the Norwegian Shelf to invest elsewhere. The misallocation of interest expenses gives oil companies an advantage in business where they compete with non-oil companies and therefore works adversely against 'fair' competition in several markets.

We see that the system was not neutral with respect to how economic activity is organised. It created a strong incentive to include other economic activity in the oil company, directly or through subsidiaries.

Interest deductions against 78 per cent tax, as opposed to 28 per cent[10] tax on the corresponding interest income, imply that the petroleum tax system is not neutral with respect to financing decisions. The most tax effective behaviour is to debt finance as much as possible. In the case that interest payments concern only companies' Norwegian Shelf activities, the 'thin capitalisation rule' seems reasonably effective, however, in limiting the scope for high debt financing.

Treatment of Losses

Another easily recognisable deviation from neutral taxation was in the treatment of losses. The petroleum tax system did not treat net income and loss symmetrically. Losses were carried forward without interest compensation and thereby lost some of their economic value. Therefore, the system lacked a full deduction for income risks. Full loss offset is of particular importance to newcomers who enter by receiving a concession and typically incur sizeable costs before income can be

---

[10] This is the tax rate that pertains to capital income in Norway. The rate varies somewhat across countries. Several countries apply a higher rate on this type of income.

expected. The tax system may have imposed barriers to this type of entry. Tax barriers will not be directly present, however, if companies enter the Shelf by acquiring a share in an already producing licence. But such interests are not necessarily readily available, and it could be that entrants were paying up for the benefit of the tax paying position. The Commission made no judgement on how important the tax barriers are compared to other barriers, for example in the licensing policy.

Lack of loss offset may also create different attitudes between licensees towards investment opportunities due to differences in tax paying position. There is a risk that companies that expect not to be in a tax position for a long while may discourage activity in the licence if expected returns are not highly favourable. The Commission concluded that lack of loss offset could be harmful.

For companies that were not in a tax paying position, the tax system may have discouraged profitable investments depending on how long it takes before deductions will be effective against income. In this case, investment-based deductions may have been too small because there was no interest compensation for losses carried forward. It has already been mentioned that it is not desirable that the tax system has a very different impact on project economics depending on tax position.

The Commission's Proposals

The suggestions made by the Commission were all within the main structure of the existing tax system. The objectives of the recommendations were to make the tax system more targeted towards Norwegian Shelf income, to diminish distortionary effects on investment decisions and to encourage exploration and development irrespective of the tax position of the individual company.

The structure of the proposed tax system follows the design of 'ideal' tax bases. Depreciation for tax purposes should follow economic depreciation more closely. Interest on debt is deductible in the corporate tax base but not in the special tax base. This will eliminate the subsidy to debt financing and therefore diminish the possibilities for exploiting the petroleum taxes regime when companies invest outside the Shelf. The 'thin capitalisation rule' may be abolished. Furthermore, the Commission proposed a new allocation rule for interest deductions between the petroleum and other activities pertaining only to the corporate tax.

By bringing depreciation for tax purposes as close to economic depreciation as possible the corporate tax will fully tax normal returns. Economic depreciation also means that the special tax aims at taxing the pure profit in each period. Deductions for financial costs in the special tax base were given by a common deduction for debt and equity computed as the risk-free interest rate multiplied by the tax-written-down value of depreciable assets.

Both taxes were given full loss offset for future losses (losses accrued after changes in the tax system have been effected). Due especially to this, transfers of licences between companies that do not have carry forward losses established prior to the introduction of the new rules were suggested no longer to be subject to individual rulings by the Ministry of Finance (section 10 rulings).

In summary, the Commission's suggestions were:

- Today's deductions for net interest payments and uplift in the base for the special tax to be replaced by an allowance for return on capital employed. This allowance will shelter normal returns on capital from the special tax, irrespective of how the investments are financed. The allowance to be computed on the basis of depreciable assets on the Norwegian Shelf assessed at the written down value for tax purposes. The applicable return on capital shall be the risk-free rate of interest before tax.
- Actual net interest payments still to be deductible for corporate tax purposes, but according to a new allocation rule. Net interest payments to be allocated between the petroleum and ordinary fiscal regimes according to net asset values, on the basis of written down values for tax purposes. The petroleum tax act, section 3 h on 'thin capitalisation' no longer to be applicable.
- The depreciation rules to be changed so that the depreciation period for tax purposes becomes a closer approximation of the economically useful life of the assets. Depreciation may start only when assets are delivered or completed.
- Abolition of the possibility to deduct up to 50 per cent of losses from mainland Norway against Shelf income for purpose of the corporate tax.
- Future losses, in the bases for the corporate income tax and the special tax, to be carried forward with interest using the after-tax risk-free rate. Future losses are defined as losses occurring after the implementation of the new rules.
- Future losses in a company that ceases its activities on the Norwegian Shelf to be transferable in case the assets are sold or in case of a merger with another company.
- The principle of tax continuity to be applied in the case of sale of assets with associated licences.
- Sale and purchase of licences involving companies with losses established prior to the introduction of the new rules, to be subject to section 10 rulings by the Ministry of Finance as before. This will also be the case in transfers where SDFI (State Direct Financial Interest) is a party to either side of a transaction.

In line with the mandate, the Commission saw a clear case for continuing the special tax at a high rate, but the Commission did not recommend a specific rate. The Commission presented computations showing that the special tax could be lowered by four percentage points following the proposed widening of the tax bases without diminishing the value of the tax receipts in a long run perspective.

Since a special tax of the proposed type is equivalent to a cash flow tax, one may ask why the Commission did not propose a cash flow tax. There are three main reasons for this. The first is that in general it seems like a good tax policy rule to tax profits as they occur. Front loading of deductions, as is already the case in the current system, may stimulate strategic behaviour, on the part of companies as well as tax authorities, in harvesting periods. The second reason is that it would seem an unnecessary complication to have, in effect, two sets of depreciation rules, one for the General Tax and one for the special tax. This would complicate the computation of gains and losses when disposing of assets or licences. The third reason is that a cash flow tax could easily raise questions with respect to the creditability of the special tax.

Reactions from the Petroleum Industry to the Proposals

The Commission's report, NOU 2000: 18, was handed over to the Minister of Finance in June 2000. The Ministry sent the report for comments to industry and other interested parties.

On behalf of the petroleum industry, the OLF (the Oil Industry Association in Norway) expressed disagreement and concern with the Commission's proposals, and asked the Minister of Finance to ignore the suggestions. The industry had several objections.

Is the Proposed System Neutral?

One important objection was that the proposed system was not neutral, but highly distortionary, seen from the industry's point of view. The confusion over the neutrality of the suggested system has to do with the idea of a special tax that strikes only extraordinary returns. A risk-free rate as compensation for deferred tax deductions, and therefore as 'normal returns', was not seen as adequate. The industry's view confers with their practice when evaluating projects.

Companies usually base their calculations on a required rate of return from expected net cash flows after tax. All elements making out the net cash flow are discounted using the same rate irrespective of the risk characteristics of the individual cash flow elements. Furthermore, the companies may use the same required rate across different tax systems in different countries irrespective of how the tax system splits the risk between the company and the government, and across different projects irrespective of the split of risk in these projects. The discount rate companies apply clearly includes some risk premium. When the certain tax reductions are discounted by this risk-adjusted rate the companies see the present value of postponed deductions as less than intended by the Commission. Therefore, a company which uses this type of capital budgeting and profitability calculations will tend to be in disagreement with the Commission's neutrality result. The industry's point of view is in accordance with earlier academic literature on rent taxation, strongly influenced by Garnaut and Clunies Ross (1975) and their proposal for a 'Resource Rent Tax'.

The tax policy question that arises is if a tax system should rely on sound theoretical results or base itself on current industry practice for investment decisions. The Commission felt that it would not be advisable to disregard the theoretical results, which are both logical and straightforward. To compensate postponements with a risk-adjusted cost of capital would incur the risk of overinvestment and the undertaking of sub-marginal and too risky projects. Being at odds with capital budgeting procedures in many companies, as the suggestions are, they may point to a better, although somewhat more demanding, practice.

The industry mistakenly took the Commission to imply that the cost of capital in the industry was the risk-free rate. This is of course not the case. The Commission makes no judgement of the appropriate level of return for the industry or for specific projects. In designing the tax system there is no need to characterise the risk of the net cash flow to the company. The proposed system will be neutral irrespective of the risk attributable to elements of the cash flows other than the certain tax reductions.

It is important to point out that the Commission's conclusion that the system in place before 2002 was not neutral does not require splitting cash flows with different risks in the analysis. Traditional analysis using one common discount rate implies non-neutrality of the current system as long as this rate is not extremely high. That investments are treated favourably is acknowledged by the industry in their arguments for a special tax treatment for rented production facilities. The aim of this provision is to make rental as favourable as in-company investment. If oil companies' investments were not stimulated by tax rules, there would be no need for this special provision.

Does the System Have Full Loss Offset?

The industry also challenged the view that deferred losses would uphold their value in all circumstances. Losses carried forward might lose their value in the unlikely event that there are no buyers for a loss position. It is also conceivable that a company will not receive the full value of the losses, due to insufficient competition among potential buyers. Thus, there are some arguments that may point to less than full certainty for the tax reductions. The risk that is left, however, is quite small and substantially less than the risk in a company's after-tax cash flows. The remaining risk is also partly non-systematic risk of no importance to the shareholders.

The Demand for Financial Volume or 'Materiality'

In the neo-classical framework, neutral taxation will lead companies to simultaneously maximise the before- and the after-tax value of any set of potential projects. This requires that society and the company value projects in the same way. An objection from the industry is that oil companies behave differently than implied by value maximising in the neo-classical framework. Specifically, the industry suggests that companies demand financial volume or 'materiality'. This seems to mean that they require some minimum net present value in a project in order to undertake it. If this is the case, small but profitable fields might not be developed. This would be unfortunate from society's point of view.

The requirement for 'materiality' may have to do with company-specific transaction costs connected to the company's specialisation or economies of scale in the administration of projects. Neither of these reasons would justify subsidies for small fields. Rather, the Commission suggested reduced barriers to entry for newcomers and stronger competition. It could also be that companies incur some costs that are not admitted in the tax base or accounted for in the project analysis. A better solution would then be to include these costs.

Another possibility pointed to is limited supply of the most qualified technical personnel, and a need to allocate these to the potentially most profitable tasks. It is quite clear that companies will experience shortages in supply of certain inputs from time to time. In general, such shortages will be reflected in input prices and therefore taken account of in taxation and project analysis. But it may also be the case that certain inputs do not earn the value of their marginal productivity or their potential market value. If this is a transitory event, it is not so clear that the issue can be resolved in a taxation system. The virtues of a more stable and lasting system will most certainly override possible benefits that could only come about at substantial administrative costs. The possibility that under-supply in certain input markets may persist cannot be ruled out, but a more realistic assumption seems to be that in the long run most factors are replicable.

In conclusion, both the underlying reasons for 'demand for volume' and its consequences for taxation policy are unclear. Although the Commission took a sceptical and cautious stance, in practical terms one must agree that a set of extremely many small interests in real projects is much harder to manage than a set of fewer, but larger interests. Partly, the companies themselves could attain more focus through the sale and purchase of licence shares. The concession system should also aim at licence shares of reasonable sizes and a sufficient number of qualified licensees.

Tax Competition

The oil companies also claim that they can achieve a high degree of 'materiality' in other producing provinces. Thus, the industry has pointed to tax competition as a factor that restricts the tax level in the Norwegian petroleum sector. The idea is that a company can move its capital and personnel elsewhere even though the resource itself is immobile. This does not answer the question, however, why profitable projects would not be undertaken, possibly by another company. The reasoning must rest on some limit in the supply of inputs. As previously mentioned such scarcity tends to be reflected in market prices. The input would then be subject to the normal rationing of the market. It seems hard to accept the persistence of a situation with under-supply across existing companies and potential newcomers in the business. Nevertheless, Norwegian taxation does not aim at capturing all the economic rents, but leaves a substantial part of it in the oil companies. The going tax rate could be seen as a compromise where problems defining a truly neutral tax, risks of transfer pricing and a willingness to award returns above market price to some limited input or competence are factors that act to restrict the level of taxation.

If the issue is that the government wants to attract certain oil companies which it considers to be especially well suited for tasks on the Norwegian Continental Shelf, more lenient taxation is probably not the way to go about it.

Taxation does not discriminate between taxpayers. In order to favour especially qualified companies there is scope to do so within a concession policy based on open and objective selection criteria.

Changes in the Petroleum Tax Act

Based on the Commission's report, the Ministry of Finance proposed changes to the petroleum tax system in Ot. prp. nr. 86 (2000-2001). Although the Ministry gave support to the Commission's analysis, the proposals were not as extensive as suggested by the Commission. The Ministry chose to maintain the deductions for uplift and interest payments in the tax base for the special tax. In deciding to keep the deduction for interest payments, an important consideration was to ensure that the Norwegian petroleum taxes could still be credited against taxes in the oil companies' home countries.

In order to restrict financial costs from other activities from flowing into the petroleum tax regime the Ministry proposed to change the allocation rule for interest payments. According to the new rule financial costs are allocated based on written down tax values in the two tax regimes following the principles set forth by the Commission. In addition, an adjustment is added to ensure that it will not be necessary for a company engaged in activities outside the Continental Shelf to maximise the allowable debt under the 'thin capitalisation' rule in order to enjoy maximum interest deduction in the offshore tax base.

Following the Commission's suggestion, deficits in the petroleum income tax bases can now be carried forward increased by interest. This should stimulate the participation of new entrants on the Continental Shelf. Furthermore, the government proposed a new rule to allow losses in case of disposal of the business activities or merger of companies to be transferred to companies acquiring the business.

In Ot. prp. nr. 2 (2003-2004) the government proposed to abolish the act concerning costs of decommissioning. Decommissioning costs were not tax deductible, but instead the government paid a grant to the companies based on the historical average tax rate for the respective companies. The system proved to be administratively burdensome and recent changes in the petroleum tax act also made the act redundant.

The Petroleum Tax Act was changed at the same time making decommissioning costs tax deductible. In addition it was proposed that the government should pay the after-tax value of deficits arising from decommissioning costs for a company that ceases its activity on the Norwegian Continental Shelf. The purpose of the proposal was to reduce the risk for the companies.

Further Work

It is fair to say that the Commission concentrated on a few, but very important, features of the tax system. Other topics are treated very superficially or barely mentioned at all. Among these, there are certainly several topics that deserve more attention. One is the huge issue of transfer pricing. A tax jurisdiction with a marginal tax rate as high as 78 per cent may attract more costs than should strictly be allocated to the Norwegian Shelf. Little is said by the Commission on this topic. More work on the scope of the petroleum tax regime must be expected in the event of more sub-sea installations and onshore treatment plants. A case in point is the change in the petroleum tax act for investments when the purpose is to produce LNG (Liquefied Natural Gas), implying that investments can be deducted over three years (cf. Ot. prp. nr. 16 [2001-2002)]. Snøhvit in the Barents Sea qualifies for the shorter depreciation period. For this development the Ministry of Finance has issued a ruling with the effect of including the onshore LNG plant in the petroleum tax regime.

Next to nothing is said by the Commission on the norm price system. As from 2002 the Gas Negotiating Committee (GFU) was abolished. Up to then the GFU was responsible for all sales of natural gas from the Norwegian Continental Shelf and consequently the gas prices have been arm's length prices. Individual companies are now responsible for the selling of gas. This implies that companies can sell their gas to a related company at artificially low prices. By setting the price low the profit will arise in a tax regime with lower taxes and this type of income shifting is therefore very profitable for the companies. In order to avoid this, the Oil Taxation Office needs to closely examine each sale and justify too low prices. The burden on the Oil Taxation Office can be relieved by an extension of the norm price system for natural gas as well. The establishment of a system for the tax treatment gas sales of will be an important task for the authorities in the near future.

In autumn 2003 the oil industry made several tax proposals through the so-called Kon-Kraft project. The industry pointed at the low exploration activity on the Norwegian Continental Shelf and claimed that this was mainly due to the high tax rate in Norway, but also a lack of prospective exploration acreage. According to the industry, the high tax rate in Norway is the major reason why oil companies do not consider many projects to be sufficiently profitable, even though they are beneficial to society at large. The claim for 'materiality' or 'financial volume' discussed above is still a crucial argument. The oil industry proposed a reduction in the special tax rate for new projects combined with a production allowance for new production.

In the Revised National Budget for 2004 the government announced certain amendments to the Petroleum Tax Act which will be put forward in the budget for 2005.

The proposals are:

- The state will pay in cash the tax value of deficits arriving from exploration in connection with the yearly tax assessment.

- The state will pay in cash the tax value of deficits if a company ceases its activities on the Norwegian Continental Shelf.
- A simplification of the tax treatment connected to selling and buying licences.
- The uplift will be accelerated to 7.5 per cent over four years.
- An improvement in the tax rules for depreciation of investments with a shorter economic life than six years.
- Less strict rules for deeming contractors as participants in exploration and extraction (and subject to special tax) leaves greater scope for incentive contracts between oil companies and contractors.

The proposals will increase fiscal certainty for new companies and improve the profitability of investments in tail-end production and improved oil recovery. The proposal will also simplify trading in licences on the Norwegian Continental Shelf.

References

Boadway, Robin W. and Neil Bruce (1984), 'A General Proposition on the Design of a Neutral Business Tax,' *Journal of Public Economics*, bd. 24, 231-239.

Bulow, J.I. and L.H. Summers (1984), 'The Taxation of Risky Assets'. *Journal of Political Economy* Vol. 92, no. 1.

Fane, George (1987), 'Neutral Taxation under Uncertainty'. *Journal of Public Economics*, bd. 33, 95-105.

Garnaut, R.G. and A.I.C. Ross (1975), 'Uncertainty, Risk Aversion, and Taxing of Natural Resource Projects', *Energy Journal*, bd. 85, 272-285.

Hall, R.E. and D.W. Jorgensen (1967), 'Tax Policy and Investment Behaviour,' *American Economic Review* 57, 391-414.

King, M.A. and D. Fullerton (1984), 'The Taxation of Income from Capital – A Comparison of the United Kingdom, Sweden and West Germany', Chicago University Press.

Sandmo, Agnar (1979), 'A Note on the Neutrality of the Cash Flow Corporation Tax', *Economics Letters* 4, 1973-1976.

Index